T0114598

"This is a deeply moving account of what it meant to be a Jew under Hitler's rule and, equally brutal, Stalin's rule. Masha Gessen, a talented writer with a human touch, has brilliantly used her grandmothers as a way to bring to life a grim era of East European history."
    —Daniel Schorr, senior news analyst for National Public Radio

"Masha Gessen has written an indispensable history of Soviet Jews as seen through the eyes of two unforgettable women—her grandmothers. The scope and complexity of their characters rivals anything you will find in contemporary fiction. Their lives, underscored by hardship, compromise and hope, are rendered both with a granddaughter's love and a journalist's insight. A beautiful book."—Gary Shteyngart, author of *The Russian Debutante's Handbook*

"*Ester and Ruzya* is an example of what's best in Russia's literary tradition—a beautifully written personal story with universal significance."
    —Nina Khrushcheva, Professor of International Affairs,
        New School University

"Beautifully written and deeply felt, Masha Gessen's *Ester and Ruzya* tells the story of the two totalitarian regimes that reigned in twentieth-century Europe from a completely fresh perspective. Gessen's description of the compromises people made to survive should force those of us living in a luckier era to think harder about what we mean by 'morality.'"
    —Anne Applebaum, Pulitzer Prize–winning author of
        Gulag: A History

MASHA GESSEN is a staff writer at *The New Yorker* and the author of several books, among them *The Future Is History: How Totalitarianism Reclaimed Russia* and *The Man Without a Face: The Unlikely Rise of Vladimir Putin.* The recipient of numerous awards, including a Guggenheim Fellowship and a Carnegie Fellowship, Gessen teaches at Amherst College and lives in New York City.

Ruzya and Yolochka

Ester and Sasha

ESTER

and

RUZYA

How My Grandmothers Survived Hitler's War and Stalin's Peace

MASHA GESSEN

DIAL PRESS TRADE PAPERBACKS

ESTER AND RUZYA
A Dial Press Trade Paperback

PUBLISHING HISTORY
Dial Press hardcover edition published November 2004
Dial Press trade paperback edition / November 2005

Published by Bantam Dell
A Division of Random House, Inc.
New York, New York

Book design by Laurie Jewell

Library of Congress Catalog Card Number: 2004045472

Dial Press is a registered trademark of Random House, Inc., and the
colophon is a trademark of Random House, Inc.

ISBN-10: 0-385-33605-5
ISBN-13: 978-0-385-33605-5

Printed in the United States of America
Published simultaneously in Canada

www.dialpress.com

146938060

THIS BOOK IS FOR MY CHILDREN

ACKNOWLEDGMENTS

The first third of this book was written while I was in Vienna as a fellow at the Institut für die Wissenschaften vom Menschen, and I thank the Institute for its generosity. The second third was written while I was a guest at my father's house on Cape Cod, and I thank Alexander Gessen for his hospitality. The final third I wrote at home in Moscow, while my baby daughter was asleep, so I thank Yael Gessen for sleeping through the night between the ages of two and four months—and express the hope that this habit may one day be reestablished. My brother, Keith Gessen, is always my first reader and best critic. This book owes a great deal to the efforts of my agent, Elyse Cheney, Dial Press editor Susan Kamil, and Beth Rashbaum, the closest of readers and the most patient of editors. But most of all, I am grateful to my grandmothers, Ruzya Solodovnik and Ester Gessen, who, incredibly, told me their stories and let me not only write but actually publish a book about them.

Contents

PROLOGUE

MARCH 1991

I was not traveling light, or lightly. I was terrified, which was to be expected after ten years (exactly) in exile: I admitted to being scared that I might not be allowed to leave the Soviet Union, but this was a red herring of a fear. I claimed not to know what had frightened me so much that I squeezed my companion's hand until her knuckles turned white as we touched down. I feared I would recognize this country and I feared I would not know it; I feared I would dislike it and I feared I would love it; I feared that my clear and certain opinions about the world and Russia in general and about my relationship to them in particular would be turned inside out—which, of course, was precisely what was about to happen.

What did I see when I imagined Russia? Snapshot memories of a few buildings and streets. The interiors of my grandmothers' apartments. My parents' drawn faces when they explained to me why we had to leave the country where I was born, and their growing exhaustion as they took each of the endless steps required to emigrate. February 18, 1981: a day that ended in the gray early morning, as the plane slowly gained altitude over an expanse of snow. I remembered our relatives, eyes red from sleeplessness and crying, lined up in two crowded rows against the chrome barrier that marked the border zone at Moscow's Sheremetyevo-Two Airport, watching two customs officers go through our belongings, packed into our "emigrant's suitcases"—cheap cardboard affairs designed to withstand exactly one journey, one way. I ran back to hand one of my aunts my drawing box, barred by customs. I ran back again to take a drag off another aunt's cigarette. I was fourteen, but this was the most difficult day of my life. We finally stepped through customs, sideways and backward so as to keep looking at their faces, receding now. They waved. Two-thirds of the way to passport control, just before their features became indistinguishable, my mother drew my head close and whispered, "Look at them. You will see all of them again, except Great-grandmother Batsheva. Look at her." What she said was absurd: everyone knew there would be no return and we would never see any of them. But she turned out to be almost exactly right: I saw all of them again, except for Great-aunt Eugenia, who died later the same year, and Great-grandmother Batsheva, who died in 1987.

As the plane began its descent now, I imagined they would be right there, pushed up against the same chrome barrier, unmoved and unchanged save for being ten years older. I tried to make out their faces in my memory, but I visualized, instead, the face of an actor I had seen in a recent Russian film, or the shadow of an old photograph. I studied every face once I stepped into the terminal, and I suspected every one of being my relative. But I saw them once I got through passport control: they really were there, behind the chrome barrier, and I recognized them immediately.

This is perhaps the place to explain family. The Russian culture and the Russian state have conspired to make the family a tight and almost immutable structure. Your family are the people who will always have to respond. A second cousin twice removed who comes to Moscow to try to get into college or to get medical help for her baby will be your houseguest and your charge no matter how small your home or how limited your means. When she leaves, you may not speak for months or years, but when the need arises or the occasion presents itself, you will simply pick up where you left off. Family consists of people one can trust—and one had better be able to, for the Soviet state held everyone responsible for the deeds not only of his parents and siblings but also cousins, aunts, and even those whose connection was hard to pin down. Thousands of people grew up during the Stalin era in special orphanages for "children of enemies of the people": having a parent arrested branded them for life. Even in later, gentler times, such as the era in which I grew up, the mere fact of having a relative who lived abroad disqualified one from any number of ostensibly sensitive jobs. Relatives could have disagreements, of course, fights and arguments, but unlike friends, they could not simply drift apart. A rift in a family was almost always a tragedy, and its consequences could be grave.

Growing up, I knew there was a large number of people whose presence in my life was a given. Our exact relationship, as determined by blood or marital ties, was often a mystery to me—I still cannot seem to retain this sort of information, interrogating some more knowledgeable cousin or another only to forget, within weeks, everything I am told. In any case, when I was young, my grandmothers' relationship hopelessly confused the picture: they were friends long before two of their children—my mother, Yolochka, and my father, Sasha—married each other, challenging the women's friendship but cementing their bond. To

me, the family as a combination of their two clans seemed to go
back unimaginable decades: their relationship, since it preceded
my parents' union, was eternal. In fact, they met seventeen years
before I was born. I had heard only one story of my parents' in-
teracting as children: my twelve-year-old father had taken my
fourteen-year-old mother sailing and gotten her soaked. This im-
plied a kind of intimacy, and I inferred that my parents had grown
up side by side—fated, clearly, to produce me. Their childhoods,
as well as the pasts of all the many other ever-present persons, occurred in an imaginary structure the pillars of which were, of
course, my two grandmothers. What I understood to be family
was very clearly two-headed. Long after I learned that this was
not the usual way of things, my grandmothers remained my two
reference points, my anchors.

I had been unanchored for ten years now, and the world's two
most important women were waiting for me at the airport; no
wonder I was scared.

My two suitcases were stuffed with things for other people:
overalls for a two-year-old cousin and a simple camera for a five-
year-old cousin, neither of whom I had ever seen; colognes for
cousins and uncles who were boys when I left; and impersonal
pretty things for their wives, whom I had never seen and who were
all, for some reason, named Natasha. For my grandmothers I was
carrying big, soft American terry-cloth towels, and panty hose. I
had never shopped for panty hose before, so just before the trip I
discovered its imprecisely descriptive sizing system. I now mentally referred to my grandmothers as "queen-size" and "petite."

In the hours on the plane the physical difference between the
two women had, in my mind, increased absurdly. I was now prepared to be met by a giantess and a midget. But the first person I
saw was my uncle Sergei, my grandfather's son from his second
marriage. He was maybe five or six years older than I, and I was

fascinated with him when I was a child. He never seemed to know I existed. And then there were my grandmothers. Ester turned out not to be quite so much bigger than Ruzya. She had recently had two hip operations, which made her shorter and slowed her down. She was not an old woman—two years to go before her seventieth birthday—and she had a penchant for bright colors. Her lipstick was a glossy fuchsia. Her skin was always the shade of a good tan, and this was more noticeable now that her hair had gone gray—tight silver curls piled high. She hugged me quickly, and just as quickly—before I had a chance to introduce my companion or say anything at all—ran through her plans for me: it was clear she had not entertained the possibility that I might have made my own. She had planned dinners and visits with relatives, and she had bought theater tickets.

My other grandmother seemed to get lost in the haste and shuffle as we filed out of the airport and piled into my uncle Sergei's car, an ancient Soviet-made Fiat, a tiny square tin box with bald rubber tires and a cracked windshield. We had a flat before we were out of the airport parking lot, and I helped Sergei change the tire as my two grandmothers looked on with awed pride. We drove to Ester's apartment, where she handed me ten rubles and a metro pass and packed me off to bed. In the days that followed, Ester proceeded to track my comings and goings with a benign intrusiveness. I submitted, for the most part, with pleasure.

After about a week I went to stay with Ruzya in the small town where she lives with her husband, Alik. I am told that she was striking as a young woman; she rarely acknowledges this. She was still beautiful at seventy-one, when I met her again. Her most remarkable feature, eyes of unlikely gray on the whitest of white—eyes from a child's drawing, the pure concept of eyes—could still turn heads. When I stayed with my grandmother Ruzya, those eyes looked at me across the table as one looks at a treasure or an unexpected, extravagant gift. She made me meals from my childhood—cabbage pie, mushroom soup, gefilte fish. She told me things about my childhood that I remembered differently or—more often—did not remember at all.

These women knew me. And what did I know about them? I remembered Ruzya's smell, but I think it was just the smell of fresh air and the thick suede jacket she had often worn. That jacket had long since worn out, and the air was never that clean anymore. I remembered Ruzya's white-gray hair, straight and light as down, and her brisk, impatient walk, and I recognized this. I remembered Ruzya's affection and the hard, cracked skin of her fingers stroking my cheek. Or I thought I did. I remembered Ester's lilting tones and the funny way she pronounced some words, and I recognized this too.

I also recognized the country to which I had returned, and this recognition changed my life. This was a country I had hated for all the anti-Semitic taunts I had heard as a child, for my parents' constant pained worry that my brother and I would be denied a future for being Jewish, and most of all, for forcing my family to break into two parts—the four of us who went to America, and everyone else, who stayed behind. This was also the place I had loved easily and unconsciously as a child, then tragically, as only a teenager can, for the three years it took us to get out. I felt the full force of this pull on my first trip back.

On my first morning in Moscow I woke up on the low bed in the smallest of my grandmother Ester's three rooms. The twelve-foot ceiling—ceilings are high in prerevolutionary Russian buildings—made me feel like I was at the bottom of a well-lit well. I remembered the feeling, and I remembered being scared by it as a child, but I liked it now because I knew it. It was about eight in the morning—two hours before Ester would be awake—and I wanted to go out right away, to test the familiarity alone. I dressed quickly, suddenly aware of the conspicuous foreignness of my long pointy shoes. (As anyone who has traveled knows, footwear is always a good indicator of belonging. Most Russians at the time were wearing rounded-toe shoes on thick rubber soles.) I ran down the eight flights of stairs.

Ester lives in the very center of Moscow, in a narrow court-yard off the wide avenue that had just been renamed Tverskaya after decades as Gorky Street. This was the part of Moscow I had known and loved most intensely as a child. I remembered once, when I was twelve or thirteen, making an unauthorized escape from the dacha where we were spending the summer to travel the one hour into Moscow, coming up the long escalator at the Pushkinskaya metro station, emerging at Tverskaya and being hit by the sweet, dry, dusty smell of the Moscow summer, knowing then that this was the place I belonged. I wondered what I would feel now. I wondered, in fact, whether I would feel anything at all. It was early March, which in Moscow falls just outside the dead of winter; there was snow everywhere, in unsightly frozen lumps, old and black. But the morning was sunny, and the sidewalk under my silly shoes was dry and dusty; the dust rose with the warm air, and I felt the smell. I was home. The problem was, I had spent ten years trying to convince myself—and everyone else—that this was not my home. A country that had treated us so badly could lay no claim to that title.

Over the following few days I learned that the problem was even deeper than I had imagined. Not only was this strange and frightening country the place where I felt most at home, it was, in March 1991, undisputedly the most exciting place on Earth. The collapse of the Soviet regime was bloody around the edges of the country, and endlessly sexy in the center, where debates on the most important issues of history and the world were rushing forward, colliding, zigzagging—and producing clear and apparent consequences in the life of the actual country. I had taken a story assignment to get myself to Moscow—it was more of an excuse than a reason to travel, since the magazine seemed to have little actual interest in the article—but now I quickly became engrossed in the reporting. After this trip I would take more and more assignments that brought me to Russia—until, three years later, I would move back permanently. Like many other journalists, I fell in love with the story. But the story often confused me. How much of the past needs to be exposed and examined before there is a future? How much can be forgiven? How much can we understand?

Many years after my first visit I met a historian who had spent the early 1990s going through KGB archives. A former dissident, he had planned to publish the documents he unearthed but ended up keeping most of the secrets he found. He had entered the archives with a clear set of standards and a simple goal: to learn how the KGB had really functioned and then to tell the story. He soon understood that the story foiled the standards and refused to be told. A famous poet's two best friends turned out to be informers, but in their regular reports to the secret police they painted a picture of her as an avid Stalinist—and this ultimately kept the poet out of prison. A dissident exiled to Siberia finally agreed to denounce his subversive activities just before his term ran out—or so an agent's report claimed—but as it turned out, he had told the agent he was sick to death of the KGB's nosing around and felt like returning to his old profession. A prominent pianist agreed to sign on as an informer—only to be dropped as "useless ballast" a few years later, after failing to supply a single bit of information. After reconstructing several such stories, the historian gave up on all the information he found—the relationship between these documents and the lives of those they concerned was impossible to decipher.

The Soviet system aimed to strip its subjects of the ability to choose. The course of history was preordained, and so was the course of human life. Any Soviet citizen who sought to control his own destiny came up against false trade-offs. The poet's friends secured her safety but sacrificed their own integrity. The dissident and the pianist sacrificed their reputations in exchange for temporary peace of mind. Most Soviet citizens, I think, never questioned this system or their own role in it. But many of those who did spent years and lifetimes in search of a decent compromise—only to discover, sooner or later, that there was no such thing. Each of my grandmothers was burdened with a conscience, which meant that both of them at crucial points in their lives tried to find a way to make an honest peace with the system. They had vastly different ways of doing it: Ruzya made conscious compromises while Ester, most of the time, remained defiant.

In early 1994 I moved back to Moscow. My grandmothers argued about my move, told me that it was a terrible idea but welcomed me and proceeded to worry that I would change my mind and leave again. Once, I almost did. When I moved, I set a limit for my stay in Russia, one that aimed to calm my own fears, as well as my father's and my friends'. I said I would stay as long as the country did not go back to what it had been. It was an unintentionally vague standard: certainly the process of breaking away from the Soviet past would sooner or later be reversed, and just as certainly, the Soviet regime as we had known it would never be restored. I would have to decide for myself whether the reversal went so far that I had to become an exile again. In January 1995, standing in the shower in my grandmother Ruzya's Moscow apartment, where I was living the first year back in Russia, I considered whether the week-old war in Chechnya meant I should end my love affair with the country and go back to the United States. Was there a way to remain in Russia without entering into a compromise with the state, which was killing people? This was how I became a war reporter.

I did not tell my grandmothers I was going to Chechnya that time—or any of the dozen or so times thereafter. They would have worried too much. Whenever I was in Moscow, they called me at least once a day to check on my whereabouts. They worried about my safety and sanity and otherwise tried to take up grandmothering where they had left off. I pushed back gently, securing my independence. And I went over for tea and asked endless questions. In return, they told me their lives—and the confusing story I am trying to write. The story of a country that does not know when to forget and when not to forgive became the story of two women. There is also the story of Jakub, Ester's father, who made his own choices and his own compromises, living in a ghetto in Nazi-occupied Bialystok. And there is my own story. It is all of a piece.

PART ONE

DREAMS

1920–1941

Ruzya

Ester

CHAPTER ONE

Like any place that has been lost, Bialystok was heaven on Earth. Or the center of the universe. That, in fact, it was—or at least it was a sort of universal crossroads. It had been ruled by Prussia, Russia, and Poland, and its streets rang with Yiddish, Polish, Hebrew, Belarusian, German, and Russian: this was perhaps why Esperanto was invented there. It was also—no, it was most importantly—a center of Jewish life in Poland between the two world wars, when Poland was the center of Jewish life in Europe. More than half of its one hundred thousand residents were Jewish; and Jews, having lived there for five centuries, dominated the city's business, political, and cultural life. The current crop of Judeophile Polish historians is fond of claiming that Bialystok in the interwar period was spared the ugly anti-Semitic incidents that grew frequent in the rest of Poland, but this is not so. It is nonetheless true that Bialystok had more synagogues per capita than any city in the world, that in addition to Jewish schools and the world's first Jewish ambulance service it had Jewish old-age homes and soup kitchens, an orphanage and various other charities, and that all of this earned it the moniker "The City with the Golden Heart" among European Jewry.

Bialystok was neither particularly flat nor especially hilly. It had a broad main promenade and a web of crooked cobblestone streets. It had a Jewish quarter that was largely poor, and it had other, more affluent neighborhoods, where the landlords were mixed and the tenants were mostly Jewish. It had ambition. Forty years after the city was destroyed, Jewish survivors living in New York published a memorial book that overflowed with pride in the city's prewar accomplishments: "Bialystok's streets grew more beautiful. . . . Electric cables were laid under the ground, streets were widened, avenues were lined with trees, and a new sewer system was installed. Large new apartment buildings and four-family homes were constructed."

In one of these four-family homes on Zlota Street lived the Goldbergs, my grandmother Ester's family. The name of their street in Polish and their surname in Yiddish meant "golden," and they might have joked about this without a trace of embarrassment, because they really were one of Bialystok's golden families. Her father, Jakub, was a big man. Physically, he was hulking: nearly two meters tall, and robust to the point of appearing about to burst out of his suits. Politically, he was imposing. A member of the General Zionist organization, he was an activist of European stature, which certainly commanded respect locally. And locally, too, he was active, as a member of the municipal council—the city's main governing body—and, later, of the *kehilla,* the board elected by the Jewish community. Financially, chutzpah was his main capital. A bank he had inherited from his grandmother went bust in the worldwide economic crash of 1929, but Jakub refused to scale back: the fancy apartment, one of the city's few phone lines, Ester's governess, and the other help—none of this would be given up. "If I die tomorrow, do I want to be remembered as the

Goldberg who paid his debts on time?" He apparently preferred to be remembered as the Goldberg who knew how to live well. He would ultimately be remembered as neither, but he was basically right: life would not go on like this much longer, and, anyway, he did not mind the gaggle of creditors following him around. He briefly tried going into business by buying a train car's worth of candles he planned to resell, but the merchandise arrived without wicks. He ultimately found a job selling insurance for a large Italian company, but he never did pay off all his debts. Nor did he buy an insurance policy—a fact his wife discovered when their apartment was robbed while they were away on holiday, and his descendants learned about six decades later, when the company in question began paying on the life insurance policies of Holocaust victims.

Jakub's wife, Bella, on the other hand, was short, even tiny, and held to an entirely different set of political beliefs. She was a member of the Bund, the Jewish workers' party. The wife of one of Bialystok's most prominent Zionists worked as, of all things, a Polish teacher at a Yiddish school. That is, while her husband devoted much of his life to promoting the study of Hebrew for the Jews' eventual return to Palestine, Bella earned her daily bread by helping Jewish children become that much more assimilated by learning the Polish language. But then, her independence did him proud, for she was a university graduate—an anomaly among Polish women at the time, especially Polish Jewish women, especially women from Chasidic families. Yes, they were both from a Chasidic family—they were cousins—and they were both atheists.

Those are the facts, as best they can be established. What could they mean? Perhaps that the Goldbergs formed that rare happy union of two people who continue to grow, independently, in more or less the same direction, conquering the world together. Raised strictly Orthodox, together they gradually mapped their path away from religion until one day Jakub shaved off his beard and exchanged the wide-brimmed fur-trimmed hat and long coat of a Chasid for a generic European suit.

Or they may have lived the uneasy union of two people who, while each is driven to act on his convictions, view the world in fundamentally different ways. As a Zionist, Jakub was convinced the Jews belonged in Palestine. Bella, a Bundist, would have subscribed to a different utopian vision, that of Jewish autonomy within Eastern Europe. She was a socialist; he was a banker. He belonged to a party that aimed to establish Jewish national unity as a far more important factor than class; her party opposed any political initiatives that were based solely on the Jewish issue. The argument between their two parties was constantly fought on the floor of the municipal council. On election day Jakub and Bella walked the streets of Bialystok with their respective placards, and he denied her his customary courtesy of walking on the pavement while she walked on the sidewalk (to lessen the nearly two-foot difference in their height).

History, in its way, has since settled their argument. The Zionists—that is, those of them who had the will, money, and luck to move to Palestine before World War II—survived. The assimilationists, or, as the Bundists were known, the "localists," died where they lived. But then, murder, even systematic and ideologically driven murder, is a function of circumstance more than anything else. Witness the Goldberg case. He was killed; she survived.

In the years leading up to his death and her unwitting escape, the arguments may or may not have subsided, but they did reach agreement on one thing. Aside from matters of politics and matters of religion, they lived a single joint project: their daughter, Ester, who was born in 1923 and grew up, as only a child of total love and devotion can, knowing that she was the smartest, most beautiful, and luckiest girl, who happened to live in the center of the universe.

MAY 28, 1936

This is easily the best day of the year. For the holiday of Shavuot, the Bialystok Hebrew Gymnasium suspends classes and marches its entire student population of several hundred from its imposing brick headquarters on Sienkiewicz Street, down Lipowa, the main street—decorated in lavish green for the holiday—through the park and past the staring occupants of the Forty-first Infantry Division barracks, and into Pietrasze Forest for an entire day of campfires, singing, and eating cheese, honey, and triangular kreplachs. The small kids—the three- to five-year-olds—are brought along for their traditional introduction to Jewish schooling, and they run around sticky with the honey meant to sweeten the taste of scholarship. The older kids—Ester is thirteen, which places her in the dignified middle of the gymnasium's age spectrum—throw themselves into the forest silliness, running around and screaming, only to slow down after a bit for some earnest confessions out of earshot of all but a few close confidantes and for the occasional argument on the political (read: Zionist) issue of the day.

It is still a couple of hours till sundown but the air is starting to cool and some of the children are already casting about for their things when Ester sees a girl from one of the upper classes running awkwardly from the edge of the forest. She is a big girl, with strong legs and thick arms and a mane of light brown hair that is now undone, flying away from her face in a way that somehow, to Ester, signals fear. She stops when she reaches a smoldering campfire and, standing firmly now, starts screaming, her words apparent nonsense: "We are surrounded!" It takes a few minutes for the mood to shift and her words to begin making sense. The soldiers from the Forty-first Infantry Division have encircled this part of the forest and are swearing not to allow any of the "little kikes" out. The two boys with whom Hanna—this is the messenger's name—tried to leave the party have been so severely beaten they are still trying to make their way back here.

The rest of the day leaves no room to be a thirteen-year-old. The teachers and some of the upperclassmen huddle, while the other older students herd the small kids into a clearing and proceed to count them obsessively, every two or three minutes. A boy from the graduating class is dispatched to try to sneak out to alert the authorities. The authorities are personified this time by Jakub Goldberg, who, being an atheist, is ignoring the holiday and working in his office in the municipal council. For the following five hours he feels very much like his thirteen-year-old daughter: his first, overconfident call to the police elicits a satisfied chuckle on the other end of the line. His calls to leaders of the various Jewish organizations succeed only in raising the level of hysteria. As the news seeps into Bialystok's tiny telephone network, crying women and shouting men start running through city streets toward the Pietrasze Forest. Perhaps the spectacle of these parents, desperate and immobile at the edge of the forest, in plain view of the Forty-first Infantry Division barracks, moves someone. Or perhaps whoever thought up the joke is satisfied with having reduced the Jews to a state of agitated helplessness. Or perhaps the soldiers get tired and want to go to sleep. It is eleven o'clock when the soldiers finally disband, allowing the children to run through the darkness toward the receiving line of weeping parents.

AUGUST 1936

A couple of hours' drive from Bialystok, Brok is a resort town. Its joys are quiet. A river, a terrace on which to take the air, an occasional visit from a young man. The suitors began to come last year, when Ester was just twelve. Uncommonly well developed for her age, she had attracted the attentions of a college student. Her mother warded him off with unwitting deftness, though, when she shouted from the balcony, as the young couple prepared to board a ferry, that twelve-year-olds rode free. The poor student not only abandoned his wooing immediately but left the resort altogether, so frightened he apparently was by this brush with potential sin or even crime.

This year's routine—the daily forays to the beach, the Saturday visits from Jakub, who stays in Bialystok during the week—has lately been enlivened by the appearance of another suitor, a Polish officer in training, a slim but dashing character in his military uniform. Bella and Ester have taken a room with a terrace in a large private home, since far too many of the pensions now announce, alongside their name, "No dogs or Jews." Ester is sipping tea with the young officer on the terrace; she must stay home this Saturday morning because Jakub is due in from a neighboring town where he has been visiting his sister. He takes the three-hour trip from Bialystok weekly, often stopping off at the house of one of his more progressive relatives, someone who would not frown upon his traveling on the Shabbat.

As Jakub approaches the house, he waves to Ester and visibly picks up speed. He bounds up the stairs and traverses the terrace in two leaping steps, then grabs the young man by the collar and holds him suspended in midair like a small animal, for a split second, before stepping back toward the stairway and sending the charming conversationalist tumbling down.

He plops down in the chair that was just a moment ago occupied by the officer. Ester, who must have leaped up when her date was so rudely ended, continues to stand awkwardly, half expecting an explanation, half wondering whether she overstepped an unspoken boundary by entertaining a grown man.

"I saw that little snake just yesterday," Jakub offers. "In one of those pickets."

Those pickets have been plaguing the Jews of Poland. Young men have been lining up in front of Jewish-owned shops in all sorts of towns, holding placards calling for a boycott of Jewish businesses. Customers—even Jewish customers, terrified at the thought of crossing picket lines with no one (certainly not the police) there to protect them—have been scared away. Jewish stores have been closing.

"*Prec z zidami, zidovecki z nami,* eh?" Jakub asks, quoting one of the picketers' favorite slogans: "Off with the Jews, but we'll take the Jewish women." He is trying to make sure his daughter is on his side. He does not need to do that. She has been thinking a lot this summer, ever since the incident in the woods, and she has made some decisions. First, she is happy that her father won the argument with her mother and she was sent to the Hebrew school rather than the Yiddish one. But more than that, she has to leave this country. They all do. She is now a hundred percent behind the plan her father laid out for her years ago: they stay in Poland until she graduates the gymnasium, in 1940, and then she will travel to Jerusalem to attend the university there, and this will help her family get vouchers to enter Palestine. (Though Jakub could use his position within the Zionist establishment to angle for vouchers sooner, this seems to all of them like an altogether more sensible plan.) In Palestine they will all work—surely Bella will see the need for this soon, perhaps even today, when she hears of the officer incident—to build a Jewish state. Meanwhile, Ester has resolved that when school resumes she will become an ever more active member of the Ha-Shomer ha-Zair organization, a leftist youth Zionist group, and will double the time she spends walking door to door with her Keren Ka'emet box, collecting money to buy back her homeland from the Arabs.

By the mid to late 1930s, Polish Jews had come to live with a constant sense of danger, perhaps even doom. Though only a few would have suspected that the ultimate threat would come from outside the country, most Jews had the sense that life as they had known it was ending. Pogroms were coming in waves. Even in Jewish-dominated Bialystok, things were changing fast. As a result of the anti-Semitic economic boycott and a number of state-enforced measures—including one mandating stores to stay shut on Sundays, a measure intended specifically to ban the Jewish-owned stores from reopening right after the Shabbat, as they had always done—the number of Jewish-owned stores in Bialystok dropped from 663 to 563 between 1932 and 1937, while the number of Christian-owned ones rose from 58 to 310. The state quashed the Jews' attempts to retreat farther into their quasi-autonomous existence. The government controlled the budgets of the *kehillot,* the Jewish councils, reducing them to largely symbolic functions. As for the Jewish schools, not only did they receive no state support but their diplomas were not recognized by the state, forcing graduates to stand for humiliating, openly discriminatory exams if they wanted to continue their education at universities—which, in their turn, imposed quotas on the number of Jews admitted. Jews who were accepted to universities were required to sit separately, on the so-called ghetto bench (instead, they stood in protest). Nor did those who chose not to seek higher education fare any better. In a time when the state was increasingly taking control of the economy, Jews were banned from jobs in state institutions of all sorts, from government agencies to tobacco factories. Protests elicited more restrictive measures—like when Ester's Bialystok Hebrew Gymnasium went on strike in response to a pogrom in a nearby town and promptly had its license taken away. From that point on, final exams were administered by a state commission that brought a Catholic priest along as the Hebrew interpreter. Students took pride in their defiance and the small ways they found of getting around the rigged system—like when they contrived to speak ridiculously fast Hebrew to show up the priest, whose Hebrew was evidently rusty. Their parents, meanwhile, were coming to the realization that they could no longer live where twenty generations of Jews had made their home.

People rarely choose change when other options are available. By the mid to late thirties, Polish Jews no longer saw an alternative. Their decisions stemmed from despair, and their main hope was to survive. Contrary to the often-cited view of Jews politely and naively accepting their doom in Europe, the truth in Poland, at any rate, was that Jews had lost their illusions. Moderate Jewish political parties were edged out by the radicals: on the one hand the Bund, which wooed supporters with its increasingly forceful rhetoric of resistance, and on the other hand radicalized Zionist parties, which supplanted Jakub's once-popular party, the General Zionists. Where the old Zionists devised extensive educational, cultural, and propaganda programs aimed at encouraging the Jews of the Diaspora to become interested in someday making their home in the place known to them as Erez Israel (and to the rest of the world as British-ruled Palestine), the new organizations were dedicated to transporting the maximum number of people there in the shortest possible period of time—no easy task, considering the increasingly heavy restrictions placed on immigration by the

British authorities. Arab-Jewish tensions in Palestine by the end of the 1930s verged on war. Following the Arab revolt of 1936, the number of Jews allowed to enter the country dwindled every year.

Not that there was any other place to go—even for those who were willing to risk leaving one country only to encounter anti-Semitism elsewhere. The most popular destination for émigrés of the pre–World War I period, the United States, had suspended its hospitality. With anti-Semitism there on the rise, as it always is in times of hardship, America issued a total of just thirty-three thousand visas to European Jews in the five years following Hitler's ascent to power in Germany in 1933. Neighboring Soviet Russia was, for the new generation, a terra incognita: the mainstream papers reported on the famine and then the purges and show trials there, while the leftist press wrote of equal opportunities for all classes, religious and ethnic groups—but all of them may as well have been writing about a different planet and not about a country that literally could be reached by foot: the border had been sealed for over fifteen years, so Russia was not so much a neighboring country as the end of the world. That left dreams of Erez Israel.

Thanks largely to the efforts of the "pioneering Zionist" parties, as they were known, a sort of Jewish autonomy was increasingly taking shape in Erez Israel, whose Jewish population reached about six hundred thousand by 1940. In Eastern Europe, meanwhile, the struggle focused on the distribution of immigration certificates: the quota was set by the British, but the coveted papers were handed out by the World Zionist Organization, which made its decisions in accordance with a convoluted set of criteria aimed at maintaining a semblance of political stability in both Erez Israel and the Diaspora. As a ranking member of the General Zionists, Jakub could have claimed a certificate whenever he chose. But Bella's younger sister Helena, an agronomist, had gone to Erez Israel and returned to Warsaw disappointed: she had not found work. And who would hire a Polish-language teacher in Palestine? Jakub and Bella had decided to wait until Ester finished high school. Staying in Poland past that point was not an option—not unless they wanted their only daughter to claim a spot on the ghetto bench. Ester's organization, Ha-Shomer ha-Zair (Hebrew for "Young Guard"), was one of the "pioneering Zionist" groups with a distinctly socialist political orientation. Jakub cringed at the leftist rhetoric but supported his daughter's activities in the interests of the greater good: Zionism. Bella, who had resigned herself to her family's Zionist path, could at least rejoice in her daughter's choice of leftist politics. The group was a kind of heavily ideologized training camp for making *aliyah*—emigrating to Palestine. Shomrim, as its members were known, most of them middle-school and high-school students, were assigned to units of about twenty people each. After graduation these children of Jewish teachers, merchants, and factory workers lived together in their small communes, learning the skills necessary to work the Holy Land, where, once their immigration certificates finally arrived, they would go on to found kibbutzes.

Ester herself, coming as she did from a relatively well-to-do family, assumed she would go to university rather than join a commune—a proposition that required money both in Poland, where she attended the private Hebrew gymnasium, and in Erez Israel. Still, the life of the Ha-Shomer ha-Zair, with its uniforms, its songs, its heroics, and its dreams, was supremely, overwhelmingly, consummately appealing. The uniforms? They were vaguely military in style, with neckerchiefs—the more or less generic uniform of scouts and "young guards" everywhere, with the ideological advantage of erasing class distinctions in dress and the practical advantage of making shopping trips and tailor visits with Bella superfluous. The songs? There was the one in Hebrew that said that "the Jordan River has two banks, this one is ours, and that one is ours too." It was the anthem of a different, more militant Zionist organization, but it sounded good, so they sang it anyway. The heroics? One had to be willing to live for the organization and carry out its orders, no matter how difficult. The organization could, for example, choose to separate couples: that happened to an older girl Ester knew, Chaika Grossman, whose fiancé was dispatched to build the future in Erez Israel while she stayed behind to organize—for a total of twelve years, as it turned out. And the dream? It was a perfect dream, of a land unseen and a life barely imagined.

Life, in other words, was elsewhere. The universal theme of teenage existence—the present as prologue—was magnified manifold by both the wretchedness of life as it was and the hurdles and uncertainties on the way to the imagined future.

The dreams were all the more powerful for Ester because she had someone with whom to dream them. The star of Bialystok's Shomrim was a boy named Isaj Drogoczinski. He came from an unconscionably poor family—he had had to stop schooling after seventh grade to go work at a leather factory—and he was fiercely articulate. By the age of sixteen he had become the group's main ideologue; as Ester would later find out, he was also the author of most of the unsigned editorials in *Unzer Lebn* ("Our Life"), the leading Yiddish-language daily in Bialystok. He and Ester had become a couple when she was fourteen and he fifteen, sometime during the year following the summer of her unlucky Brok affair, and from that point on their future was never in doubt: "There was never a question in our minds that we would marry. He was, naturally, also planning to go to Palestine."

Jakub and Bella were less than thrilled with Ester's early and firm choice of a match from such a poor, uneducated family, but they resigned themselves to the fact about a year into the relationship. That spring the leather factory where Isaj worked burned down, and the boy, luckier than some of the workers, ended up in the hospital with horrible burns all over his body. He was hospitalized for about two months, and Ester spent her days by his bedside the entire time, eventually moving Bella to start visiting him in the hospital as well. By the time he was released, half emaciated boy and half scar tissue, his place in the Goldberg household was no longer questioned.

There is perhaps nothing so expansive as teenage romance with an ideological foundation. Isaj and Ester's romantic moments were shot through with their politics. On the way to a Zionist summer camp in the Carpathians in 1939—the year Ester turned sixteen—they read the stories of Yosef Hayyim Brenner to each other; Ester had given Isaj the book. Brenner's biography, which they knew by heart, was a study in the history of Eastern European Jewry. He had been born and studied at a yeshiva in Ukraine, become a Bund activist in Belarus, lived briefly in Bialystok, served in the Russian army, fled to London during the Russo-Japanese war, become a socialist Zionist, and emigrated to Palestine in 1909. There he wrote in Hebrew, describing the Jews' blood-drenched existence in Russia, their sweat-soaked life in London, and still more bitterly, their humiliated position in Palestine. He was killed in the Arab riots of 1921. Like thousands of Eastern European Jews of their generation, Ester and Isaj adopted as their manifesto Brenner's story "*Hu amar la*" ("He Told Her"), the monologue of a Jewish youth addressing his mother on the eve of a pogrom. He tells her the time has come to stop relying on the anti-Semitic authorities for protection from the hoodlums and to wage "a war of the poor sons of Yankel against the powerful descendants of Chmielnicki." Chmielnicki was, in the seventeenth century, the Ukrainian Cossack leader who presided over the massacre of more than one hundred thousand Jews. Yankel, a name Brenner picked to represent a generic Jew, happened to be Ester's father's Yiddish name. Isaj had been just as poor and as desperately angry as the narrator. Clearly, this was their story, and their future.

CHAPTER TWO

1925

Moscow, for a five-year-old, is a cramped, stuffed apartment full of little things and little smells, surrounded by big places and big smells. This place, where her mother has brought Ruzya and her brother, Yasha, smells like the zoo, or perhaps like the circus. Ruzya has been inside the circus only once, but the big domed building is just around the corner from their house, and the smell, sweet and repulsive at the same time, drifts and catches her when she goes to the store with her mother or for a walk with her brother. But no, this smell is more like the zoo: it does not come in waves and does not mix with street odors like the smell from the circus; it sits still and heavy and resists letting you in at first, before grabbing you and sticking to you from all sides. And there are bars everywhere, on the windows and the doors, making it all look a little bit like a cage. This is definitely more like the zoo than like the circus.

This is the Butyrki. The name sounds like the Russian word for "bottles," but Ruzya knows that it is a place rather than a thing, and an important place. Her mother, Eva, has been coming here every week for a long, long time, and she has always taken a large bag of food with her. She says it is for Uncle Lev. Ruzya has never seen Uncle Lev. Of all the relatives she has vaguely heard about, Ruzya knows only a couple of cousins on her father's side. Most relatives, she knows, belong to the family's "other side," a collection of people who are all somehow connected to her but whom she has never seen. These are Eva's wealthier relatives. Ruzya knows that some of them are doctors, and all of them seem somehow more important, better, than her little family, which consists of her mother, Eva, her father, Moshe, and her older brother, Yasha, who is ten years old to her five.

Uncle Lev is confusing: her mother keeps going to see him, but Ruzya gets the sense that he is one of the "better" set. That is what makes this visit unlike a trip to the zoo or even the circus. Ruzya has a distinct sense that it will be Uncle Lev who will be doing the looking. She and Yasha, dressed in their best suits—both a variation on silly sailors' outfits—are being shown off. Even though Uncle Lev, as it turns out, is the one sitting in a cage.

It takes a long time to get to his cage: first a woman checks their papers and opens a heavy door with a clanking lock to let them into a tiny corridor. Then Ruzya and Yasha have to stand in the corridor, smelling the smell and feeling a wet chill creep through their bones, while their mother goes into a little room with a man in uniform. Then more clanking doors.

"Mama, what is Butyrki?" Ruzya asks, grabbing Eva's hand so she can keep pace while her mother answers.

"*This* is Butyrki," says Eva. She often answers questions like this, without really giving an answer. Ruzya wishes she knew how to ask questions that made it clear what she wants to know. Mostly, though, she just tries to ask her father things.

"Butyrki is a jail, stupid," says Yasha, wedging himself between

Ruzya and their mother. This is a scary answer, and Ruzya looks up at the uniformed man who is walking them down the corridor—but no, he does not seem angry with Yasha. Maybe it really is a jail.

Uncle Lev is a tall man, meaty and beautiful like their mother, but at first he seems small, sitting at a large gray table in the middle of his cage. The uniformed man lets them into the cage and stands by the door, arms crossed on his chest, while they talk. Uncle Lev smiles a lot and hugs them, and touches their faces, saying they are so soft, so tender. He smells horrible, and his hands and his face are hard and prickly. But Ruzya decides she likes him, because he has a kind smile and he asks questions she likes answering.

"Do you want to study?"

"Yes!"

"Do you want to learn to sing and dance?"

"Yes!"

"Can you sing a song for me?"

Ruzya loves to sing, but Eva hates it when she does. Eva can sing beautifully. Adults, especially men, often ask her to, and she leans against a wall and makes music with her voice. Ruzya decides to impress Uncle Lev with one of the songs from Eva's repertoire.

" 'I once loved you / And love may still . . .' "

Uncle Lev leans back in his gray chair and laughs happily, loudly, and Eva laughs along with him. Yasha snickers. No one seems annoyed. Ruzya is happy.

She never saw Uncle Lev again. A member of the Socialist Party, he was exiled to the Urals following his lengthy internment at the Butyrki prison in Moscow. His punishment for holding the wrong set of political beliefs—he was not a Bolshevik—was mild by Soviet standards, a function of the relatively benign period when he was arrested and who knows what sort of good luck. He and his wife were allowed to live in the big city of Sverdlovsk (formerly and now again known as Yekaterinburg) and to work. What they did for a living, Ruzya does not remember—or may never have known—but they apparently made more money than their childless family required, so every month Uncle Lev sent his sister money so that her children might have music and language lessons.

Yasha danced with their father's confident grace and sang with their mother's ease. Ruzya, big-boned like their mother but short, moved with a heavy uncertainty that infuriated dance teachers. Her attempts at singing caused instructors to declare her unteachable. In language lessons, though, she proved she had a steel-trap memory and a learner's logic. German—the most popularly studied foreign language at the time—came so easily she hardly thought of it as either a calling or a worthy hobby. She envied Yasha his music lessons.

Ruzya attended a remarkable school in the center of Moscow, the enclave of the educated if not always the privileged. She was born in Ukraine, in the old Pale of Settlement, but her family, like so many others, moved to the big city almost as soon as the new regime allowed Jews finally to choose where they lived. She was too young to remember her old home, but it had been in a small town with a single main street where horses moved in clouds of dust. Ruzya's new home, in Moscow, was a semibasement apartment, its windows just level with the sidewalk. First Kolobovsky Lane was not exactly a central avenue—just a crooked side street with a slight incline, lined with old three- and four-story apartment buildings—but it was only steps away from the most important places in the new Russia, so the sidewalks outside Ruzya's windows were always crowded. The Kremlin, recently reestablished as the seat of power—after the revolution the capital was moved back to Moscow from St. Petersburg—was no more than a twenty-minute walk. The headquarters of the secret police was even closer, as were the old luxurious hotels where the country's new rulers had taken up residence. Thousands of people in Moscow at the time were starting their lives anew, with new roles in the new society. They moved into the city, forcing its old residents to make room, quite literally, by giving up their apartments to the newcomers. The four-room apartment Ruzya's family shared with a lone, quiet elderly woman had a couple of years earlier also belonged to someone. But so had everyone else's home: this was a time that had no past.

Eva and Moshe adapted to the big city no worse than anyone else. They were not your usual shtetl Jews but educated people— he an accountant, she a nurse—and they found work easily. They did not have a lot, but neither did anyone they knew, so, even as they grew accustomed to a permanent gnawing hunger, they did not think of themselves as poor: they simply thought of the epoch as cruel. There were those who had more—Eva's relatives, who had lived in Moscow for years—but they rarely saw these people, and in First Kolobovsky Lane everyone's clothes showed signs of wear and everyone's stomach was concave.

Life was difficult, but it had always been so for Eva and Moshe—not because of poverty or hunger but because, Moshe had come to believe, his wife had not been born to be happy. She had survived several major illnesses, she had lost a baby girl— Yasha's twin, the first Ruzya—at birth, she had been robbed of her beauty by a thyroid disorder, and she seemed to carry the pain around with her: it came out in constant explosions, major and minor. Perhaps because her health was so precarious she never felt fully settled anywhere, and their apartment, even as over the years it filled with children and belongings, never ceased to feel like a place that was occupied temporarily and accidentally. Moshe was afflicted with a clarity of vision that made him aware of all the cracks in their existence, but he felt as helpless to do anything about them as he was to stop loving Eva desperately and fully. Had anyone asked him, he never would have complained, for he had what he was sure no other man could have: a daughter, his own little girl, who was smarter, prettier, and kinder than any other. He had given her an unusual name in honor of his beloved stepmother, who was Polish. Little Ruzya's every step felt like his personal accomplishment, and the fact that she was attending school in Moscow made Moshe a successful man.

Ruzya's entering class, owing in no small part to the good graces and residual ethnocentrism of the Jewish first-grade teacher, who handpicked her group, comprised mostly the children of the Jewish intelligentsia—engineers, teachers, doctors, and more than anything else, accountants. They made a point of not thinking about their Jewishness. Stripped of religion—Ruzya's parents had given it up with apparent ease—sprung from the Pale, and relieved of the myriad discriminatory laws that governed Jewish life in czarist Russia, they really did not see much point in even a secular Jewish identity. True, Soviet documents always specified the bearer's "nationality," which really referred to ethnic origin, but the new generation believed this was done in the spirit of diversity. This generation was fated to live through World War II, and after it, through a viciously anti-Semitic period in Russian history, but most of them, just like Ruzya, retained only the vaguest identification with their Jewishness and found things that seemed too clearly or vocally Jewish consistently distasteful.

In sixth grade, Ruzya and about ten of her classmates grew into a group of friends that would hold together for six decades. They adored most of their teachers, but one was incomparable. She punctuated her history classes with a single expression: "And this is no mere coincidence." Ruzya, therefore, knew she would be a history teacher. She would teach school—never college—and inform her youngsters that nothing in the world's memory was "a mere coincidence."

She would indeed study to become a history teacher, but even before she graduated university she would come to think of that decision as the first and biggest mistake of her life. By the time she became an adult, she would begin to see it as a dream from a different era, the era of her childhood. The people of her generation recall the 1930s, and especially the 1920s, before the purges and show trials, as a time of unrelenting romanticism. The first generation born after the revolution, Ruzya and her friends believed they would build a future of equality, where the good things, from food to literacy, would be plentiful and universally shared, and the bad things, from poverty to anti-Semitism, would be but a memory. Every undertaking, be it organizing, building, or teaching, they imagined as heroic.

Most members of Ruzya's generation lost their illusions slowly, or not at all. Some managed not to notice or question the purges, even the arrests of friends and relatives: these began when they were children and reached into every apartment building by the time they were teenagers. Some continued to believe every word from the government even as their lives filled with secrets. Ruzya was a doubter, and a lucky one, because every member of her gang seemed to lose his illusions at about the same pace, and this helped keep all of them safe. It was a gradual process, although Ruzya would remember several incidents as eye-opening; in any case, by the time she received her historian's degree, she was sure that most of what she had been taught was a lie.

MAY 1933

Ruzya is strolling with Boba, one of her classmates and also one of the gang. He is stout, round-headed, very talented in the sciences, and very happy, always, to discuss their respective dreams of future heroics. Like all of their friends, they have no doubt that, personally and collectively, they have a giant job of future-building ahead of them, and they consider it their duty to engage in some rhetorical practice as often as possible.

"I am sure I'll be posted to a rural school somewhere," says Ruzya.

"Probably."

"And do you know something? I am not scared one bit."

"Why would you be?" Boba asks importantly.

"Well, it will be uncomfortable, no running water or indoor sewage."

"True."

"And the children—you know, the children will be ill-prepared. They have a shortage of teachers in the rural areas, and some children may not have attended school at all."

"I know that."

"But these are challenges. I do not expect things to be easy. And these problems do not scare me at all."

"Of course," Boba says, forcing his voice into the lower octave from which it keeps slipping. "If I thought you frightened of those things, I would not respect you."

In another four decades they will have a long and tortured love affair that will ultimately collapse under the weight of their mutual stabilities, but for now their passion is reserved for the Soviet future. Standing in front of Ruzya's building, just to the right of her apartment's basement windows, they say good-bye to each other, then nod, acknowledging the gravity and righteousness of their mission and their conversation. But this does not seem to convey the emotion that fills them. So they shake hands.

CHAPTER THREE

MARCH 1934

Food shortages are the rule now, the peasant markets are prohibitively expensive, and it is difficult to buy anything in the common shops anymore, but many institutions ensure a subsistence diet for their staff by letting them shop in proprietary stores. The store to which Ruzya's father is "attached"—where he is registered to shop, courtesy of the large industrial plant where he works as an accountant—is absurdly far away, very nearly all the way across town. Ever since the twins were born four years ago, it has been Ruzya's proud duty to make the two-tram journey to buy food while Eva stays home with the little boys. At first Ruzya used to pass the time staring out the window; now that she is practically an adult, she reads the paper on the tram—and then stares out the window.

She has had the sense that something was missing since she left the house. Her mother calls this "the feeling of an iron left on." But only now that Ruzya is inside the store has she figured out what it was: she forgot to take a bag. How dumb. Good thing she has the paper: she quickly separates its four pages from one another and fashions each into a small conical paper sack. She extends the first of them to the saleswoman, asking that it be filled with buckwheat. The woman, a supersize blonde in a stained white coat, quickly presses Ruzya's extended hand down on the counter with her own. "You want to get me arrested?" she snarls, though her voice is barely audible. "Put that away."

On the page Ruzya used to make a sack there is a picture of Sergo Ordzhonikidze, a member of the Politburo, the top ruling body of the Communist Party. Using a Politburo member's face to pack buckwheat may easily be interpreted as counterrevolutionary activity.

JANUARY 1937

When class gets out, she is right there waiting for Ruzya. But it does not occur to Ruzya that she is waiting for her specifically, so she starts to walk past the girl, who then falls right into step with her.

"I'd like to talk to you," the girl says. Ruzya does not like her. She is good-looking, to be sure, in that just-right way that has always intimidated Ruzya. She has that perfect part in her thick dark hair, that blue sweater over a crisp shirt—just looking at her makes Ruzya feel all wrong. The girl is the school's Komsomol— Communist Youth League—organizer; this is her official title: every school has one of these. This is not the reason Ruzya dislikes her: after all, she, too, is a member of the Komsomol, as is everyone else, really. In fact, as a top student, she was among the first in her class to be inducted. But this girl goes overboard.

It has been four years since Ruzya and Boba walked the streets

of Moscow conjuring the Communist utopia. A lot of things have
happened in that time. Last year, the school began talking about
the arrests. Ruzya can allow that all of those arrested were guilty.
Or most of them. In any case, she has not spent that much time
thinking about their guilt or innocence. It's what's been going on
at the school itself that has frightened her—the all-school meetings, the loud proclamations, and the children who have so easily
denounced their parents. It seems almost routine: an adult is arrested, and the next day the entire school gathers in the assembly
hall. A child is called to the stage; some days there have been several students going up one after another. He or she says, "My father [name, surname] is an enemy of the people. I denounce the
man, whom I no longer consider to be my father. I apologize to
the Komsomol organization and the Communist Party for not
having been alert enough to recognize the enemy living alongside me. I shall forever serve the Party with utter vigilance."
Sometimes the denunciations have sounded bland, tired, and
forced, but on the really frightening days they have sounded inspired. Every once in a while—maybe twice, maybe three
times—students have refused to denounce their parents. These
students never came to the school again: the lucky ones were suspended; the unlucky disappeared—either to an orphanage for
children of "enemies of the people" or, if they were older, to
prison. Members of Ruzya's gang have somehow been spared the
worst of it—all of their parents are home for the time being—and
they have comforted one another in their resolve to remain hon-
orable and loyal should disaster strike. They have been spending
time at one of their apartments and discussing this; at the end of
every gathering someone, most often Boba, stands up on a chair
and shouts into the air chute: "Glory to the Soviets! We thank
Comrade Stalin for our happy childhoods!" It has become their

tradition to assume that the listening device is planted in the air chute.

While they were at this, the girl who is now walking alongside Ruzya has been organizing the denunciation meetings and has provided their loudest voice and shrillest presence, browbeating her fellow students into admissions of guilt on the rare occasions when pressure was required. Now she is asking, "So what are they saying about the trial in your class?"

"Oh, not much," Ruzya responds nonchalantly. "They mostly feel sorry for Piatakov."

Yuri Piatakov is an old-time Bolshevik, a Soviet industrial executive who was arrested last year on charges of treason. Yesterday the show trial began. There are seventeen defendants, four of them well-known Bolsheviks. All are accused of organizing acts of sabotage and terrorism under the direction of the exiled Leon Trotsky; all have confessed—as those arrested usually do. It is not that anyone in the class has expressed particular feelings about Piatakov outside the requisite rhetoric, just that last summer Ruzya stayed at a friend's dacha and one of the neighbors had mentioned this Piatakov as a wonderful and capable man. This was before Piatakov was arrested, but now Ruzya repeats that neighbor's words. "He was such a good executive," she laments. "That's what everybody says. And now look what's happened."

And look what is happening to the Komsomol organizer. She is losing her famous composure; she is sputtering; her face is turning blotchy. "You must come to the Komsomol room with me now!" she squeals.

Ruzya assents easily. This is her moment, the day she refuses to be a snitch by saying something at once defiant and obviously absurd. She is not herself sure where she got the inspiration for this, but she is glad she did. Then it all goes very quickly. The

Komsomol room serves as the setting for an extraordinary meeting of the presidium of the school's Komsomol organization. All of them—seven? nine? she is not sure, she is so exhilarated—take their seats around a long table for just the few minutes required to vote on the "personal question of R. Solodovnik." She is expelled from the Komsomol on the spot.

Ruzya went home excited that night. She told her father of her courageous stand and her consequent expulsion. Moshe was devastated. That night and for many nights afterward he could not eat or sleep. He was certain he would be arrested. The way he worried, with that certainty that they would come for him any minute, meant that terror had now entered their home. Ruzya and her father lay in separate rooms, staring at the ceiling, the wall, with the blankets pulled overhead in an attempt to hide from the insomnia, and Ruzya imagined her beloved father among the men whose faces were now published in the newspapers alongside the articles about spies, saboteurs, and traitors. She realized that she had known all along the accusations were lies.

With that knowledge came the certainty that it could happen to anyone. Moshe was the chief accountant at a major industrial plant. In the next few years he would be the only executive there to avoid arrest. There was no apparent reason for this. Just luck, perhaps. Or, perhaps, he simply lacked enemies, for no one seems to have denounced him. Even an anonymous denunciation, no matter how absurd—he could have been reported as a Japanese spy, for example—would have landed him in prison. Or perhaps some secret-police clerk carelessly misplaced a piece of paper that should have led to Moshe's arrest. Even though the number of arrests had been growing for years, 1937 is generally considered the first year of the Great Terror—the period in Soviet history that began with the purges and mass arrests, continued with the show trials and the relentless media campaigns against individuals, organizations, and entire ethnic groups, and cost tens of millions of people their lives by the time it ended with Stalin's death in 1953. The Great Terror was a mammoth production that, in one way or another, involved the entire country, and Moshe must simply have fallen through the cracks.

Certainly, Ruzya's carelessness could have led to Moshe's arrest. With thousands of people going to jail for no apparent reason, expressing support for a confessed spy and terrorist was reason enough. But the Komsomol organizer at Ruzya's school must have felt that she and her comrades had handled the matter honorably and sufficiently and did not need to report it to higher authorities. No one came that night for Moshe, or for Ruzya, or for Boba or anyone else in the gang. But Moshe continued to wait, and so did Ruzya, just as thousands of people in the Soviet Union waited every night, unable to sleep, think, or make love, always listening for the car engine in the courtyard, the steps on the stairs, and the banging on the door. For some, the wait commenced when they heard that a friend or colleague had been arrested; for others, when they realized they had let a careless word escape. That first night Ruzya waited for them to come must have been the night she first knew she had no choice. The moment when responsibility for your loved ones' lives comes into conflict with your aspirations of honor, you choose for the last time. Ruzya could never be reckless again. Her aspirations became her dreams—the dream of staying honest, the dream of staying as far away from the state and its deeds as she could and still survive.

CHAPTER FOUR

JULY 23, 1939

Ester and Isaj have been so taken with reading Brenner aloud to
each other—the resistance manifesto was followed by the touching story of a London shopkeeper saving to move to Erez Israel,
this story more grounded in daily detail but inspirational nonetheless—that they have not noticed the train slowing nearly to a
standstill and darkness descending outside. It seems they will not
make it to their campsite in the Carpathian Mountains tonight, so
arrangements have been made to sleep in a barn not far from the
railroad tracks. They pile in, about eighty Shomrim, arranging
themselves on the barn floor in the manner of warehoused timber.
Isaj and Ester end up very nearly on top of each other, and though
they are wearing their uniforms and bulky sweaters on top, and
are surrounded by their giggling comrades, their kissing is inti-
mate. Afterward Ester wonders if this is how women become
pregnant; but in fact, all they did was kiss.

AUGUST 25, 1939

The eighty Shomrim, their uniforms a touch dustier and tighter for the wear after their month in the Carpathians, board the Warsaw-bound train. The plan is to reach Warsaw in about four hours, change for the Bialystok train, and be home before sundown. They very nearly fill up the train car, staking out places on the wooden benches, where they plan to spend the summer holiday's precious last hours.

But the train screeches to a halt almost before it starts moving. A few Polish peasants, one wearing an old military uniform, all toting large bags, get on. They eye the young Jews with a familiar mixture of curiosity and hostility, and sit down. The train starts and halts again. More men board. Some of the Shomrim exchange questioning glances and shrugs. In this odd stop-and-go fashion the train reaches a regular station, where a large and loud group of men gets on. There are no seats now, and these men stand in the aisle, leaning on the benches and on one another, and speak in the overly expressive way of people who are jittery with fear and anticipation. They talk about their wives, the food supplies they are apparently carrying, and the mess the authorities have made, so that these men do not even know where to report for duty.

"Excuse me, did I hear you say 'report for duty'?" Isaj surprises Ester by addressing a tall, pimply-faced blond youth standing closest to their bench. The young man quickly glances at his companions, who are older, looks Isaj up and down in a way that leaves no doubt how he feels about skinny young Jews who dare open their mouths, but then apparently decides against confrontation.

"I guess you did. So?"

"I apologize, but we've been away," Isaj explains, clearly a bit too ceremonious for the other boy's liking. "Would you mind telling us what's going on?"

"Where have you been, the moon?" the youth asks, and he and his buddies guffaw. "General mobilization's what's going on. All grown men fit to serve must stop any available means of transport and get on. The likes of you have to get off." Isaj is seventeen, a year short of conscription age—none of the Shomrim traveling together today are old enough for the army: they were schoolchildren on vacation.

"The Germans?" Isaj asks, more because he does not want to let the conversation end with a put-down than because he has any doubt that it is the German army that is about to invade Poland.

"The Germans," the young man confirms.

The train crawls along, the Polish men with their bags keep piling in, and soon the male Shomrim have to start disembarking to make room for the conscripts. The girls are allowed to stay on. Isaj takes his leave quickly, perhaps even sooner than necessary— there is still some air around their bench—with a quick "bye" to Ester and a peck on the cheek. Wedged in among Jewish girls and Polish men, Ester sits dazed for what might be five or ten hours, until the overburdened train pulls through the pitch blackness into Warsaw's well-lit railway station, where the pale faces of Bella's two brothers appear in the window before Ester has had a chance to move. Bella has apparently been calling them for hours, making them sick with her worry, and now they drag Ester away to visit her grandparents—the entire family, which has remained religious, is ignoring bans on traveling on the Shabbat, and this only adds to the chaotic, frightful feel of the day.

The visit is a blur: Ester is exhausted, and no one is making much sense anyway. The next day she is put on the train to Bialystok, which takes about six hours instead of the usual three, and this time she is picked up at the station by Bella, who refuses to try to hold back her tears. "I will never, ever, let you go anywhere without me," she shouts, for all of Bialystok to hear. "You hear me?"

Ester looks for signs of change or danger or something. But Bialystok looks the same as ever. Over the last two days people have stocked up on the panic essentials—matches and salt and grains—and now everyone is just waiting. The whole city is quietly sick to its stomach, but you cannot see that out in the streets.

SEPTEMBER 3, 1939

Two days after the German army invaded Poland, the Shomrim hold a meeting. This is a reunion of sorts: this summer's male campers have just finally reached town, having traversed the country by foot, buggy, and the kindness of strangers. The mood is what it has always been, only more so, the point of the meeting being to reinforce the members' resolve to stay faithful to their mission. "War is coming, sure," Isaj proclaims, attempting a somber tone to disguise his excitement. "No one knows what tomorrow may bring. But we have chosen our path, whatever the circumstances! Everyone may be hiding in cellars, but we won't be frightened! We shall carry on despite the war." Applause all around, then some talk of the work units and certificate applications, and then it is back to the cellars, the waiting. That night German planes circle the city for the first time.

SEPTEMBER 15, 1939

The small crowd that has been gathering in the Goldbergs' apartment for the last three weeks to listen to one of the city's few radios is now fast dispersing. Today's news is that the Germans are about to enter the city, so everyone is to go home, close the shutters, bar the gates—as though the German army were a hurricane, a force of nature to be weathered, waited out. The Polish army is offering no resistance in these parts—this is the east of the country, and the military's strength was spent in the west, where the Germans first invaded—so the Germans' entrance seems almost casual: they drive in on their odd motorcycles with the high seats and the sidecars, with no tanks for cover. Still, though the logic of their entrance might dictate a sort of peace, they do descend on the town like a force of nature, proving that conquerors, even German soldiers with their legendary love of order, are universally trigger-happy. People who happen to be in the street are shot, and those who do not die immediately lie in the street slowly bleeding to death as their neighbors watch through the cracks in their shutters. The city's famed ambulance cannot make it out of the gate. Most of the dead are Jews, and many of these are the observant men and women who hear the news in the synagogues, where they have gathered to pray on the second day of Rosh Hashanah. They run out into the streets in panicked clumps and continue to run as the bullets fly, the men losing their wide-brimmed hats, the women getting tangled in their skirts, falling, dragging their children so their feet barely touch the ground, falling again. "What a way to start the year," says Jakub, and Bella glares at him. *To be flippant at a time like this,* her look says. *There will be plenty of time yet to be morbid,* he looks back.

Ester is glued to the shuttered window of their apartment, but the view of the intersection with Sienkiewicz Street—the bigger street where there is much more action than on their small road—is skewed, full of black shadows that can only be interpreted through the sounds that accompany them. There is shouting in German, screaming in the assorted languages of Bialystok, the clatter of hobnailed boots and occasional snaps of gunfire. Later in the day, the gunfire starts coming in bursts, and there is the sound of glass shattering: with the Bialystokers now hiding in their homes, the soldiers start shooting through windows, then barging into the houses to remove valuables. A neighbor is killed for refusing to part with her rings, which the soldiers then leave stuck on her fat fingers. This information comes from a neighbor boy who takes the senseless risk of running from house to house to report the news: two murders on this block, one robbery, and now they have posted a notice saying curfew is in effect from eight in the evening till five in the morning. Not that anyone besides this madman would consider going out.

SEPTEMBER 16, 1939

Is she expected to stay inside forever? It is not as though the Germans were going anywhere. Sooner rather than later the Goldbergs' modest food supplies will run out and they will have to venture outside, if only for food. And anyway, one can die from boredom or go insane before any real danger presents itself—if one insists on staying inside, that is. Bella's objections and Jakub's silence ignored, Ester goes out. At the last minute Bella manages to convince her not to wear her Ha-Shomer ha-Zair uniform: she puts on a dark blue dress that is too small—a consequence of having refused to accompany Bella to the tailor's for over two years now—and she is gone.

Sienkiewicz Street is quieter than usual but by no means deserted. There are few men out—rumor has already spread that any male risks being conscripted for bizarre duty like washing the sidewalks or lugging dirt from one place to another—but there seems to be something vaguely festive in the manner of the women strolling the street. Ester supposes that is what happens when going outside becomes a special event. She laughs inside at how little it takes, but she feels excited, too, and proud of this wide tree-lined street, already cleared of the shattered glass from two days ago. She has not quite decided where she will go, and by default she is readying to turn a corner onto a side street leading to the Jewish quarter when one of those large black German cars screeches to a halt at the corner and a green-uniformed officer— well, she just assumes he is an officer if he is riding in the backseat of a car—jumps out and grabs her by both elbows. Now she is in the car, in the backseat, between two Nazis barking something— at her? at the driver? at each other? Are they going to kill her now?

"Do you understand German?" is what it turns out they are asking.

"Yes," she answers in Yiddish.

"Drive," one of the officers says to the driver.

They continue down Sienkiewicz, past several Jewish shops, now shuttered, and stop in front of a Polish-owned food store. She gets out of the car with the officers, who make no particular effort to make sure she is following them—but she is anyway.

"Bread," the older of the two says in German when they enter the store.

"Bread," she repeats in Polish.

"Bread." The shopkeeper nods and places a loaf on the counter.

It takes no more than an hour to visit three stores, buying food and wine for the officers' dinner and a pair of hats for their wives. After Ester regains feeling in her legs, she is able to translate easily, even adding a polite word or two to her companions' barked orders. The shopkeepers show no surprise at the odd union of two Nazi officers and a Jewish girl: apparently, this method of procuring translation has been practiced widely the last two days. When her services are no longer needed, the German car dumps her on the side of Lipowa Street, and it is all Ester can do to walk rather than run home. She rushes past German soldiers putting up notices on lampposts, but she learns their meaning only when she gets home, from the neighborhood's self-selected messenger. The curfew hour, it turns out, has been changed from eight to six in the evening.

About an hour later, over fifty people who did not learn of the curfew change are shot dead in the streets—without warning, just as the notice said they would be. Ester, still shaking from her encounter with the German officers, has resolved to stay inside as long as she possibly can.

It was probably impossible to gauge the danger, to separate the fear of any aggression, any army occupying your land—and the Jews, whatever dreams they had for their future, did consider Bialystok their land—from the specific fear of the Nazis. Bialystok's and Warsaw's Jewish newspapers had reported on the Third Reich's racial politics, but these stories always took second place to reporting on anti-Semitic activity in Poland itself. And what really made German policies so different from Polish ones? Both countries had for years been subjecting their Jews to a state-sponsored economic boycott. Both states openly discriminated against Jews in education and the professions. Only in the year leading up to the German invasion of Poland had there been news reports that may have indicated that the horror of Nazi policies would exceed what Jews had known in Poland—or anywhere else.

In addition to the news reports, there were about seventeen thousand Polish-born Jews who had been exiled from Germany in October 1938. Most of them had settled into a nightmarish existence in the borderlands, but a few had made their way east as far as Bialystok, and their fear of the Germans was the most convincing argument that the occupation would bring unimagined terror. But when the occupation came, it did not proceed according to the usual rules of such things, though few Bialystok Jews had the experience and the presence of mind to realize this. The Polish army had given up this part of the land without battle, yet the occupiers did not seem to be acting like they planned to stay. They murdered, raped, and marauded, but they preferred to do this, oddly, under the cover of night, as though someone could have stopped or reprimanded them.

In fact, the Germans were not planning to stay in Bialystok. According to the secret agreements signed by German foreign minister Joachim von Ribbentrop and his Soviet counterpart, Vyacheslav Molotov, on August 23, Bialystok, like the rest of Eastern Poland, would be annexed by the Soviet Union, while the rest of the country would become part of Germany. The specifics, however, had not been ironed out by the time Germany entered Poland a week later, and two and a half weeks into the Nazis' faster-than-expected offensive, Stalin still had not made up his mind on the date, manner, and justification for the Soviet attack on its neighbor. So the German army pushed on, while the German government was secretly urging Stalin to hurry and take his part of Poland. While he hesitated, the Nazis took Eastern Poland. The Jews and others of Bialystok—those who had bled to death in the streets, the fat woman killed for her jewelry, the fifty unwitting curfew violators—were the casualties of imprecise planning, caught in a sort of no-man's-moment in history.

At two o'clock in the morning on September 17, Stalin received German ambassador Schulenburg, to inform him that Soviet troops would cross into Poland four hours later. A gentlemanly telegram exchange followed, with the Soviets asking the Germans to hold their planes west of the designated territorial-division line, and the Germans, citing short notice, asking the Soviets to take care not to fly too close to the line themselves, lest someone get hurt.

The Jews of Bialystok learned of the Soviet advance into Polish territory on the morning of September 17 and shifted into a state of relieved anticipation. Little as was known about the country to the east, the Soviets were believed not to be consistent Jew-haters. After all, they even had Jews in their government. Jakub Goldberg, for one, had his doubts—he had always distrusted Communists—but there could be no arguing: after the German occupiers, the Soviets appeared as liberators. The first of the Soviets arrived the next day, and the handover of the city was completed in four more. The process was bizarre: officers of the two armies shook hands when encountering one another in the streets; the ostensibly defeated Germans took time readying themselves for the road, and departed, in plain view of their supposed enemies, with trucks full of looted goods.

Still, the city had been occupied by the Nazis and now liberated from them, and no one—not even a consistent anti-Communist like Jakub—could argue that this was not cause for celebration.

OCTOBER 8, 1939

These are days of joy. The Soviets have set up movie screens in several of the city's squares and parks and have been showing films. In the rush of relief and gratitude, Bialystokers have set upon the liberators with endless questions. "Will there be a war between you and the Germans?" "Will you move farther into Poland?" "Can you save all the Jews?" "Are there Jewish officers?" "Do you have enough food?" The soldiers' answers are cheerful, slick, and alarmingly free of substance. "The situation must be stabilized." "Order must be restored." "Everyone is equally valuable as a contributing member of society." "We have everything aplenty." This last response becomes a refrain, and the younger people test the Russians' comprehension and sincerity by asking, "And cholera? Do you have that too?" or "And consumption?" They continue to insist they have everything aplenty, but the officers betray themselves in the shops of Bialystok.

"Do you have men's shirts?"

"Yes."

"I'll take them."

"How many?"

"All of them."

Shopkeepers jack up prices daily, but this is no deterrent: the officers seem to have nothing but money and need. In a particularly grotesque episode about three weeks into the occupation, the Red Army officers' wives relieve the shops of all the floor-length silk nightgowns, which they proceed to wear to the opening show of a visiting opera company from Minsk.

The initial celebration has coincided with the Jewish high holy days, but now is the time for the traditional autumn slow-down, for getting back to school. On the first day of her last year at the gymnasium, Ester has discovered that her school is no longer the Hebrew Gymnasium but Bialystok Secondary School with Instruction in the Yiddish Language. Hebrew, which is banned in the Soviet Union, shall no longer be taught, read, or spoken in Bialystok. A few students' in-class protestations that they will continue to study the language and work for the dream even if they have to go underground are cut off by the teachers with uncharacteristic swiftness.

On the evening of the first day of school Ester and Isaj are strolling on Lipowa Street when they encounter the gymnasium's Hebrew teacher, a single-minded pedant known for chastising his students whenever he encounters them speaking a language other than Hebrew, in school or outside of it.

"Shalom," Ester addresses him, opening her mouth to add something in Hebrew in a show of good faith and solidarity.

"Good evening," the teacher responds in Yiddish, anxiously. "I will see you in school tomorrow for our Yiddish lesson." He scampers off.

Ester expects Isaj to say something appropriately deprecating, but her boyfriend is oblivious. He is in a relentlessly great mood. In the last two weeks he has added a joyful skip to his walk, and his talk has mixed his favorite socialist rhetoric with the propaganda spouted by the Soviet soldiers. The changes in his own life have been remarkable: his father has been given a job in a newly nationalized factory that never used to hire Jews, and Isaj himself has left his job as a pharmacist's assistant (a charity post he got after the leather factory fire) to enroll in a newly formed high school for future teachers.

"You shouldn't get upset about small things," he tells Ester. "Look at the bigger picture. The Soviets have to restrict all other political movements, including Zionism, in order to advance their policies of equality and opportunity for all. Can't you see what that means for us? We can leave Poland; we will go study in Moscow together!"

Moscow has never been a part of Ester's geography, but Isaj's enthusiasm, coupled with the rapid disappearance of all other options, will reorient her: she will gradually grow accustomed to the idea that she will go east.

There were those who refused to accept the new dispensation, who scrambled for a way to reach Erez Israel. They bought counterfeit passports, took advantage of early wartime confusion to cross borders, and some of them ultimately did make it to Palestine. Jakub Goldberg's general inability to scheme and his sense of responsibility conspired to make him stay in Bialystok. He gave refuge to relatives who fled from the other side of the Bug River—the dividing line between newly Soviet and newly German territory—and tried to maintain the ways of his existence for as long as possible. He added his voice to Isaj's, encouraging his daughter to travel into the Soviet Union proper, farther away from the Germans and the arrests that were becoming more frequent as the Soviets rushed to bring their new lands into line with the rest of their purged and scorched country. "If we survive all this," Jakub promised, "we will move to New Zealand." Why? "Because there will never be a war there."

For many Jews in pre–World War II Poland, Zionism was a politics of despair and Israel itself purely a dream of escape. For all their talk of destiny, Erez Israel was merely a destination, one that could be exchanged—for New Zealand, for Moscow, for any place that seemed to offer a future.

It was an accident that, while many of her classmates courted colleges in Belarusian Minsk or Ukrainian L'viv, Ester found a listing of Moscow colleges in the Bialystok city library. It was a matter of ignorance that she picked one of the most prestigious and competitive colleges on the list, the Institute of History, Philosophy and Literature, or IFLI. And it was a matter of unchallenged chutzpah that she, now an aspiring literary scholar, wrote IFLI asking to be relieved of the obligation to be tested on her knowledge of Russian. Then it was a matter of a simple misunderstanding that she took a letter from the college instructing her to report for her entrance exams no later than August 1, 1940, as a granting of that request. In any case, it was a matter of luck that she went to Moscow: the slip of paper from IFLI served as a railroad pass out of the restricted occupied zone and into the Soviet mainland.

CHAPTER FIVE

MAY DAY, 1941

This is not Ruzya's usual crowd. Gathered in someone's large apartment, most of them are students, like her, but some are apparently from different schools. There are many unfamiliar faces, and she feels a bit constrained without anyone from the gang around.

"Why are you so sad?"

It is the man sitting across from her. He is beautiful, a bit too beautiful for her liking: his reddish brown hair, wavy and over-long on top, is brushed over just so, his brown suit is made of unusually thick cloth, and his thin tie is arranged in the tiniest knot possible. He is tall, too, and Ruzya always notices tall men. She saw him when he walked in, an equally chic girl on his arm, and she felt a little annoyed when he was seated across from her.

"Your turn." He smiles. He has thin lips.

They are playing a stupid game, bouncing a copper five-kopeck coin around the table, and she did not notice it land in front of her. She sends it on and looks around for something to eat or drink or otherwise occupy herself.

"Let's dance," he says, and when she looks up he is already standing, extending his hand to her across the table. She hates to dance, but she likes the way the invitation has been extended. She extends her hand, and they walk the length of the table holding hands, forcing everyone who is still sitting to duck awkwardly. Like most songs played at parties these days, this is a tango, and she and the young man perform a shy, toned-down version of the dance. "Oh, those wondrous eyes / Captured me," the record player hisses. He says she has beautiful eyes, such mysterious pure gray. She looks up and sees that his eyes are very light, almost watery. He says his name is Samuil and that she has a beautiful smile. She registers that his name is Jewish, and she momentarily resents the sense of comfort she derives from their shared ethnicity; still, she is proud of herself for not having noticed his Jewish looks from the start. She smiles, and he says he especially likes the space between her teeth. She smiles again, but the suspicion lingers: she thinks he might be mocking her.

"I know where the wine is," Samuil announces in a stage whisper as the song winds down. "Will you come with me?"

She is not sure she likes being drafted as his coconspirator, but she follows him. He is thinner than she thought, and he looks dangerously fragile as he weaves through the party crowd, at one point extending a long arm into the kitchen to fetch an open bottle of red wine and a single glass. He opens the balcony door for her, and once they are both out there, he drops, laughing, to one knee. He pours wine into the glass and extends it to her while pressing the bottle to his heart.

"Allow me to give you this so you may never be sad again!"

"I shall never be sad again!" she promises.

He rises and invites her to gaze from the balcony. He actually says "gaze," and she would suspect again that she is being mocked if the view were not so spectacular. They are looking out over the Moscow River, and they see building lights, bridge lights, boat lights—all reflected manifold in the black water.

"You didn't come here alone," Ruzya says, instantly regretting she had ruined the moment but relieved to have broken the spell.

"I really didn't care where I went today or with whom," Samuil says, turning to her. "There are many parties tonight, and I didn't know what brought me here. Now I do." He takes her hand. "Do you like Mayakovsky?"

Of course she likes Mayakovsky. Who does not? Even Stalin called him "the best, most talented poet of the Soviet epoch," which seemed simply a statement of fact. But as this boy starts to recite a popular poem, holding her hand with one of his and gesticulating wildly with the other, still holding the bottle, she understands something about him: he is a believer. He means what he says, and he trusts what he hears. He could not mock anyone if he tried.

Ruzya had her doubts, which, by the time they met, had hardened into permanent skepticism and an ever stronger defense against faith of all sorts, but especially the unquestioning fervor of young Stalinists. Samuil had a penchant for extolling the "knights of the revolution," who included, first and foremost, Stalin and the founder of the secret police, Feliks Dzerzhinsky. He believed, and that meant Stalin was his ideal and the "enemies of the people" were his enemies. Their ecstatic courtship did not leave space for disagreements about such matters or any other: they were preoccupied with discovering their perfect match in each other. Had their relationship ever matured past its honeymoon stage, or had

Samuil ever made it out of his boyhood, perhaps they would have argued. Or perhaps Samuil would have grown into a disillusioned man, someone who shrank from responsibility and, eventually, thought. Or he may have put his passion and his knowledge of the law to the service of another ideal, becoming a critic of the regime. What they could have made of their life together was their dream and anyone's guess. Fact is, he was twenty-two in 1941, a year older than Ruzya, and he would be dead a year and a half later.

He had applied to college in 1937, the same year Ruzya, still a high school student, was expelled from the Komsomol. That was also the year when the Soviet military, decimated by the purges and beginning its prewar buildup—the nonaggression pact with Nazi Germany was still two years away, and talk of war was in the newspapers and in the air—drafted all eighteen-year-old men. Samuil had not even begun his studies at the Institute of Jurisprudence when he entered military service. He did extraordinarily well, however; singled out for his abilities, he was shortly shipped back to Moscow to take a job as personal assistant to the dean of the Military Law Academy, where he also became a student. Therein lay an additional source of his fervor: by the time Ruzya met him, he had been serving his country for four years, and, like the best of soldiers, he was readying himself for ever greater battles.

CHAPTER SIX

For all Ester could comprehend of her new surroundings when she finally arrived in Moscow in August 1940, she may as well have traveled to another planet. She was joining the Soviet Union's most wretched generation at what may have been its worst moment. Nineteen forty was the fourth year of the Great Terror. IFLI, the Institute of History, Philosophy and Literature, was just like Ruzya's school, the site of regular meetings in which young people denounced their freshly arrested parents—or, rarely, refused to do so, usually to disappear themselves. And some of those who performed just as they were expected to, denouncing their parents and swearing their unending loyalty to the Party, were arrested anyway. At the height of the hysteria in 1937–1938, the table at which the Komsomol presidium sat took up permanent residence on the auditorium's stage, the meetings were held nightly, and some nights as many as fifteen students had to face the crowd to account for a parent's fictitious misdeeds.

Like every institution in the Soviet Union, the college was steeped in paranoia: the enemy was everywhere, and anyone could at any moment be exposed as an enemy. Many of the students had been the conscious witnesses, victims, or perpetrators of the first stages of Soviet repression. Some—the children of peasants—had had their lives turned upside down by the collectivization of the 1920s. Others had served as members of the "collectivization brigades," which went around robbing peasants, or of similarly unsavory Stalinist enforcement bodies. Still others had come to Moscow from Siberian cities where their families had been exiled. These were, of course, the lucky ones: most children of "enemies" were banned from pursuing higher education.

"We were weaned on hatred," wrote an IFLI graduate decades later. "We were weaned on novels, poetry books, songs, plays, all of them called 'Hatred.' Humans had for centuries been weaned on love. And here we were weaned on hatred. Such was our youth, with its springs, its theaters, concerts, arguments, paintings, poems, sports—rowing competitions, volleyball in the college courtyard."

IFLI was founded in 1934 to supply a new generation of teachers to replace the ones lost to Lenin's and Stalin's policies of systematically persecuting, imprisoning, exiling, and killing members of the prerevolutionary intelligentsia. Unlike the grand and prestigious Moscow State University, which had undergone a thorough ideological cleansing, IFLI was never intended to be anything but a teachers' college: it was given a building on the outskirts of Moscow, reachable only by way of a long chain of trams. But circumstances combined to make it an island of rarefaction. Old professors who had long been kept away from sensitive young minds were dusted off and sent to prepare the new breed of teachers. They were joined by a few remarkable young instructors, and together they created a college that very quickly became a magnet for the most talented poets, writers, and critics of their generation—and a thorn in the regime's side. By the time

Ester arrived in Moscow in August 1940, what was known as "an ideological takedown" was being prepared for IFLI, whereby the college would be closed and its professors arrested. But these things could take a surprisingly long time in Stalin's Russia: IFLI felt increasing pressure but lasted into 1941, when the war began and, without ideological fanfare, the college was merged with Moscow University.

Some of the professors had vanished in the late 1930s, often on the basis of a student's report to the authorities about something the instructor had said, in class or outside. The interpretive fields of study were riddled with potential pitfalls. One of the older teachers noted that ancient Greece "had the sort of democracy that has never been reproduced since and never will be." The following evening, he was called upon to retract his careless statement with demagogic flourish at the Komsomol meeting. This was a relatively slight penalty—likely because none of his students had found it necessary to report the misstep to authorities outside the college.

Discipline bordered on paranoia. One of the generalissimos' recent decrees made tardiness and absences from work criminal offenses, punishable by imprisonment. The decree did not specifically apply to students, but no one was going to risk setting a precedent. Professors tended to arrive for classes exceedingly early, and, with the meanness of youth, students wished the less-popular instructors would fall victim to some fateful public-transport breakdown.

But by the time Ester arrived, the main topic of discussion at IFLI was the impending war. The college population was feverish with anticipation. The Soviet media had suspended its anti-German and antifascist rhetoric after the nonaggression pact was signed in 1939, but for the dreamy poets and writers of IFLI, the possibility of war continued to promise a chance at reclaiming their idealism: it promised to redefine the enemy as the person on the other side of the front line, implicitly exonerating teachers, parents, and friends. "Romanticism is the future war with fascism, in which we will triumph," wrote one of the college poets. (All the IFLI literati considered themselves Romantics.) Of another, his widow would later remember, "Like many of our contemporaries, he breathed a sigh of relief when the war started and the line between friend and foe was redrawn: it now lay at the front."

Of course, in 1940, the year when the Soviet press tirelessly trumpeted the country's friendship with Nazi Germany, few IFLI students dared speak of the war dream. Silence was a matter of habit, a way of life. This was a community of writers, virtually none of whom kept a journal: private notes could be, and often were, used to convict the author of treason, espionage, or whatever other absurd charge happened to be advanced. Instead, they wrote romantic poetry, often extolling love of labor and of their country, and edited whatever subtext there may have been out of the creative process.

So Ester arrived in a world of profound silence. And pervasive poverty. "I remember the IFLI cafeteria," writes one alumna. "A standard day's diet consisted of, for breakfast in the college cafeteria, a starchy drink made from concentrate, a slice of black bread with jam, and a small saucer of beet-and-potato salad; and for supper at home, a precooked hamburger that was half meat, half starch. And there were quite a number of students who could not afford even this level of subsistence." IFLI memoirs often contain detailed descriptions of the students' outfits: most students owned only one dress or pair of trousers and one pair of shoes.

Ester loved it.

AUGUST 15, 1940

The first two weeks of Ester's stay in Moscow passed like a dream sequence of goodwill and good luck. Ever since she got off the train at the grand green Belorussky Station in the center of Moscow and froze in disoriented awe, things have been going her way. One person after another asked her where she needed to go, and people boarded subway trains and trams with her to deliver her to the out-of-the-way college, where she was given a chaperone to see her to the dormitory. An embarrassing incident followed—she was dispatched to the bathhouse, where she was apparently expected to strip and wash in the presence of other women, a behavior that fell entirely outside the realm of possibility. After she refused, a concerned dormitory nurse inquired about the nature of Ester's presumed illness, and laughed her big blond head off when shame was finally revealed to be the culprit. If rumor of the misunderstanding spread, it only added to Ester's newfound status as an exotic attraction, the star foreigner everyone wanted to befriend.

If anyone had any doubts as to how different she was, she laid these to rest during her first exam, the English orals, when she answered with a confidence and mastery unparalleled by her Russian peers. She got a five on a five-point scale. But the pièce de résistance was the second exam, the world literature orals. As soon as she faced the examining professor, the still-young but eminent Abram Belkin, Ester issued several Russian phrases she had rehearsed with her dormitory roommates. Her grammar and pronunciation were still hopelessly mangled, but the kindly Professor Belkin managed to grasp the meaning: in light of her Polish education, Ester was asking not to be questioned on Russian literature.

"Shakespeare, then," the professor ruled. "Let us begin simply with summarizing the plot of *Hamlet*."

"Indecision makes beginning," Ester began confidently enough. "Early ghost—host," she stumbled and halted.

"Why don't you speak German." Professor Belkin smiled, offering relief that Ester could not accept.

"I speak English," she advanced as a counteroffer.

"I don't." The professor seemed not at all annoyed.

Ester remembered the incident with the German officers who used her as a translator and, without further negotiation, launched into a Yiddish summary of *Hamlet*. "The prince of Denmark is visited by the ghost of his father, who was murdered some months before. The crime has remained unsolved, but the ghost tells Hamlet that the murderer was actually Hamlet's uncle Claudius, who in the meantime has married Hamlet's mother and is now sitting on the throne—"

"Did you study Hebrew?" the professor suddenly asked in German.

"Of course," said Ester, who, even after nearly a year of living under the Soviets, had not developed the habit of editing her past and taking care with her answers.

"You know, I studied the language a quarter of a century ago. I wonder how much I have forgotten. Please continue in Hebrew."

Ester continued, relieved to switch into the language in which she had stood most of the exams in her life, forgetting that the use of this language in this country was a crime. Belkin listened with evident pleasure, squinting, his gray head tipped slightly back, for about fifteen minutes as she summarized *Hamlet* and proceeded to analyze the characters. Finally he gave a satisfied sigh and said, "Very well," lifting his pen over his examination charts. "A five."

At the classroom door, where other applicants kept their vigil, looking for clues in the eyes of exiting comrades, Ester was ambushed by three young men. They seemed older than the applicants, perhaps simply because they were so much more confident. They had the IFLI look: hair slightly disheveled, longer on top and parted on the side, long shirt collars laid over well-worn suit jackets. "Anatoly Korkeshkin," the first one introduced himself. "Secretary of the Komsomol organization."

"Semyon Krasilshik," a second man picked up. "Reporter for *Komsomolia*." This is the college "wall newspaper," a biweekly publication that is produced by hand and posted along one of the hall walls; IFLI is famed for having the longest wall newspaper in the city.

"Vasily Kuznetsov," finished the third man, blond and ruddy-cheeked. "Ordinary student."

"Hello." Ester laughed, mostly at the last introduction.

"We are going to be your mentors," declared the one named Semyon, a lanky young man with brown hair.

"My what?" A Polish speaker can generally understand spoken Russian, but this went beyond Ester's comprehension. A mentor, as she soon learned, is a peculiar Soviet institution, a way of setting up a big-brother-type relationship between an experienced worker and a novice, a senior student and a freshman, the entire staff of a factory and the school body of an elementary school. The trio did not manage to get this across just then, but Semyon issued forth with a tirade from which Ester was able to deduce that they would from now on be showing her the way. "So you be my guides," she concluded.

"Yes," Vasily piped in enthusiastically. "We'll show you Moscow too."

That was two weeks ago. Since then these three, together and separately, have been by Ester's side almost constantly. Semyon is intense and always holding forth on something or other—Ester can only occasionally understand what, exactly; Vasily swoons, blushing intermittently, and, in contrast to Semyon, grows less coherent with each passing day; and Anatoly is cool, collected, remote, and usually the first to leave their nighttime gatherings. As it turns out, all three are fourth-year students who were present at Ester's literature exam as observers in preparation for their teaching practice. In their capacity as mentors they negotiated with Ester's examiners before each test, so she sailed through her remaining two orals—by wordlessly pointing out countries, capitals, seas, and continents on a map for her geography exam and by writing dates on the blackboard by way of answering the history questions. The last and most important of the exams, the Russian essay, is the one from which Ester asked to be excused back when she first wrote to the college. So she did not go. Now she has a couple of idle days before the college posts the final admission results—not that she has any doubt she has made it, what with fives in all her subjects. She is trying to read Russian in the afternoons—one of her temporary dorm roommates, another applicant, has said, "How I envy you the opportunity to read Pushkin for the first time," and Ester has devoted herself to this task, though it far exceeds her mastery of the language—and in the evenings she is out with the three mentors.

But this afternoon as she lies on her bed with a book and a stubby black pencil, a sweaty and now genuinely disheveled Semyon barges in, with no apparent regard for whether Ester is dressed or whether any of her three roommates might be present (in fact, they are not, but two are out on dates wearing Ester's dresses, which leaves her in a housedress and rather embarrassed by Semyon's sudden appearance).

"I've just sat in on the admissions committee meeting!"

"What happened?" It does not occur to Ester that whatever outrage Semyon has witnessed may have any connection to her.

"They've decided not to admit you."

She stares at him.

"There is a deputy dean named Zozulya—he just wouldn't hear of it. 'Very nice she has done so well on her exams, but she still didn't take all of them,' and so forth. 'Let her take a year to study Russian, then she can come back and stand for her exams again, and surely we will admit her.' Pretty much everyone else there tried to argue your case, but he had veto power and, technically, an incontrovertible argument."

The word *incontrovertible* reduces Ester to tears: helpless, suffocating, ugly, and endless tears.

"Don't you think we are going to let this drop," Semyon declares, provoking, quite predictably, more tears. "We will write a complaint to the Committee for Higher Schooling, and the decision will be overturned. It must be overturned!"

There is no time less appropriate for oratorical fervor than when a woman is crying. Semyon's overblown confidence only convinces Ester that all hope is lost. Suddenly the prospect of returning to Bialystok seems barely better than death, compounded as it is by the expense of her ticket to Moscow and her stay here— money her parents could have spent on helping relatives in the German-occupied territories. She cries and cries.

The following morning the Lobby of Three showed up in Ester's room all business and no tears, three completed—even typed— letters in their hands. One was signed by the college Komsomol committee, another by the editors of *Komsomolia,* and the third was to be signed by Ester herself. All three made the same argument, spectacular in its demagogic flare. Essentially, they argued, Ester had come to Moscow to apply to university because the Soviet Union offered the sort of equal opportunity she had never seen in the old Poland, where Jews were relegated to the ghetto bench. But instead of being welcomed with open arms, she was once again turned away because of her ethnic origin! For had she been born in an ethnic Russian family in Poland, she would have learned the language of her ancestors. But because her parents were Jews and spoke to her in Yiddish, she could not write an essay in Russian and was therefore denied a fine Soviet education. The argument appealed to Ester: it made her desperate personal fight—she has to go to college this year!—seem principled rather than selfish. She signed, the trio delivered the letters to the Committee for Higher Schooling and reported back that they would have to come for the answer in two days' time.

The day has arrived. It is post-exam–high-anxiety season, and the courtyard of the Committee for Higher Schooling is filled with screaming mothers and their sulking offspring. The mothers wave their letters of appeal in the air like flags, and shout their arguments to no one in particular. Each has a child—more often a son—who is brilliant and was given an unfair grade. "He has had all fives his whole life!" "He must be given a chance to retake the exam!" "The spelling of this word is variable!" "This problem wasn't in the school program!" Even Semyon stalls slightly at this scene: the simple task of pushing their way through to the building entrance appears impossible.

Suddenly one of the doors opens and a graying doorman in an old military uniform sets one foot outside. The crowd hushes momentarily. "Is there an Ester Goldberg here?" he shouts out.

"Yes!" screams Semyon.

The sea of applicants and their mothers parts silently to let the four of them through. The doorman separates Ester from her support group, nodding to the young men to stay put, and takes her upstairs to the office of Comrade Kaftanov, the committee chairman himself. Kaftanov is a stocky man also dressed in something vaguely military, in accordance with the old postrevolutionary fashion. He says hello and, without adding another word, takes Ester by the hand and leads her out to the balcony off his office. This building in central Moscow must have been a wealthy merchant's house before the revolution, and the massive semicircular balcony with a squat stone railing speaks to the former owner's royal aspirations.

"I want to tell you all something," Kaftanov blares, and the crowd outside falls silent once again. "The Committee for Higher Schooling will interfere in the affairs of a learning institution only under extraordinary circumstances. Here we have one such case." He nods in Ester's direction. "This girl grew up in the old Poland." He proceeds to repeat, almost word for word, Semyon's interpretation of Ester's story. "Clearly, what happened at the Institute of History, Philosophy and Literature smacks of a prerevolutionary sort of anti-Semitism, which cannot and will not be tolerated in the Soviet Union!" The crowd actually, incredibly, applauds.

Kaftanov leads Ester back into his office, hands her a typed letter to the IFLI authorities, and wishes her luck. Now the four of them run to the college administration with the letter, then to the central telegraph office to fire off a jubilant telegram, and finally to the railroad station to buy Ester's ticket home for tomorrow, for a quick trip to pick up her things. In the evening they walk endlessly, round and round on the city's central green boulevard ring, reciting poetry, eating ice cream, and every so often quoting Comrade Kaftanov, each time sounding more overwrought than the last. Life is beautiful, and life is just.

There is a line with which my grandmother Ester likes to finish some of her stories. She always pronounces it with a note of wistful amazement: "There really was no anti-Semitism in the Soviet Union at that time." This is one of the few points on which she and Ruzya are in complete agreement. To be more precise, though, there was no state-enforced anti-Semitism of the sort that prevailed before the revolution and that came into being again during and after World War II. Still, in the interwar years the regime succeeded in annihilating the institutions of Jewish culture and criminalizing the use of Hebrew—but this fit a pattern of destroying all non-Bolshevik groups, an effort to root out any potential source of resistance to Soviet officialdom. Eventually, as tolerance for difference of any sort shrank, individual Jews, too, came to represent a threat and, as a result, became targets. But before World War II, the rhetoric of what was known as internationalism ruled. To a girl coming from Poland, this seemed like a miracle. Ester was endlessly amazed that none of her new acquaintances even asked her about her ethnic origin. (In all likelihood, this was because, never having seen a foreigner in the flesh, they assumed that Ester's Semitic features were typical of Poles.)

I have seen no photographs of my grandmother from that time, but there are later pictures, taken around the time the war ended. She is all thinness: hands with thin fingers holding her baby, a long thin nose on a pale face framed by long tight curls. A hat cocked not so much coquettishly as consciously, for the photographic occasion. She looks like a starlet. Back in 1940 she had perhaps more youthful plumpness, less of an air of sophistication and more of unequivocal enthusiasm. She had, after all, found the Promised Land, the land of no anti-Semitism.

During winter break, in January 1941, Ester returned to Bialystok for the first time and found a city filled with terror. The fear had moved in while Ester was still there, but the change struck her only after she had been away. The relationship between the Red Army saviors and their saved had long since lost its sheen. The arrests had begun almost immediately after the Soviets entered; the deportations soon followed. Decades later, researchers of Soviet crimes would come to the conclusion that Polish citizens made up one of the most numerous groups among the victims of Stalinist repression. Though the Soviet Union never declared war on Poland, in 1939 the Red Army captured 240,000 Polish military men. Some of them were soon handed over to the Germans, some were released, and 15,000 were executed.

Arrests of civilians followed. A week after Soviet troops occupied Eastern Poland, the Politburo adopted a resolution calling for the abolition of all Polish institutions of governance and the establishment of Soviet order in the occupied territories. They rushed to bring the newly annexed lands into uniformity with the rest of their country, where arrests, executions, and purges had been systematically carried out over the previous two decades. The resolution translated into the arrests of officials at all levels, businessmen and other representatives of the bourgeoisie, and political activists of all sorts. Two-thirds of all those arrested in the Soviet Union between September 1939 and June 1941 were Polish citizens. About 108,000 Polish citizens—more than the entire population of Bialystok—were accused of "counterrevolutionary activity," terrorism, espionage, and the like, and sentenced to prison terms; 18,000 were executed. Most of the arrested were men. Starting in February 1940, members of their families, as well as a variety of other civilians, were summarily deported to Siberia and other northern regions of Russia. About 320,000 Polish citizens were forced to labor there under secret-police oversight.

By the time of Ester's visit, Bialystok was a city of gaps and ghosts: everywhere she looked, people and entire families were missing. The city's population had nearly quadrupled in 1939, when the border with the Nazi-occupied territories, where Jews were already being herded into ghettos, was still open, and a steady stream of Jewish refugees had flowed across it. Now these people were gone, deported by the Soviets, who first attempted to hand them back to the Germans, but when the German authorities declined, sent them to work in lumber production in the Far North. Among the deportees were Ester's uncle Zalman and his family, who had come from Warsaw to stay in Jakub's home. They were taken away one night in the summer, along with over seven thousand other refugees from the Bialystok area. Uncle Zalman died. Years later his son came through Moscow on his way to Poland from the Far North. He stayed with Ester, but told her little about what he had experienced: the only thing he wanted to think about was getting out of the Soviet Union.

All told, in 1940, between 211 and 215 trains carrying refugees turned deportees traveled the route from the occupied territories to the Russian Far North. Many of them froze or starved to death. The Jews among those who reached their final destination also found that many shops refused to serve Jews during regular hours, setting aside a special time when they were allowed to enter. Their police supervisors complained in reports that "they have never done physical labor" and concluded that "Jews can never be taught to work." So much for the utter lack of anti-Semitism in the Soviet Union.

The winter of her visit, Ester found Jakub, now working as a bookkeeper at a nationalized shoe factory, preoccupied with the weekly task of putting together food parcels for Uncle Zalman and his family in Russia and for the innumerable relatives now living in the Warsaw Ghetto, and coolly certain that it was a matter of time—in all likelihood, not very much time—before the Soviets came to arrest him. Indeed, though he had not been elected to the last prewar municipal council, he still served on the *kehilla,* the Jewish council, which made him a sort of representative of the old authorities. Even worse, he had been a very active member of a non-Communist political party. The men of Bialystok—the Jews, the politicos, the small-business men (the local tycoons had long since been arrested)—had by now grown accustomed to this state of waiting. Those of them who had grown children focused on getting the children out of Bialystok. Most had figured out that the only way to escape was to run behind the firing line, to Moscow, the seat of the evil that was plaguing the occupied territories. The best way to secure a pass on the railroad to the Soviet mainland was to be a recent high-school graduate traveling for college entrance exams. The young people of Bialystok were glued to their textbooks, studying for exams that would get them into Moscow colleges. Friends, and especially the parents of friends, envied what they assumed had been Ester's extraordinarily prescient planning in this regard.

Isaj was getting ready to go to Moscow too. His family's good fortune, which began with the arrival of the Soviets, had continued. His extraordinary aptitude and knowledge had been noticed at the teaching school, and he had been allowed to transfer to a teachers' college without earning a high school diploma. Now he would be able to transfer to a college in Moscow, and Ester had already made arrangements for him to join her at IFLI in the next academic year. He was studying Russian and writing to Ester daily, sometimes two or three times a day, often trying to insert a Russian word here and there, and always trying to ape what he perceived to be the Soviet style. For a while he even folded his letters in triangles—a habit he must have noted among the Red Army soldiers—until Ester's roommates sent him a joke poem teasing him about his "fashionable" envelopes.

Isaj's letters were written in Yiddish on small pieces of bluish and brownish paper, ink-stained in places. My grandmother Ester kept these letters without rereading them, in a small drawer of an old rolltop desk. She did not mean to keep them secret: they were simply part of another life. She even grew convinced she had forgotten Yiddish. I talked her into reading some of the letters to me, translating as she went.

My dear,

I have received your letter. Its every word literally made me shiver. I was so happy that you are so close to me, despite the physical distance. . . .

I have started reading the book by Brenner which you gave me. This same book you and I were reading together that time when we were going to the camp at Brok. Do you remember that? It's been less than two years, but what a colossal difference in what I find in this book now! Back then I was more taken with his story about a shopkeeper in London who is saving money to move to Erez Israel to settle there. To open a shop there. Tusia, please excuse my language, but now when I was reading this story I thought it stank. All of this is so old, so foreign to me. Every story is so far from real life, so pale and forced. The author reminds me of yeshiva students I used to encounter at the city library.

Maybe my earlier impressions of the book were influenced by the situation in the world in which I lived when I read it then. The atmosphere in the book is soaked in the awareness of property, profit-seeking. I had the impression that all the characters, aside from how they portray themselves, have another dimension that shows through, that I don't like.

Ester, what do you say to all this? . . . Write me about your impressions, too, and I repeat how I strive to be with you. Write me, my dear.

This was one of the letters written at the beginning of Ester's stay in Moscow. Another, one of the last letters my grandmother received from her fiancé, was inspired by one she had written, describing, with her characteristically excessive candor, one or more of the suitors who followed her everywhere in Moscow. She never so much as kissed any of them, but this was a fact that Isaj, stuck in the provincial hell of Bialystok, could hardly have trusted.

It's not every girl who will tell things like that to a guy she is planning to marry. This is why I never touched on this subject the entire time you were here in Bialystok, though I don't know if I was right not to. But you see, I believe everything you write, including what you say about your flirtations or longer or shorter affairs. Of course, I feel a certain resistance to this. I didn't tell you, but now I have to admit that I find this, as they say in Russian, obidno, hurtful. I am writing this letter bit by bit because I keep stopping to think about this.

Do you remember, when you were leaving for Moscow for the first time, I asked you if you think that life in the big city may not pull you away from me. You said a very decisive "no." When you were in Bialystok again for vacation, I asked you again, and again you said no—but with much less certainty, or so it seemed to me. How would you answer that question now?

Maybe everything I am writing has a shtetl flavor to it. I feel it myself, and I am ashamed.

I am going to finish, primarily because electricity will be turned off in a few minutes. I received the psychology book yesterday. I am very grateful to you for it. I was reading it today and literally jumping up for joy. . . . Well, I wanted to add something else, but I can't because the lights are already off.

CHAPTER SEVEN

JUNE 15, 1941

In the last six weeks Ruzya and Samuil have walked the length
and breadth of Moscow. They have exhausted their repertoire of
Mayakovsky poems. They have carried out comparative studies of
ice cream served on street corners citywide. Like all young
Moscow couples, they conduct their relationship in the street.
Ruzya is still living in the cramped basement apartment with her
parents and the twins, who are now eleven years old. (Her older
brother, Yasha, is by this time a married man, no longer living in
Moscow. A professional pilot, he has been test-flying planes in
Sverdlovsk.) Samuil, his parents, and his teenage sister occupy two
adjacent rooms at the end of a communal apartment's corridor.
On the one occasion the couple spent time there, when the rest of
Samuil's family was occupied outside the home, they overheard a
neighbor's loud lament regarding Ruzya's too well-worn coat, left
carelessly to hang in the entryway: the neighbor would have to
report to Samuil's mother that the boy was keeping inappropri-

ately shabby company. From the pinched look on Samuil's face, Ruzya gathered that, much as he would wish otherwise, his beloved mother was not above such concerns. They have stayed out-of-doors ever since.

There is no better time to walk the streets of Moscow than the months of May and June. An occasional chill provides the excuse needed to press close to each other, but it is never too cold to stand still and stare endlessly at the lights in the distance or at each other, struggling finally to say the obvious and finding no relief even after releasing the words that have crowded out all others. They have done all the known routes: the romantic Boulevard Ring, the animated Garden Ring, the foreboding, vast granite embankments of the Moscow River. They have lingered on bridges, under streetlamps, and next to monuments. They have taken that extra circle around the block, that extra ten minutes on the bench, that extra moment just inside the entryway of her building before parting. They have told each other about their exams—they are both finishing the fourth year of five-year programs—the pressure and the cramming, but still school has receded into a haze. They have told each other they are in love. Somehow, using interjections, silences, and sighs, they have now come to a new agreement: their relationship should pass into its next stage.

Their initial plan's elaborate nature betrayed their fears. They decided to take a boat down the Moskva-Volga Canal. Samuil said it was an appropriate choice because the new channel, which connected the Moscow River to the Volga four years earlier, making the Soviet Union's landlocked capital into a world-class port city, symbolized that in the future nothing would be impossible. What he meant, they both knew: their plan called for leaving town. Once aboard one of those beautiful new white boats, they would choose a stop—they all had names like Sunny Meadow and Green Harbor—to disembark and wander until they found seclusion in one of the parks that, according to the papers, lined the canal. They went to the river port early that afternoon—it was their day, they knew, because neither had exams on a Thursday—and stood in line for two hours. They felt a bit out of place among the white-shirted and straw-hatted families with shiny children whose very presence seemed designed for the neoclassical splendor of the port, with its alleys of round streetlamps lighting the approach to the white boats. Ruzya, at Samuil's request, wore the rust-colored dress she had had on at the party where they met; he, for utilitarian reasons best left unspoken, had donned a trench coat. Trying hard to ignore the moms, dads, and nannies, all of whom, they felt certain, could plainly see their intentions, they engaged in that sort of regressive chatter couples in love easily fall into. He called her "Puppy" and held her large hands and told her he was ecstatic to be in her paws. She told him he had peas in his eyes and made a production of calculating their number: "4,817 little ones and 599.5 large ones."

The line was cut off no more than ten people in front of them. There would be no more boats that day. It was as if some force had pushed them apart—they let go of each other's hands and breathed their separate sighs of relief at the collapse of their thrilling and frightening plan—then allowed them to reunite, their bond cemented now by the momentary lightness of separation. "I now consider us husband and wife," Samuil whispered, putting his arm around her.

They walked most of the way back into town: four or five hours, sore feet, and a new kind of planning. Now that they considered themselves married, what would they do? His parents were leaving for the dacha the following weekend, but the prospect of facing their friendly and nosy flatmates frightened Ruzya, who after that single visit to Samuil's home was convinced his family would reject her. Her own parents and younger brothers were planning to leave in just over two weeks to spend the summer at a dacha Moshe had been building for years. He had a dream, a most bizarre one for an urban, educated Jew—he wanted to have a vegetable garden. This summer, finally, following years of scrimping and saving and countless arguments with his wife, he was going to commit his family to three months of digging, watering, and fretting. Once they were gone, Ruzya and Samuil could set up housekeeping in her parents' apartment.

Today, three days after their failed boat expedition, they feel a new legitimacy. Separated for days by their exams, they meet now in town, she in the rust-colored dress and he in the trench coat, and they take the tram to Sokolniki, a giant park whose carefully trimmed alleys give way to what, in urban Russia, passes for complete wilderness: a mixed forest where squirrels and even moose wander virtually undisturbed. Ruzya and Samuil venture far enough to feel that it is unlikely they will be seen by anyone other than the animals. They lay down Samuil's trench coat, and they become husband and wife.

PART TWO

WAR

1941–1942

Ruzya and Samuil

Chapter Eight

June 20, 1941

Salomea is running. She is a student at the Textile Institute in Moscow—she came here from Bialystok a year ago—and she is running to see her friend Ester at IFLI, because Salomea has just received an urgent unsigned telegram: ESTER'S PARENTS GONE TO VISIT UNCLE ZALMAN STOP SHE SHOULD GO VISIT FRIEND STOP. Salomea knows that Uncle Zalman is the Goldbergs' refugee relative whose family was deported to the Russian Far North last year. The telegram means Ester's parents have been arrested. Salomea is scheming as she runs, imagining Ester can move to Salomea's dorm room to evade the secret police.

They hold a silent war council in Ester's room at IFLI. Salomea hands her the telegram, and Ester then hands it on to Eda, her roommate, a Jewish girl from Grodno. All three of them have relatives interned on both sides of the border, in the ghettos in the German-occupied part of Poland, and in the forced-labor settlements in the Russian Far North. All have been expecting just this sort of news about those in their families who remain free. All know, of course, that walls have ears and they cannot discuss the matter at hand out loud; nor do they need to.

Eda and Salomea look at Ester questioningly. She scoffs: "I am here, anyway." Translated, that means: *I am far enough away, and surely they won't come looking for me. There is no reason to hide.* Eda and Salomea nod their agreement. Now Ester sits down on her bed and weeps, and her two friends sit on either side of her, holding her hands and occasionally wiping away her tears. She is crying for her parents and for her home. Going back to visit, as she planned to do in just over a month, is no longer possible: that would mean risking arrest. Not that she has anyplace to go: their apartment and everything in it have surely been confiscated. Every time she stops crying she thinks of Isaj, who was clearly the one who sent the telegram and whom she may not see for a long time, and the tears come again. She is so alone in the world now, it is as though she could feel herself swaying in the winds from every direction. By evening, she has a chill.

JUNE 22, 1941, MORNING

Another message, a small triangle, this time delivered by the post. *My dear beloved daughter, I am passing through Moscow. Papa is not home, so do not go there yet. Papa is well, but he is not with me. I'm in a hurry because the train is about to move. I will write again as soon as I can.*

Ester thinks of Isaj's triangles: they were an affectation, his version of fashion. She has never had to consider the idea that a triangle in place of an envelope means that the letter writer was lucky just to have a piece of paper on which to write. Ester has heard that when people—some people—find a triangular piece of paper with an address written on it, they will affix a stamp and drop the missive into a mailbox. It is the least—or perhaps the most—they can do for those who are being taken away. Ester understands that Bella has been sent into exile while Jakub was kept in Bialystok, presumably to face trial.

The last wave of arrests and deportations swept through the annexed Polish territories on the night of June 19, 1941. According to secret-police documents, ten categories of "unreliables" were targeted, among them "participants in counterrevolutionary parties and anti-Soviet nationalist organizations" (category 1) and members of their families (category 8). Jakub, as a Zionist, would have fallen into category 1, which numbered 2,059 people in the region that had been designated Western Belarus. They were separated from their families at so-called concentration points—what amounted to transit camps—and placed in prisons on June 21, the day before Germany invaded the Soviet Union. Bella, despite her Bund membership, must have fallen into category 8, which was why she was among the 22,000 to 25,000 people placed on the trains going through Belarus and Moscow on their way to Siberia. Five of the twenty trains never made it: German bombs destroyed the railroads ahead of them, and the deportees were allowed to disperse—a sort of liberation that almost certainly spelled death for the Jews among them, for they were released into open fields that would become German in a matter of days. Bella was lucky: she was on one of two Bialystok trains that arrived in the Siberian city of Biysk on July 4, 1941, bringing 3,002 deportees, most of them educated people, who were to be put to work on the collective farms. Without a trial, all of them had been condemned to twenty years of forced labor.

JUNE 22, 1941, MINUTES AFTER NOON

The twins come bounding back in just after Ruzya has sent them out the door and settled in for an afternoon of studying. The minute the eleven-year-olds return, they are shouting in agitation. The boys, both sporting the schoolboy's regulation stubble on their heads, are inexplicably short and pudgy—no one else in the family has their build—and they look frankly ridiculous when they put on a show of boyish joy and bravado, or whatever it is they are trying to portray at the moment. "War!" they scream over and over. "Hooray!" "War!" They start skipping around the room.

"What are you talking about?" Ruzya asks, alarmed. She has put them under strict instruction not to return home before dusk, and this may or may not be the reason she suspects their screams are not just part of some game they have dragged in from the street.

"War!" they shout again, in unison. "There is a war on!" They point toward the street, as though war had just erupted right there on First Kolobovsky Lane.

Ruzya attempts to look out the window, though, of course, she cannot see anything from the basement. A few people run past, and that could mean anything. She turns on the radio. The foreign commissar, Vyacheslav Molotov, is explaining that, just over eight hours ago, Germany broke the terms of the bilateral nonaggression pact and violated the borders of the Soviet Union. Ruzya feels tears start to pour down her face, and she pushes aside the stupid twins and runs out the door. "Our cause is just," Molotov is intoning. "The enemy will be beaten. We will be victorious."

She is running along the crooked lanes of her neighborhood to the huge Garden Ring, where she turns left and keeps running, breathless, inhaling her own tears mixed with the diesel fumes of trucks stalling at an intersection, until she reaches the large building where Samuil lives. There are others running up and down this street, each person on a separate path, and there are smaller and larger crowds everywhere, surrounding the radio loudspeakers mounted on lampposts, but none of them sees one another. She does not manage to catch her breath in the elevator to the fourth floor, and she is still wiping her face with a white handkerchief when Samuil opens the door. He is already wearing his uniform, dark green-brown trousers tucked into tall boots and a long shirt belted with a leather contraption meant for a gun he does not yet have.

"I'm on my way to the academy," he says. If there is a war, certainly all of the Military Law Academy's students and staff are expected to report for service.

"I'll walk you there," she says, and a sudden fear that he will be taken away from her today, that he will go to the front as soon as he reaches the academy, crosses her mind.

In fact, he will not go for nearly eight months—but the fear stays with her from this minute on. That, and the fear that Moscow will be bombed.

JUNE 25, 1941

Eda is running into the dorm and up the stairs, storming into their room and grabbing Ester, dazed and half-dressed, to drag her out into the street.

"What happened?"

"Come quickly, now!"

They stumble out the door of their redbrick building, and Eda takes a quick moment to orient herself. It has been three days since the war began, and everything is different: the trams are no longer running and even the crowds are changed, thick and anxious. She struggles to get her bearings on the street where they have been living for nearly a year.

"This way." She pulls Ester along.

"Why? What is going on?"

"Listen, your Isaj, he was walking down the street. Maybe he is looking for you."

Now Ester is silent and they run up Stromynka Street, zigzagging around people dragging heavy sacks—some with supplies of grain or other food, some with their radio receivers, which everyone has been ordered to turn in, some with whatever they have deemed worth hiding away from their home—until they are just behind a man in a wrinkled dark suit and a flat cap, carrying a leather travel case. Eda points at him. It is not Isaj's back—too broad and fleshy, even under the suit—but Eda's conviction moves Ester to skip a few steps ahead of the man and turn abruptly around before shaking her head "no" to a disappointed Eda.

Eda, of course, has seen Isaj only in a couple of photographs, and these were group photos of Ha-Shomer ha-Zair, which made everyone look generic. Maybe she thought the man looked foreign—with his leather case he did, vaguely. Maybe she thought she had noticed some feature that made Isaj stand out in any crowd. Maybe she just thought anything is possible in this city, where nothing is the same anymore.

Ever since the first announcement three days ago the radio has been broadcasting instructions on how to behave during the air raids: turn off the lights and go down to the bomb shelter or into the metro (this is the cable radio on lampposts and in those buildings that are wired; wireless units are illegal now: the more the Germans advance, the more radio frequencies they can put to their own use). By the first night all the streetlamps had been turned off and lightbulbs in courtyards and entryways changed to dim blue ones, which are said to be invisible from the air. Black curtains or any dark cloth that happened to be available went up over the windows everywhere in the city. Practice air raid alarms began on that first night. Many people now carry gas masks wherever they go; Eda and Ester have no idea where they might be procured.

And if only the gas masks were the only change in the streets! The Russians, so sullen and resigned ordinarily, have been supercharged with anxiety. They line up outside grocery stores and savings banks, and more and more of them are crowding the waiting halls at the railroad stations, trying to get themselves and their belongings on any train going east. And then there are the conscripts. General mobilization began June 23, and suddenly every other man seemed to be wearing a uniform. That day, or the next, they first started marching through the streets—to and from railroad stations, or their barracks, or draft offices—sometimes with song, always out of sync, and always alongside them are women running, sometimes with children, all faces streaked with tears. Dogs run, too, and then linger in confused clumps after the women disperse.

Tomorrow the war effort will take over Ester and Eda's dormitory building, which is being turned into a barracks and conscription point; the residents will be moved to a school building elsewhere in town. Ester and Eda have, of course, resolved not only to move but to join the effort. Ester has been making the rounds of draft offices, telling the story of two girls from Nazi-occupied Poland who made their way to Moscow specifically to join the Red Army and fight the Nazis. She repeats this version of their histories so frequently and so insistently that she has already grown to believe it. So far they have had no luck: the draft officers seem not to know quite what to do with women, and foreign ones at that. Yesterday she was asked if she was a member of the Komsomol. Most Soviet young people joined in high school, when Ester was attending the Hebrew Gymnasium in Bialystok. "Join the Komsomol, and then we'll talk," the officer told her. She will join today.

JULY 5, 1941

An entire week has gone by, and Ruzya has only just learned that it happened. A friend of Grisha's, someone she has met once or twice, came by to tell her. Grisha Petrosyan was the smartest boy in Ruzya's school gang, and one of her best friends—nothing romantic, but he came over every day, to see her and play chess with her mother, for Eva counted supreme mastery of the game among her many talents. In a group of brilliant and hopeful young people, he was the star. In 1938 he was admitted simultaneously to two faculties of Moscow University, and he was among the first students to be awarded the Stalin Stipend, the highest honor bestowed on young scholars.

On June 23 and 24, when his classmates gathered at the university to be assigned to People's Militia regiments, Grisha had the flu. He reported as soon as he could, and, though he had brought no clothes and no food with him, was immediately put on a bus with a group from a different faculty. The bus took them to a train station, and they piled into cattle cars, and they traveled. It may have been two or three or four days—however long it takes to start passing out from hunger, the lingering effects of the flu, and the heat and odor of the cattle car.

The account Ruzya received from Grisha's friend was short, and delivered in a monotone—*overrehearsed,* she thought, even as she listened to it. But the speech contained enough details to en-able Ruzya to imagine what happened—and keep imagining it, obsessively. First, she imagines him running. He is running, or he thinks he is running, because he cannot keep up with his comrades, who are marching off the train. Wherever they are now, this place must have gotten a lot of rain lately, because there are puddles everywhere. Grisha's shoes and socks quickly become waterlogged, which makes it even more difficult to run. It is slippery too: the ground, a glistening light-brown color, must be pure clay. He slips once but manages to break his fall, landing on his knee and his right hand, and he gets up again, but it is even more difficult to run now because his trousers, wet from the fall, are heavy and slipping down, and he has to hold them up with his hand, which hurts. He lifts his head to look around for the first time since they got off the train. He is looking for something—a sympathetic face, an end to this road, a patch of dry land—when he feels he is slipping again, falling forward, and he cannot land on his hand because he is still holding on to his belt, and he hears the splash when his face hits the puddle. He should lift his head, but he manages only to turn it. The clay feels warm against his cheek. There are people marching all around him, some of them already wearing heavy army boots. He puts his hands over his head.

Grisha Petrosyan is Ruzya's first war death.

It had been less than twenty years since the Russian Civil War ended; that had followed World War I virtually without interruption. For the purposes of collective memory, twenty years is a short time: all adults knew the devastation of war. There were also the more recent experiences of disastrous warfare: the Soviets' failed intervention in the Spanish Civil War and the 1939 war with Finland, with its meaningless and massive carnage. At noon on June 22, when the Soviet government finally acknowledged that the country was at war, though German troops were still hundreds and thousands of miles away from most Soviet cities, the people knew enough to expect the worst. The Soviet leadership's ill-concealed state of disarray, indecisiveness, and fear added to the general sense of dread.

Stalin had clung to his belief in German good faith and the nonaggression pact to the last—and then some. This placed the Red Army, already outnumbered and outgunned, at an unimaginable disadvantage: not only had the military failed to mobilize for a potential attack, but for the first several hours of the German incursion Soviet troops were forbidden to defend themselves. On the first day of war, the German military succeeded in destroying twelve hundred Soviet military planes, most of which were bombed in the airfields before they had a chance to take off. By the end of the second day, two thousand aircraft had been destroyed. After another three weeks, that number had tripled.

Four days into the war, German troops had advanced nearly two hundred miles into Soviet territory and taken more than three hundred thousand prisoners. A week after the fighting began, the Belarusian capital, Minsk, had fallen; nearly two million Soviet soldiers, including many officers, were dead—a loss all the more devastating for a military force already decimated by Stalin's own purges, which had taken nearly forty thousand officers. This was when Stalin finally emerged from his apparently catatonic state to address his nation on the radio. He acknowledged that the enemy had penetrated deep inside Soviet territory and called on the people to mobilize to defend their motherland.

Even before his call came, men and women all over the country were besieging draft offices. Women, especially students, were shipped to dig trenches outside any number of large towns and cities—an assignment in which many got stuck for months, dying in the trenches they were digging, of hunger, cold, and German

bombs. Those who did not qualify for regular military service—
men who were too old, too young, too frail, untrained, or even
exempt from conscription, as well as those who, like Grisha
Petrosyan, fell victim to bureaucratic accidents—joined the ranks
of the Narodnoye Opolcheniye, or the People's Militia. Over
three hundred thousand people from Moscow alone joined the
militia. These unfit soldiers were armed with antique rifles literally pilfered from museums, with trowels, and often with nothing
at all, and were used to form what amounted to human shields.
The British military historian Anthony Beevor writes of the militia, "The waste of life was so terrible, it is hard to comprehend: a
carnage whose futility was perhaps exceeded only by the Zulu
king marching an *impi* of his warriors over a cliff to prove their
discipline."

By mid-October the Moscow People's Militia had been destroyed. The vast majority fell on the battlefield, which saw no
battle—only killing; some, like Grisha, died before they ever got
to the battlefield; the rest were taken prisoner and herded west,
which, for the many Jews among them, meant a slower and more
painful death. German troops were just outside the Soviet capital.

OCTOBER 16, 1941

Cars and trucks are roaring down the streets of Moscow, all
headed east, east, east—fleeing the Germans. The vehicles buckle
visibly under their various burdens: all carry people and their possessions, some of which fly off the backs of trucks, but this does
not make their owners stop: nothing can. A rug here, a batch of
documents there—what the fleeing see fit to salvage. What was
prized yesterday has now been reduced to trash: piles of books
have grown in the courtyards—the complete collected works of

Lenin and Stalin, Marx and Engels. No one sees any reason, anymore, to doubt that Nazi occupation of Moscow is now just days, if not hours, away, and Muscovites who have not found a way out of the city are unloading whatever may compromise them in the eyes of the occupiers. This morning the radio announcer, whose reports are usually peppered with reassuring phrases like "retreat to strategic positions," "heroic effort," and "heavy losses sustained by the enemy," stuck grimly to the point: "During the night of October 14, the situation on the western front deteriorated. The Germans, with a large number of tanks, broke through our defenses."

At the Military Law Academy, Ruzya collects more news: roads leading east out of the city are clogged with people traveling on foot, lugging backpacks, wheelbarrows, and baby carriages; some of those who are staying have begun compiling lists of Jews living in their buildings—presumably to get in the occupiers' good graces; some academy staff have disappeared, likely having assumed civilian identities; there is widespread looting of abandoned shops and homes.

Ruzya has come to the academy today to make the final arrangements for the job she has managed to get: she will teach German to the academy's military lawyers, who will need the language to interrogate prisoners. The job means she, too, will be leaving Moscow, following Samuil to his posting in Ashkhabad. After months of waiting for an assignment, he finally left about a week ago to accompany the academy commissar, the two of them part of the advance guard charged with making arrangements for the academy's imminent evacuation to Central Asia.

This is not how Samuil and Ruzya planned it. They wanted to go to the front, not to Ashkhabad. For the almost four months since the war began they have been writing appeals asking to be allowed to volunteer. As they envisioned it, he would be a *politruk,* or "political leader," a Soviet-era equivalent of chaplain, and she would be a translator: translators were needed at the front to debrief prisoners. But the academy refused to release him in advance of the evacuation—and military institutions are among the last to be evacuated.

Meanwhile, Ruzya and Samuil have been making their life together right here, in the heart of the disaster. Both sets of parents left the city back in the summer, part of the early wartime exodus. Before they left, in the shocked first days of the war, Ruzya and Samuil conducted a quick round of introductions: she brought Samuil home to meet Eva and Moshe, and he dragged Ruzya out to the dacha to meet his parents, Batsheva and Lev. As usual in Ruzya's house, no one knew quite how to behave: Eva was preoccupied with some sort of scuffle between the twins, and with worry about what would now happen to Yasha the pilot; Samuil and Ruzya sat in the kitchen for a while with a hospitable but restless Moshe before finding an excuse to leave. At Batsheva's dacha the next day, it was all homey food, hugs, a bit of crying, and a ready dose of reproach for Samuil's transparent soldiering plans. Ruzya found herself thrilled at becoming, finally, a part of what felt like a real family with a real home.

Then, within a couple of weeks, they were alone: both their fathers worked as accountants at large industrial plants that were moved hastily to the Urals. Although Moshe never made it to his dream dacha, as he had been so determined to do that summer, his letters soon, bizarrely, boasted of his vegetable-growing feats in the East: his squash even fetched a prize at a country fair. Meanwhile, Samuil and Ruzya made a home in the basement on First Kolobovsky Lane and learned the basics of being a couple. At some point they registered their marriage at the civic registrations office down the street, but neither of them thought enough of the occasion to fix the date in memory: they agreed it was a mere formality. The art of deciding jointly without speaking came with the choice to stop running the half mile to the metro during the air raid alerts: they were in a basement anyway. They did not budge, even after the practice alerts were replaced with real ones on July 22 and, one by one, familiar buildings started to disappear from view. The knowledge of being joined inextricably came in early autumn, during the weeks of worry after Samuil shot himself in the foot while cleaning his handgun. Terrified of being accused of deserting by maiming himself, he sought care underground, from a doctor friend of a friend, and to everyone else explained away his limp by claiming to have burst a blister.

They learned something, too, that alternately thrilled and shamed them. It is possible to be ecstatically, deliriously, foolishly happy even when your country is bleeding and danger's breath is audible just behind you. It is possible to cry from helpless rage while reading the newspaper posted in the morning on the stand outside the circus building and minutes later to cry for joy while hugging your husband before he goes off to work.

Now, as the city breaks apart and away all around her, Ruzya, alone, tries to hold on to that feeling. Her daily visits to the academy help it linger. Talking to Samuil in her head while she puts away things in the apartment—wrapping the clock and the dishes in blankets and towels before stuffing them in the cupboard, to safeguard them against a partial collapse of the building—helps her too. Knowing that the academy will ship out within a day or two, as she learned today, helps her even more. She has heard all about the pandemonium at the stations, about stampedes that have killed people, but these seem like negligible obstacles if the trip will reunite her with Samuil.

CHAPTER NINE

AUGUST 1941

And now, where do they get a corkscrew? They lost sight of the
little things during their buying spree. They are Ester, her IFLI
roommate Eda, and Lena Zonina, Ester's instant best friend going
back to her first semester in Moscow (they bonded after they both
got "excellent" from an instructor known for his picky strictness).
Ester and Eda had to find a place to live about a week after
Germany invaded, when their dormitory was turned into an army
barracks and students were moved to a school building in the center of the city, where they had to sleep on desks. A friend helped
get them into a room in a communal apartment vacated by a fellow student who had already been evacuated. So Ester and Eda
moved into this room, and Lena joined them weeks ago, when
her mother was hospitalized. Lena, who alone among their friends
lived in an apartment with just her mother and no flatmates, did
not want to stay there by herself.

Today they have bought things they have not tasted in

months, maybe years, maybe ever, Georgian red wine among them. Best to keep the celebration muted, of course, for the occasion is somber. They have come into an inheritance of sorts. A young pilot has died. They never knew him, but it seems a year or so ago he saw Eda's photograph at the home of a mutual friend in the Soviet-occupied territories, so he sent her a letter. She responded, and romance ensued. About eight weeks ago he wrote that he was going off to the front, and in another three weeks he sent her the details of a bank transfer with a brief explanation: he was getting a large allowance as an air force officer, and he had no use for the money there at the front—and no one in the rear but his beloved Eda. They picked up the transfer and bought food. And now they have received news that he has been killed, and another bank transfer, an astronomical sum of money, something like a year's student stipend. They have bought wine.

Before the windfall, they had been struggling for a long time. First semester was hard enough: it seemed to Ester both she and Eda were constantly working to scale down their expectations. But once you did that—once you put words like *dessert* out of your mind, once you accepted that your selection of underwear was limited to the two garments you washed every night and put on the heater so you could put them on in the morning, once you developed the habit of telling yourself, "Look, everyone around here lives like this—and survives and even manages to have fun and create"—then you could learn to live on a student stipend. In their letters they both told their parents that the stipend afforded a perfectly suitable existence and assured them they needed nothing: everything their families could spare should go to relatives in the Warsaw Ghetto. Then, in February, Eda did not make the grade: to qualify for the stipend, students had to have straight "excellent's" on their exams, and Eda got a "good" on two of her midyears. After nearly five months sharing a room, studying

Russian together and helping each other find their way in the realities of their new country, they were practically family, so Ester said they could both live on her stipend.

Somewhere around that time she first heard the word *vprogolod'*. It means "a life of hunger"—not the crisis of famine but the habitual, year-to-year, day-to-day, painful light-headedness and sucking sensation in the esophagus—and it described their way of life exactly.

And now this wine and bread bought by the loaf and pinkish brown smoked meat must be her reward. Their reward? For a second Ester actually believes there is a sort of higher justification for the good fortune of having a full stomach for once. She lifts the wineglass—well, the thick yellowish glass with wine in it—to her mouth. It tastes kind of sour: she realizes she expected the sweet taste of Shabbat wine. She has never been a wine drinker before. But she might become one: even with Lena living with them, they can probably afford to buy wine at least once a week.

SEPTEMBER 1941

War sometimes seems all about food. Or at least Ester's life is all about food. Here she is now, behind the wheel of a truck stalled at an intersection, on her way to the front to deliver the chickens and potatoes stacked in the back of the truck. Also sitting in the back are two loaders, skinny, sickly guys in their late thirties—clearly not strong enough to be soldiers, but perfectly capable of loading and unloading soldiers' food (and loading up on it while Ester drives). Now Ester faces a choice: either get out and turn the unbearably heavy crank in the front to get the engine started, or go around the back to ask the loaders to do it. The first option is nearly impossible physically; the second, impossibly humiliating.

"Hey, young men, could you give me a hand with the crank again?" she shouts over the wooden planks that fence in the truck bed.

There is shuffling and groaning in the dark recesses of the truck, then the pair emerge in a cloud of invectives. They refer to sexual relations with the makers of the GAZ-AA truck, Ester, Ester's mother, and whoever came up with the idea of putting women behind the wheel.

This was not, of course, where Ester planned to end up. She and Eda tried just about everything else to join the war effort. They both tried to enlist but were rejected. They tried catching spies. This was Ester's friend Boris Kravets's doing, mostly. A classmate from IFLI, he is another frustrated soldier: too nearsighted to be allowed to join. But not so nearsighted as to not notice, as he stood on Ester and Eda and Lena's balcony one night, that an odd blinking light was visible somewhere in the maze of buildings across the street. This was a couple of months ago, right after the first air raids, and the radio was regularly imploring Muscovites to be vigilant, always on the lookout for people who may be directing German bomber planes to strategic objects (not that they seemed to be bombing anything particularly strategic—just a lot of different buildings). They called the police, and two NKVD officers came, set up some sort of equipment on their balcony, and stayed two nights. They came on the third night, as well, to thank them for their service: they seemed to indicate, without quite saying it, that the young people had indeed helped apprehend a spy.

Ester was beside herself with pride for a day or so, but her spy-fighting fervor lessened considerably when Salomea came by to tell them about her recent misadventure. She was apparently spotted by one of those newly vigilant Muscovites who had heard her say something on a tram—with an accent, naturally, a Polish one.

She was forced to go to the police station to prove she was not a spy. Fortunately, she succeeded. She was lucky: every foreigner was suspect, and a Pole was, to the NKVD, just someone from the other side of the front line.

The radio reports were getting more and more somber, and doing nothing was getting intolerable. Then, about five or six weeks ago, she saw a notice: YOUNG WOMEN NEEDED TO DRIVE SUPPLIES TO FRONT LINE. ADMISSION TO DRIVING COURSES AFTER TEST. Well, here was something. She and Eda ran to one of the addresses listed on the notice. The test turned out to be a cursory eye exam. Eda was done and signed up in two minutes flat. But the nurse administering the test to Ester made a discovery: the patient was just about completely blind in one eye. Had she not known? Had she never had an eye checkup? Ah, she had grown up in Poland. The woman sighed understandingly: this simply confirmed what she had been taught about inferior medical care in capitalist countries.

Ester took the results of her eye exam as something very much like a personal insult. That this should not keep her from becoming a driver seemed self-evident. There was now simply the question of how to devise a way to get around the problem. As it turned out, drugstores had eye-exam charts available. She memorized one in less than half an hour, and in another hour she had already passed the exam at a different sign-up station.

Over the next two weeks she got to know the GAZ-AA, a 1.5-ton truck with a square, long-nose cab and a flat wooden bed riding on skinny, wobbly wheels. It started with a crank that was inserted into the elliptical grille between the two headlights, and it stalled every time it stopped. At every traffic light, that is. At first she always cranked it back up herself; now she sometimes gets up the nerve to ask the disagreeable loaders.

Ester's daily routine is picking up her truck at the park and

reporting to a place grandly named Glavrestorantrest, meaning
the Head Restaurant Trust, to receive instructions on her routes
for the day. She is dispatched to a food warehouse, a fowl factory,
or some such thing, reports back to the Glavrestorantrest, and,
loaded down with prepared food and two men to manage the
cargo, begins the journey to the trenches. It is not far to the front
line, about thirty kilometers from Moscow (right around where
my grandmother Ester's dacha is now—it takes me two hours to
cycle there from the center of town), but with the stalling and the
shelling, the journey sometimes takes Ester half a day. If there is
shelling, she leaves the truck on the road and lies facedown in the
ditch until the shelling stops, and then she takes the crank to her
truck again. Even with the nights nearly white—in late summer
and early fall the sun does not set until eleven o'clock in
Moscow—neither she nor Eda can usually manage to get home
before dark. God knows they try, for they desperately want to
avoid having to navigate the darkened city without headlights,
which they are banned from turning on lest they help German
bomber pilots get their bearings.

In the early weeks, when the air raid alarm sirens sounded,
they would take small suitcases and go down into Stalin's glorious
metro, which now functioned as a giant bomb shelter. It was
crowded, standing room only, and once they started working they
gave up going there, because, though they had a friend who had
been wounded when a bomb hit her building, they needed their
sleep to be able to work. Still, they are always so tired. That is why
she would rather listen to the loaders' cursing than try to heave
the crank herself.

DECEMBER 1941

It has been nearly a month since Ester and Eda finally boarded a train to Ashkhabad, where they will join the rest of their IFLI classmates. The train is made up of stragglers—mostly students who, for one reason or another, were left behind last fall when the Institute was merged with Moscow University and the students and faculty from both schools were loaded into cattle cars bound for Ashkhabad. Ester and Eda could not go then, because they were officially working for the war effort, and Glavrestorantrest was not releasing any of its employees. They drove through the October days of panic, pushed by a sense of duty that went un-challenged as long as they both went without sleep. They assumed every day they took supplies to the front line was the last: the Germans would either break through or have to retreat, would they not? But the next day each of them would be behind the wheel again, and in the ditch again, hiding from shells, and driv-ing back into Moscow after dark again. One day Ester imagined this going on forever, and then she realized they had to try to get out. They started knocking on doors trying to find someone who could help them, and one day finally dragged a university repre-sentative to see the personnel manager at Glavrestorantrest.

"Comrade, you must take into consideration the fact that these girls are Jewish," the representative said blandly. He had the air of a man who was doing the right thing because it was his job, not because he had any particular sympathy for the two young women or, for that matter, for anyone else.

The personnel manager signed two slips of paper and silently handed them across his large desk. He looked annoyed at having been forced into a corner by an incontrovertible argument. This was when Ester realized they all expected the Germans to win.

A couple of days out of Moscow, the train unloaded them in a

snowed-under town, where a businesslike local woman distrib-
uted the students among the log cabins. Ester and Eda roomed together at the house of a woman in her forties or fifties: she made a
pastime of evaluating each of them as a potential daughter-in-
law—as a wife, that is, for her son, who was away fighting the war.
She liked Eda better: the bespectacled, small, and bony Eda was
helping her around the house when the more popular Ester was
either out with friends or resting after a late night out. These were
not wild nights: the students walked around the small town in
groups, talking and laughing in the pitch-blackness. A few times
there was a dance in the barnlike club; the students danced while
several young local women watched with awkward fascination.

After a couple of weeks, when the great wartime train bureaucracy once again remembered the students, they were re-
sorted into groups and packed back onto trains, into wooden
freight cars retrofitted with small wood-burning stoves. Ester and
Eda's train moved slowly, stopping seemingly at random—for
minutes, hours, or sometimes days. Assuming each time that the
cause was nearby bombing, the students filed out of the cattle cars
and lay down in the snow close to the tracks. Often there were
bombs, and sometimes they fell close enough to shower the dis-
embarked passengers with thick black dirt that blasted out from
under the snow. In between bomber flights, the passengers used
the stops to wash up, rubbing the snow on their hands, faces, and
necks, and then filling their small aluminum pots with it so they
would have drinking water.

They also foraged for firewood during their stops. It was easy
to find, and stops were plentiful, so the air in the cars grew suffocating, hot and heavy with smoke and the stagnant smells of the
cars' occupants. They looked forward to Central Asia, where,
they imagined, they would not always be having to fire up the
stove to fight the cold wind that got in through a multitude of

cracks. They imagined dry, warm air that would bring a sort of peace.

And it did: the bombs stopped as they got closer to their destination. Even the frequent stops in Central Asia felt better. The ground was soft and relatively warm—it was not snow they were lying on, but sand—and that made lying on it more comfortable than any arrangement they could find for their bodies inside the cattle car.

But when the snow disappeared, so did the water. It has been three days since they started rationing water. Ester feels like not only her throat but the skin on her face, and for some reason, especially behind her ears, is starting to resemble the earth here: gray, dry, cracked. A couple of days ago people started scratching themselves. They assumed at first that they itched because they could no longer wash, but then dismal rumors began to travel from car to car, and then one person in Ester's car confessed he felt like he was being bitten. Lice. Two people already have said that a boy in one of the other cars is dead from typhus.

Ester wonders if she is going to make it to Ashkhabad alive, and then she tries, again, not to think, again, about whether they should have been in such a rush to leave Moscow. It has been a month since they left, and as far as she knows, Moscow is still under Soviet control. She could be there now, sleeping in a bed instead of leaning against the wooden wall of a freight car, feeling a helpless weakness spread through her body as she wonders if that little bump on her skin is not the bite of a typhus louse.

When I was a child in Moscow I was fascinated with a weekly radio show that consisted entirely of missing-persons announcements dating back to World War II. Thirty years later, people were still sending in names, ages, and distinguishing features. A sad male voice slowly read them out, one after another, adding nothing but the briefest of pauses in between. "Kharitonova, Irina Dmitriyevna, born in 1923, is sought by her sister. She has a large oval birthmark on her left shin. Last seen October 23, 1941, at the train station in Voronezh." I imagined a train pulling out, a young woman looking at it over the heads of a thick crowd and opening her mouth in a slight, silent protest. I never really imagined that thirty-five years later this woman might find her sister again. I took the radio show for what it was: a collection of very short stories, a sort of oral history.

Soviet history is a narrative of train schedules, of the chains of cattle cars transporting desperate, cold, and hungry people from one end of the empire to another. Before the war began, these trains had taken several million—it is still impossible to give anything like a precise figure—inmates to labor camps and colonies, and hundreds of thousands of deportees to sites of forced labor. With the start of the war, the cattle cars were transporting not only conscripts of various sorts but also about twenty-five million people fleeing the advancing German troops. Many were evacuated with their factories or institutes, but as panic built, hundreds of thousands of others fled chaotically, boarding any train they could, often becoming separated from family members. The trains got stuck en route, sometimes for weeks at a time. The cars and the tracks were bombed. People died inside, of wounds and hunger; those who sought refuge from the raids outside the train died of exposure. Trains changed their destinations and often took off without warning after a stop of hours or days.

Ruzya's was a lucky train: it did not take too long, it did not get bombed, derailed, or diverted, and it took her to her husband. It also took her to the strangest place she had ever been. Like most

Soviet citizens, she had grown up with a sense of rightful owner-
ship of the vast variety of lands that made up the Union. She had
never questioned the idea that Russian speakers traveled to these
lands to bring culture, education, and much-needed structure to
the well-meaning and welcoming but disadvantaged natives. It
certainly would never have occurred to her that, to escape an occupying army, she was fleeing to an occupied territory.

Like most evacuees, she did not expect to end up in a land so
foreign. In the dusty, flat Turkmen Valley, nothing seemed logical.
Not the square clay houses with their inner courtyards hidden
from view—as though someone had turned the traditional Russian
gabled wooden house inside out and upside down. Not the odors,
as pungent in the slow warmth of late October as at the height of
summer heat: rotted melons, human waste, smoke from wood-
stoves. Not the natives' colorful multilayered dress and loud street
manner—and the women's habit of planting their feet far apart and
lifting their many skirts to empty their bladders wherever they felt
the urge.

Ashkhabad had already accepted several waves of Russian
evacuees, so a relationship between the natives and the refugees,
who fancied themselves guests, had taken shape. The Turkmens
had many reasons to feel squeezed: the lucky ones were renting to
the evacuees, but others had been summarily ordered to make
room in their homes, free of charge. Food was suddenly in short
supply: local stores could not serve the swelling population, and
with transportation and procurement networks breaking down,
the situation bordered on catastrophic.

Almost certainly the Turkmens expressed their resentment
among themselves, in the guttural native language the newcomers
neither understood nor cared to try to learn. But sometimes, especially in food lines, the frustration boiled over—audibly and unmistakably, even if the words could not be understood. There

seemed to be no better catalyst for an outpouring of pent-up feeling than the appearance of a man, a young and apparently able-
bodied one, well coiffed—Samuil still had that fashion-plate look
that once put Ruzya on guard—and, as his looks somehow made
clear, Jewish. "You yid," they shouted, "you should be at the
front, not standing in food queues with housewives!" After a
while, Samuil tried not to leave their rented room except to go to
the academy—and certainly not to stand in line at the stores. It
never occurred to him he might argue back that he was doing his
duty at the Military Law Academy, and that this was a part of the
war effort too. He never really bought that argument even when
his own boss made it, trying to convince Samuil to give up the
dream of going to war. The thing is, Samuil agreed with those
screaming women.

Ester and Ruzya arrived in Ashkhabad just weeks apart, as they
would learn eight years later, when they first met and became
friends. What both remember to this day is the hunger—more
than the heat, the local women with their many skirts, or the
crammed, chaotic housing quarters. More even than the fear,
which fades like all emotions, they remember the hunger.

Hunger is *obsosy*—literally, "suckers"—the hard candy that
replaced sugar because there was no sugar. Ration cards entitled
families to a certain number of suckers. They came in different
colors, so each person picked a color, which made it easier to
make them last from meal to meal: you sucked on a sucker as you
drank your tea, then put it back on the common plate, to pick up
again when you next sat down to eat. You just had to remember
the color of your sucker—and to keep from sucking it too hard.

Hunger is a detailed memory of store shelves. When Ruzya
and Samuil first arrived in Ashkhabad, the shops sold canned crab-

meat for kopecks and delicious Turkmen wine, and then it was all gone, within days, as all those cattle cars pulled in.

Hunger is believing that the exact measure of good living is the difference between starvation and survival. Bread was now rationed, too, and bread and "suckers" were the only food items available to ordinary evacuees in Ashkhabad.

Hunger is when all the new mothers in town are so malnourished they have no breast milk. Hunger is food named not for its ingredients but for its consistency, like *balanda,* a thin soup that could be made of anything—any combination of meat or vegetables and a lot of water. It had no fatty film on top, no solid parts to spoon up, and it had an unidentifiable flavor—but anyone who had access to balanda was lucky.

Hunger is a vocabulary tuned to the fine distinctions of need. A generation that grew up obsessed with food, which was always in short supply, always to be procured, won, deserved rather than merely bought, they know the words of their experience. In Ashkhabad, says my grandmother Ruzya, "We were not starving. We were hungry."

CHAPTER TEN

MARCH 6, 1942

"My God, but you are expecting!" This is the first thing Batsheva says after kissing Ruzya and Samuil hello at the train station. She and Lev and Samuil's teenage sister, Zhenya, have crossed the country again, north to south, to be able to say good-bye to their son: Samuil is still waiting, still begging at the draft offices, but there is no doubt that he will be called up soon. No one is exempt any longer. So his parents have left what was a tolerable existence in the Urals and come all the way here, to the dust, stink, and hunger of Turkmenia. "Welcome, you wandering Jews," Samuil said, taking their mismatched luggage—two proper travel cases and four yellow-gray pillowcases filled to bursting—off the train. Ruzya had been noting with surprise that she was anticipating their arrival joyfully, without the reservation that her shyness would normally impose. But now she finds herself speechless, stunned by Batsheva's words.

In the evening, after they have helped Samuil's parents unpack their belongings in the room they found for them a few days in advance, after Samuil has wolfed down the cookies his mother baked in the Urals and dragged across the country in a pillowcase, the men go into the courtyard to smoke and Batsheva instructs Zhenya to go wash up for sleep. Then she sits in a chair, her legs spread, her long arms hanging down between them—a simple, confident, very tired woman—and leans forward: "You didn't know, did you?"

"You know, I haven't had the monthlies," Ruzya admits, feeling already convinced by this woman, but still feeling foolish for believing her easily. "But no one has them anymore—I mean, the nerves, the hunger." She stops because she is not allowed to tell Batsheva that Samuil has not been eating well. "And I haven't gained any weight."

"You wouldn't, not at this point, little girl." Batsheva smiles affectionately.

Ruzya is quiet. She believes the older woman. Tomorrow she will start noticing changes in herself: her hips have widened, and her breasts seem to be filling out. In another two weeks, the doctor will tell her she is three months pregnant. A few weeks after that, in April, Samuil will go off to war.

Ruzya—left in a strange, foreign city to give birth to a child and try to feed him when even healthy adults were starving—never considered trying to stop Samuil. When he said it was his sacred duty to be at the front, she agreed. Samuil was going off to be a politruk, a "political leader," the job he had long wanted, which, if one believed the official word on the matter—and Ruzya did—was the most important job in the military. The troops had to be motivated if the country was to be saved.

When Samuil finally went off to war, the Red Army's crisis of motivation was at its height. Less than a year into the fighting, vast territories and millions of lives had been lost, and troops were retreating haphazardly, disobeying orders to hold their ground and sometimes deserting en masse, going over to the enemy. The Soviet leadership flailed in search of a force, an instrument, a mechanism for motivating the troops. It backtracked temporarily on its anti-Church stand to allow the clergy to preach to the ranks. The ministers worked side by side with the politruks, who urged the soldiers on by dangling the prospect of full membership in the Party—the province of the small ruling elite before the war. Stringent requirements for aspiring Party members were relaxed, allowing soldiers who had distinguished themselves in the battlefield to be inducted without the requisite recommendations and waiting period. About four million people joined the Party during the years of the war—more than the number of Party members before 1941—about half of them died.

Samuil was dispatched to the front after three months of training, around the time of Stalin's Order #227, one of the main ideological landmarks of the war period. In the dictator's deliriously poetic way, the order read, *It is time to stop the retreat. No turning back! This must now be our main slogan. It is necessary to defend every position, every meter of Soviet territory to the last drop of blood, to hold on to every bit of Soviet land and protect it as long as possible.* So-called fence-in battalions were now stationed behind regular troops, guns at the ready, to prevent unauthorized retreat.

A memo from the Defense People's Committee (this is what the defense ministry was called) defined the tasks that now faced the politruks. The memo proposed a brief scenario for the morale-boosting meetings the politruks were expected to conduct:

MEETING TOPIC: On the actions of Komsomol members in the battlefield.

RESOLVED: It is better to die in the trenches than to leave in disgrace. And not only must you stay but you must make sure the person next to you does not leave.

AUDIENCE QUESTION TO MEETING CHAIR: "Are there legitimate reasons for leaving the line of fire?"

ANSWER: "Of all possible excuses, only one can be considered, and that is death."

To an educated young man like Samuil—a soldier, a Jew—it must have seemed obvious that he could best serve the war effort not just by picking up a gun but by putting his mind, his training, and his rhetorical gift to work. But what did he think of the tactics he was ordered to use? Did he believe it when he told a soldier he should bleed to death under fire rather than seek help? Did he, along with hundreds of millions of his compatriots and zealots everywhere, believe that embracing a container filled with fuel (what is known elsewhere as a Molotov cocktail) and throwing yourself under an enemy tank, or using your body to clog up enemy artillery, was a supreme expression of valor? Or did he believe that a soldier is more than his body, that sometimes valor is found in trying to stay alive?

My grandmother keeps Samuil's letters—small brittle yellowed sheets—in a black cardboard folder. She has reread them only once, and resolved she would never again subject herself to that kind of pain. I have read them over and over, but they offer no clues to Samuil's opinion of the vision he worked to advance, convincing soldiers to sacrifice themselves in battle. The letters are a grating mix of heartbreaking longing and turgid rhetoric. Certainly they passed the military censors, and almost as certainly Samuil did not need censors to remind him what could and what could not be written.

Dzerzhinsk, July 2, 1942

Ruzen'ka-love,

    I am proud to be walking the ground of a city named for a knight. So what if its avenues are lined with buildings that are far-between and not too tall and that green grass is pushing its way through the sand of its squares? I can still see a city of giant build-ings and feel beneath my feet the ringing, mirrorlike surface of paved roads. And so what if the city is dark and its air circled by planes that are guarding its calm and the sirens are howling? I can still see a cityscape of bright lights and thousands of lamps reflected in the fast-flowing waters of the Oka River and feel the air, the light and fresh night air, lowering itself onto the city's shoulders, drawing in the tender and fragile moonlight that will never again be blocked by the wings of enemy planes. There will be no more sirens. People will forget what a target is. Where the riverbank is now gaping with bomb damage, young couples in love will be de-scending stairways carved in marble. The forest of factory smoke-stacks will drown in the green of gardens, parks and groves where happy little Felikses will catch dragonflies, chase grasshoppers and use sand and clay to make statues of the other Feliks, the big one, the one whose bronze bust towers over the city and whose name has been given to this city. This was a Man who had the hands of a laborer, the head of a scholar, the dress of a simple soldier.

He was writing about Feliks Dzerzhinsky, Iron Feliks, the founder of the Soviet secret police. The city named for him, about twenty miles down the Oka River from Nizhny Novgorod (then called Gorky), is home to ten large chemical plants. Today, sixty years after the letter, it is Russia's most polluted city, where nearly three out of four babies are born with congenital defects and life expectancy stands at fifty. As for Dzerzhinsky, the dismantling of his monument in Moscow in 1991 was probably the most powerful symbol of the victory of democracy—and the repeated attempts to have the monument restored are among the most troubling signs now of the past's refusal to recede.

Ruzya and Samuil had agreed to name their son Feliks. They just assumed the child would be a son.

August 31, 1942

Ruzya stares at the tiny bundled-up worm in her arms. They have brought the girl in to nurse because—miracle of miracles—Ruzya's milk has come in. The nurses of Ashkhabad have not seen breast milk in about as long as they have not had a decent meal.

It is almost five months since Samuil went off to war. Three days ago his parents walked Ruzya to the hospital. Looking at her hugely protruding stomach, the doctor predicted twins—nothing short of a disaster in their hungry Ashkhabad existence. The girl, then, came as a relief. They have already named her Yelena—Yolka or Yolochka for short; she and Samuil once agreed that would be the name if they had a girl—although he, of course, had his heart set on a Feliks.

The baby has latched on with an urgency and a skill that prompted an approving chuckle from the nurse. Now Ruzya sits uncomfortably in the bed, her back against the metal headboard, her shoulders tense and leaning forward, her elbows rigid around the baby. She studies the girl's tiny round face, or the part of it not obscured by her suddenly huge breast. The baby has black downy hair extending halfway down her wrinkled forehead, a meaty nose with splayed-out nostrils, and eyes of an uncertain dark color. She seems willing to open only one eye at a time. Her lashes and eyebrows are thick, definite, black. Ruzya looks for traces of Samuil, for anything that would remind her of the airy boy with the delicate features, the watery eyes, the faint reddishness, and she sees nothing. Her beloved is a soldier, and she is alone with this strange and separate creature.

As soon as Ruzya came home with the baby, they spent a fortune to hire a photographer so they could send Samuil a picture of his baby daughter.

October 3, 1942

My wonderful little daughter,

Goo-goo! Goo-goo, my little Yolochka! Come on, smile! You already know how to smile, don't you? Smile, and let's meet. I am your daddy. . . . I can't pick you up in my arms today, can't baby you, can't pull you out of your swaddles, can't toss you up to the ceiling, can't set you on top of the wardrobe—because there is a war on, and thousands of mileposts separating us from each other.

Your mommy, your granddaddies and grandmommies will, of course, be opposed to your sitting on top of the wardrobe and flying up by the ceiling and getting pulled out of your swaddles—but then they don't understand how particularly wonderful it is to smile from the top of the wardrobe and to make pleasure bubbles up by the ceiling. You'd like it. A lot! I know. As soon as we de-molish the fascists and get done with the war, you and I won't leave a single ceiling, a single wardrobe untouched. But for now we'll just talk, all right? You stretch your little arms—a sign of consent. Here it is nighttime, and there is cannon fire. Raindrops are hitting the top of this bunker, firewood is crackling in the makeshift stove, the oil lamp is smoking something awful and throwing a yellowish light on this piece of paper and on the faces of my sleeping comrades and on the picture of your mommy. Where you are, the sun is already coming up and you are probably stretching out of your comfortable little bed, shaking your little arms impatiently and making funny smacking sounds with your lips: it's time to eat.

You are big already. I counted: you are one month and five days old. But it was only yesterday that I found out that your name is Yolochka and you have outstanding eyelashes and feet (they compare your feet with mine, but this is clearly slanderous, baby: I barely fit into size forty-three boots!) and that you are liked as a granddaughter and niece.

How I would like to sneak a peek at you, through a crack at least, to hold you in my arms for just a minute, but I can't. This isn't the right time: I am a soldier, and I cannot leave the formation for even a minute—that would create a gap and play into the enemy's hands. He is clever, mean and dirty. He wants to take away our happiness and our lives. He is a lowlife, a nothing. He has brought grief and tears into our joyful land. He will be beaten, destroyed! The world will be cleansed of the filth of fascism. That is what the fight is for, the great fight. You came into the world in a time of gunpowder, in the days of the trenches. Fire over Stalingrad accompanied your first scream—your birth! All the brighter and finer for that will your future be. You were born on the eve of amazing events. Autumn. Winter. We will move forward and bring grief to the enemy. You will grow up a free person in a liberated land.

DECEMBER 20, 1942

Ruzya has grown so used to this view, it almost feels like home. It used to feel absurd to look out into your own courtyard, but now she finds its barely perceptible pastels comforting. She stares out the window as she breast-feeds Yolochka, then the neighbor's son.

The neighbor woman has no milk; virtually no one does. Ruzya feeds her baby, and free of charge at that: she hopes and even sometimes believes that her goodness will be repaid, and that Samuil will come home whole. With breast-feeding a barely interrupted process, she uses the time to look out the window, searching for Batsheva returning from the market, Lev coming home from the cafeteria where he has found work as an accountant, and the mail carrier walking into the courtyard with her big black leather bag.

The mail carrier is also an evacuee, a sturdy woman who stomps cheerfully along her route. She likes to hand the mail to Ruzya personally, and Ruzya always tips her in whatever currency she has available—coins or hard candy. When you get so many letters and they are so beautiful, you must reward the messenger.

Now she sees the mailwoman, oddly, before she hears her ridiculous black boots stomping. She is walking quietly, almost slinking along the courtyard, head lowered and shoulders stooped—an obese mouse in a grayish blue uniform. She steps carefully onto the terrace that runs the length of the courtyard and quickly slaps a triangular piece of paper on the table that sits out there on the terrace.

Ruzya pushes back the instant knowledge of what this behavior means, then reclaims it, quickly, for time is suddenly of the essence. With the neighbor's boy still cradled in her left arm, she jumps up and runs out to the terrace in three quick steps. The mail carrier has already vanished, which must mean that this letter cannot be returned or attributed to some sort of mistake.

Samuil Lvovich Minkin, aged twenty-three, died in battle not far from Moscow on November 30, 1942.

December 22, 1942

Four people sit in a terrace kitchen eating and crying. There is a box on the table just outside their window, open, with newspaper scraps still holding the shape of things they were used to pack: a dried melon, a huge batch of homemade nut-and-raisin cookies. They were Samuil's favorite. The package came back yesterday, marked "addressee dead." The mail carrier left it on the outdoor table, just as she had the death notice. The people brought it inside, because it was food. They took it back outside because it was untouchable. This morning at breakfast time Batsheva went outside and unpacked the box, silently. They are eating now, sweet melon and salty tears. They are hungry.

Two and a half years later, an army comrade of Samuil's, another politruk, named Ivan Gordeyev, a blond man with a ruddy face and shaved eyebrows, came to visit Ruzya. By the canon of countless Soviet war movies and books, the purpose of such a visit would be to tell the widow the details of her husband's heroic and noble death and to forge a bond, always at least vaguely romantic in nature, between the person who loved the late soldier most and the one who saw him last. As his story went, Ivan Gordeyev and Samuil had walked the front line performing the politruk's most sacred duty—handing out Party membership books just before battle to newly inducted Communists. As they walked back to their camp, Samuil was hit by a piece of shrapnel. He died on the spot, and Ivan Gordeyev was unscathed. By the time Ivan Gordeyev came to meet Ruzya, she could see nothing romantic or ennobling in her husband's death, the futility of which was made only more clear by his companion's robust survival.

I have a childhood recollection of the story of Samuil's death.

In this telling, he is warned ahead of time not to venture out of the trenches but insists he must help the men become Communists before they go to battle. This may have been my great-grandmother's or great-aunt's version, or I may have borrowed it from some other story from a book, a film, or a lecture. Wherever I got it, this tale is a Soviet literary staple, the quintessential heroic narrative used to teach us about World War II. I think I believed for a long time that the death of a man who risked his life to induct others into the Party was more meaningful than the death of someone who was shot in battle, bombed while digging trenches, executed by the fence-in battalions, or drowned in a puddle.

I have always heard that my grandfather was beautiful: my great-grandmother Batsheva said so, as did my grandmother Ruzya. She said, in fact, that when they walked down the street together, heads turned. I have seen three photographs of Samuil—I do not think there are any others. Two show a confident young man in a narrow tie, with stylishly disheveled wavy hair overhanging smiling light eyes. In the third, which has discolored to a light sepia, he is wearing a military uniform. The hair is gone, the eyes look not scared but a bit lost, and the long thin neck tells you this is the picture of a boy. Aside from the letters, these pictures are the only evidence of my grandfather's existence.

PART THREE

SURVIVAL

1942–1943

A Courtyard in Ashkhabad

CHAPTER ELEVEN

APRIL 1942

Students are most easily found in the cafeteria. Since university officials decided to attempt a semblance of a semester under the auspices of a local teachers' college, its cafeteria has become the place where humiliated professors chase down their students, alternately trying to shame them and promising to keep the lecture short enough that they will be able to return to their place in the queue in time to receive the day's balanda. But this time the dean's secretary is calling out just one name, and Ester responds instinctively, forgetting even to stake her place before she follows the thin thirtyish woman to the dean's office.

"Are you Ester Goldberg?" inquires an official matron Ester has never seen.

"Yes."

"Date and place of birth?"

"Bialystok, January 5, 1923." She is starting to feel the fear.

"We have received a letter for you." An arm extending lazily, offering a brown triangle—now triangles have become the rule, since they save money and the censors' time—a hand reaching for it, the recognition of Bella's handwriting, the scramble of fingers to open the message, the first in eight months since that letter Bella threw out the train window.

> *My dear daughter,*
>
> *I had nearly despaired about finding you. At first I could not write for five months—I will explain later, after I have received your response—and then all my letters to your institute were returned "addressee unknown." But yesterday I met a woman, also from Bialystok, who told me your institute was merged with the university and the university was evacuated to Ashkhabad. I am writing right away, to say just the main things: I am all right, living in Biysk, in the Altai. The climate is hard, but I am managing to get by. No news about your father. I hope so much that this letter finds you, my girl.*
>
> *Love, Mama*

This is a message by a writer unsure it will be read, a discreet testing of the waters. Ester runs back to her room—stopping outside the building and returning to thank the matron, who acknowledges her gratitude indifferently, then running again—forgetting about balanda and everything else except the post office's closing hour, by which she has to dispatch her letter. In the coming weeks, writing furiously back and forth, sometimes every day, their letters usually crossing en route, answers trailing questions by a half dozen missives, they will try to tell each other how they have lived through this separation.

How the cattle-car train carrying Bella and 3,001 other deportees from Bialystok arrived in the Siberian town of Biysk. The journey, if you can call it that, had taken twelve days. The sound of explosions had followed them at first, but they were more concerned with the lack of water and food. Indifference set in, dull as the sound of bombs in the distance, after they passed Moscow. Everyone in Bella's car survived, thank goodness; though, in the heavy silence of the last few days, they could not be sure until they left the darkness and the stench of the cattle car.

How they were lined up alongside the train and told, by a young NKVD officer, that all of them would be put to work for the benefit of the Soviet state and its military might—this is when they knew what they had been sure of for days: a war had started between Germany and the Soviet Union. The secret-police officer assured them that each would be put to work according to his profession. Bella did not count on a job teaching Polish, of course, but she assumed that the deportees, mostly educated and largely middle-aged, would be assigned to clerical duties. When her job turned out to be digging toilet holes, she complained, "For twenty-four years of Soviet rule they relieved themselves behind the shed, and now they need Bella Goldberg to dig toilets for them!"

The local woman to whose house she had been assigned sighed that night, "You shouldn't have said that. Not out loud. Your shift leader is a snitch." How she was right, of course: there was a loud knock on the door later that night, an escorted walk to the precinct, the first of about one hundred and fifty nights spent in a small square cell.

The story of Bella's protest has always been a family favorite. It does us proud to hail from this kind of stock: a woman who talked back to the NKVD. And this at a time when most people in the country were afraid to open their mouths on any topic at all. In the late 1990s, when certain archives were made public, I discovered my great-grandmother was not unique: it seems the Poles deported to Russia were not infected by the virus of fear that kept Soviet society so obedient. So they did things like talk back and even stage protests.

In August 1940, the deported refugees from German-occupied territories staged a mass protest—even referred to as a riot in some NKVD documents—in the Novosibirsk region. Over fifteen hundred people refused to work, demanding that they be given jobs according to their professions and be moved to urban areas in a warmer part of the country. The riot was put down, forty-five people were arrested, but less than a year later a special decision of the NKVD allowed educated deportees to live outside the so-called special settlements.

Another protest was staged by people Bella probably knew personally—deportees, most of them Jewish, taken from Bialystok to the Siberian city of Omsk at the same time she was taken to Biysk. For three days fourteen hundred deportees, temporarily quartered in the city circus building, of all places, managed to resist the NKVD's efforts to ship them to their destinations in the distant villages of the region. It took a hundred and twenty armed policemen to force them into the trucks.

The most remarkable part of these stories is that, each time, it took the NKVD days to put down protests by sick, exhausted, unarmed people. Each time, the secret police were stymied by people who thought they could do the unthinkable. So Bella's individual protest was not an isolated incident, but one that left her minders at a loss. Their ultimate solution was to sentence her to ten years of labor camps for "religious propaganda"—an absurd charge for an atheist, to be sure, but no more absurd than the charges against hundreds of thousands of Soviet citizens sentenced in those days for espionage, terrorism, and sabotage.

As it happened, just when she was sentenced, in August 1941, the Soviet Union signed a cooperation agreement with occupied Poland's government in exile and, in conjunction with that move, declared amnesty for all Polish citizens held in labor camps, prisons, and special settlements on Soviet territory. Many of them, including the future Israeli prime minister Menachem Begin, left the Soviet Union in the ranks of an army formed by Polish general Wladislaw Anders. The rest, like Bella, remained in the Soviet Union through the war.

Bella was never shipped off to labor camp, and was finally released from prison after five months—at least four months after the amnesty took effect.

Bella still has not learned her lesson, and she tells the story in letters to her daughter. But she does not write about prison; she writes instead about her search, about the overwhelming futility of looking for someone in this vast land, the absolute impossibility of finding her girl, her only daughter, her—she keeps repeating—one remaining person in the world.

By this time Bella, who had spent two years within miles of German-occupied territories, who knew exactly what the Germans did to Jews, assumed that her sisters in Warsaw and her husband in Bialystok were dead. She was wrong. Her husband, like the Bialystok ghetto itself, would survive until late 1943. Her younger sister Helena, who, after all of her Polish friends had refused to help her hide, had unsuccessfully tried to commit suicide by drowning, was saved by other Poles, who first hid her and her baby daughter and then helped her secure false Aryan documents that kept her safe until the end of the war. Helena's husband, who was a strong swimmer, had chosen a different way of killing himself: as his wife looked on, he threw himself in front of a train; he succeeded.

Ester writes about how life changed overnight—the night of June 22, 1941. How the dormitories were emptied and the students moved to a school building in the center of town, where they slept on tables. How she and Eda got jobs as truck drivers. She omits the fact of her half-blindness because, of all the things that might worry her mother, this, it seems, could be kept secret. She omits the hard facts of her work and, of course, she does not write that they stopped going to bomb shelters after a while.

She writes that a friend fixed her and Eda up with a room, and that they caught a spy.

They both write that they must be reunited, that they will promise never again to part.

They both are now—briefly, as it will turn out—entitled to move around the country freely: Bella has been amnestied, and the strict travel restrictions that will be in effect for all citizens through much of the war have not yet been introduced. They try to decide who should undertake the arduous journey: Ester, who at nineteen is certainly physically better suited for it, or Bella, who would be going to sunny Turkmenia, where many of the newly amnestied Poles have rushed following the miserable Siberian winter.

Hunger is when potatoes—rather, the promise of potatoes—decide where and how mother and daughter should be reunited. "I made a final decision only when I got a letter from my mother saying that the Poles in Biysk were not starving because at the lo-cal market you could exchange items of clothing for potatoes,

pretty profitably. That ended my doubts. In Ashkhabad we'd forgotten what potatoes tasted like. I ran and got a ticket that very
day. My friends had been telling me to do just that all along: 'How
can you think about bringing your mother here when we are all
going to starve to death?' "

Hunger is saying that the journey she began a week later was
a good one because the military men she met on the trains—she
had to take a total of four trains, each time spending a day or more
at the layover station—were always giving her something to eat.

APRIL 1942

The journey northeast from Ashkhabad to Biysk could have taken
two days, or, with all passenger train schedules suspended indefinitely in favor of military transport, it could have taken any number of days at all. It took a week, but Bella has been at the station
every day since she received Ester's telegram. She comes to the
platform in the morning and stays there, pacing up and down, sitting on a bench, ducking for a half hour into the small station
building. Wooden and unheated, it is better for a change of
scenery than for trying to warm up. She stays until the train
comes—there is just one every day, but its time of arrival is impossible to predict—and waits until it empties out: Biysk is the last
station on this railroad. Though she is convinced that she will see
her daughter from any distance as soon as Ester steps on the platform, Bella still stays until the last person has walked past her. She
looks at every face, looking for her daughter's.

They do see each other, finally, all the way across the long
platform, and in an instant they are embracing and crying and
whispering the kinds of nonsense words that long-parted lovers
might say. Bella leads Ester to the low, huddled wooden house

where she is renting a room. The landlady is a bit younger than Bella and has a daughter a few years Ester's senior; the husband and son are both at the front. The owner of the house fires up her big wood-burning stove, fills a big tin bath with freezing water from the well, and together the two Russian women heave the bath into the stove's large opening, which is usually used for cooking. Ester bathes—the last time she felt so dirty was when she arrived in Ashkhabad about five months ago—and afterward, flushed and relaxed, she sits with Bella and the Russian women at the table, drinking hot water from the samovar and receiving a stream of visitors: the Biysk population of exiled Polish Jews from Bialystok has been following Bella's search for her daughter and has been waiting with her, and now all of them are coming around to get a look at a family story with a happy ending.

When they have all gone, and the two Russian women have gone to bed in an adjacent room, Bella and Ester cry. They cry for Jakub. Ester cries for Isaj. Bella cries for her nine brothers and sisters, her parents, Jakub's seventeen siblings, and together they cry for an entire world that has died, leaving the two of them to face the aftermath.

But the next morning Ester wakes up unaccountably happy, feeling like, after months of struggle, life has resumed.

CHAPTER TWELVE

Biysk was life—with jobs, suitors, a household—which replaced waiting and writing letters, and Biysk was hunger too. But at least they had currency they could exchange for food. They had silverware, and they had a man's suits and an overcoat.

The silverware had belonged to Bella's sister Helena: her husband had brought it with him from Warsaw when he still hoped he could smuggle his wife and baby to the Soviet-occupied territories. The clothes belonged to Jakub: when the police came to arrest them in Bialystok, they instructed Bella to pack, separately, fifty kilos of luggage for each of them, and she had refused, thinking she could manipulate the Soviets into keeping them together. In the end he was left without even a spare set of underwear and Bella was delivered to the train and then to Biysk with all of her husband's clothes.

Another good Russian word, one that goes well with *vpro-good'*, is *spasat'sia*—literally, to save oneself, but to do it on a regular basis, every day, persisting, surviving, habitually balancing on the edge. My grandmother uses that word when she recalls trading her father's clothes for potatoes, then trading the silver. They thought they might hold on to the silver, sell it later in Moscow for more, but gradually it went too: the local elite, the factory directors and such, would give a cupful of grain for a silver spoon, a small bag of flour for a spoon and a fork or a fork and a knife. The flour was good because Bella learned to make bread patties with it, and they ate half and sold or traded the other half on the market, to get potatoes to vary their diet.

Ester chose to drink plain hot water instead of the carrot tea, a brew of carrot peels, that everyone drank. It always disappointed, because it looked like it should taste like tea. At least hot water tasted just the way it looked.

Some people's memories live on as fears; my grandmother Ester, a stranger to that emotion, calls her phobias "hatreds." She claims to hate driving, and she has not driven once since the war. Another thing she hates is the smell of fish frying. There was a day when all of Biysk was in an uproar: the drugstore was selling castor oil. You could fry potatoes in that, and they did, and they were delicious, but she still cannot forget that nauseating smell.

"So my father's clothes—we saved ourselves with that a little, because to work the way I worked—it was mostly physical labor—on that ration of bread alone would have been very hard."

My grandmother Ester's anecdotes of her Biysk jobs are a family treasure. There is the one about her first place of employment, a munitions-factory steel-casting department staffed by convicted criminals—the beneficiaries of early-release policies instituted to provide the rear with a workforce—and by Ester, a nineteen-year-old philology student. She still had some telltale signs of having come from the West, from a well-off family—well, maybe just one telltale sign, a wristwatch. One day she looked down and it was gone, and she remembered all the curse words she had heard her loaders use in that awful GAZ-AA, and she unleashed a torrent of words that would have made the most hardened of criminals—well, if not blush, then develop an abiding respect for her. Which they did: to show it, they returned the wristwatch—stolen, as it turned out, on a bet.

She also says she hates swear words, and just shivers when she is forced to hear them. (My grandmother Ruzya, incidentally, does not, and has been known to use them on occasion with moderate virtuosity.)

She was probably lucky to get that steel-casting job, but she was even luckier to be able to get out of it, because she could not have carried on much longer than the four months she toiled there, making casting forms out of clay and sand, working twelve to fourteen hours a day. Extraordinary measures introduced during the war outlawed worker resignations in the military industry. But the personnel manager, who was Jewish, noticed the young girl in the casting department and suggested he could get her out of the job.

Our favorites are the anecdotes from her next job, the one at the spirits factory. She worked in bottling. She learned to drink because she had to: the women—here it was all women—worked standing up to their ankles in ice-cold water, and the only way to keep the blood warm was drinking. They were allowed to drink all they could, and they could down a couple of liters a day each of so-called raw spirits, a clear liquid that is seventy-five percent alcohol. The women called it wine, and so did she, a foreigner. As a result, she nearly poisoned her future husband when he showed up for a visit blue from the minus forty outside, and she suggested they drink some wine to warm up. My grandfather was never much of a drinker, and that night he nearly choked to death on the raw spirits.

Remarkably, my grandmother does not claim to hate drinking. She can still drink. This was my salvation in 1991, during that first visit back to the Soviet Union. I was not a drinker then, and at endless family-related feasts I continually poured the contents of my vodka glass into my grandmother's, and she drank for the both of us. But what she hates is her grandchildren bragging about how she can drink anyone under the table—as if there were nothing else remarkable about her.

In any case, the job at the spirits factory, for the couple of months that it lasted, was the best a girl could wish for: she got an allotment of the clear liquid to take home, and they traded it at the market.

Until she started getting fired.

They must have noticed her right away in Biysk. Anyone and anything atypical was suspect, and here was a young woman who had left a warm place to come to Siberia, left the relatively privileged position of an evacuated university student to live among recently amnestied deportees. Among the roughly six thousand former Polish citizens now living in Biysk, Ester was possibly the only one who carried a regular five-year domestic Soviet passport, that most important document in the land. She had received it when she arrived in Moscow as a full-time student, becoming a resident of the capital rather than the occupied territories and thereby gaining all the rights of citizenship.

Over the nearly two years when its troops were occupying part of what used to be Poland, the Soviet Union did not recognize an independent Polish state. But with the signing of the co-operation treaty in August 1941 and the amnesty for Polish citizens on Soviet territory, Poland, in the official Soviet view, was once again restored to statehood and the deportees to Polish citizenship. Upon release from prisons, labor camps, and special settlements, they received temporary identity papers that indicated they would in the future be exchangeable for Polish passports. In cities like Biysk, where the deportations had created a concentrated Polish population, the government in exile set up representative offices to serve the residents with this odd status. What an unnerving proposition this must have been to the local NKVD chief, charged with monitoring and controlling the local moods and motives: he was used to subjects who were in every way cogs in the Soviet machine, and here he was responsible for watching a population that was not even really Soviet. And what an opportunity he must have seen in Ester, a bona fide Soviet citizen, a Komsomol member entrenched in the community of exiles: it was as though a ready-made agent had been sent for his convenience.

The NKVD officer's name was Gurov. Major Gurov.

NOVEMBER 1942

The knock on the door is perfunctory, followed immediately by the stomping of feet: two people are shaking snow off their felt boots in the entryway, the unheated shed that traditionally precedes the door to a Russian home. By the time they knock on the inner door, Ester is opening it: it is probably an acquaintance, one of the many Jewish Poles here. No, it is a policeman, a young man bundled in cotton-stuffed winter garb, red-faced from the cold. He is accompanied by a middle-aged woman in civilian clothing, vaguely familiar, but Ester can't quite place her.

"Your documents," says the officer.

So the woman must be a residence official, one of those low-level snitches charged with keeping tabs on the inhabitants of a particular block. She must live nearby, which is why she looks familiar. A document check is not an extraordinary occurrence—it never was in the Soviet Union, and now, with the new wartime vigilance, it has become almost routine—but there is something about this one that feels scripted. Bella and Ester hand their documents to the woman, who makes a face of feigned surprise and hands the papers to the officer silently.

"This is very strange," says the officer. "Different-issue documents. Strange. We'll have to check on this. Get dressed." He nods to Ester.

She pulls on her father's overcoat and her shoes, and she can feel, without looking, that the pair are eyeing them with distaste: city shoes, leather, where only traditional Russian felt boots are warm enough—and with holes too. She straightens up carefully— her head will spin if she does it too fast—and stands, demonstrating her willingness to follow the pair.

They walk in the night, lit only—barely—by starlight reflected off the snow, to the two-story brick building that houses the police. They proceed directly to the second-floor office, where a man who introduces himself as Major Gurov is already waiting for her.

"So you came here from Ashkhabad?" he begins.

"Yes."

"Why would you leave a warm place like that to come here?"

"Apparently you know my story, but if you want to hear it from me, I came because my mother is here."

"Your mother, let me see. Oh, yes. Religious propaganda, if I'm not mistaken?"

"She has been an atheist her entire life. In any case, she was amnestied."

"An amnesty does not annul the fact of a crime. But I'm sure you, unlike your mother, are a loyal Soviet citizen."

"I am a loyal Soviet citizen, of course."

"And a member of the Komsomol."

"And a member of the Komsomol."

"So you would, of course, want to help your new motherland in every way."

"Of course. This country is fighting fascism, therefore I want to help it." This is a declaration of conditional love, and it maddens Gurov instantly. Color comes to his otherwise bland and colorless face. He is about forty and average in every way but one: he is clearly, conspicuously, well fed. He has a thickness about him, and he has plump hands, and now he reaches into a drawer of his gray metal desk and produces a package of cookies. He puts it on the desk, unwraps the brown paper slowly, and, pushing aside the black telephone, advances the open package toward Ester.

"Would you like a biscuit?"

Hunger is accepting the humiliation of a cookie from him. She concentrates on taking small, indifferent bites.

"I have a form for you to sign. Nothing special, just a promise that, should you hear anything we should know about—you know, about the state of mind among the Poles here—you'll let us know." He reaches into a drawer again, and a blank piece of paper appears on the desk.

"I don't want to sign anything."

"It's just a formality."

"But there is no need. As an honest Soviet citizen, if I ever hear of any plot against the regime, I will certainly let you know. No signatures necessary. But, you know, there is nothing like that circulating among the people I know, because they are all loyal persons not involved in any conspiracies." This is not a lie, exactly. It is a safe generalization to say that the former Polish citizens, brought to Biysk in cattle cars, forced to dig toilets through the coldest and hungriest winter of their lives, hate the Soviet regime.

At the same time, these are Jews who credit the Siberian twist of fate with their own survival. There are, indeed, no conspiracies among them, and no vengeful plans; there is only waiting, and the hope that Germany will be defeated and they will be allowed to leave the Soviet Union. Theirs, then, is a loyalty, of sorts.

———

There was a misunderstanding between Ester and Major Gurov, and at the center of this misunderstanding was fear. Fear was the most important instrument of control in the Soviet Union. It was cultivated in every citizen virtually from birth. At eighteen Ester had happened into a life where all of her peers had grown up in a world of purges, show trials, and denunciations. Mass executions had been going on since before they were born. People were imprisoned, tried, executed, not just for what they did or may have done according to denunciations or false charges but also for who they were: clergy, landowners, intellectuals, the children of any of these groups. Major Gurov, who was in his mid-forties, had spent his entire working life in these conditions, where everyone he "controlled" was terrified of him, and where he was terrified of everyone above and below him, because purges in NKVD ranks were perhaps even more common than elsewhere. He might never before have seen a person who refused to sign. His hatred for Ester was preordained because she was, in Soviet-speak, "socially foreign," but his fascination with her stemmed from her unpredictable actions.

———

"You scum!" Major Gurov rises, placing his potbelly over his desk with unexpected agility. "How dare you even say the word *loyalty*! Maybe you don't understand? Well, you will! You will be spending the night here." He pushes a button on his desk, and an officer enters the room. "Take her to the cell," Major Gurov says, his face blotchy as he regains control.

The cell is probably a large room, but Ester cannot tell, because everywhere there are backs and bellies and other women's hair. The cacophony of voices makes her realize there must be scores of women here. Judging from the voices, they are mostly young. They are sitting on mattress-less wooden bunk beds and standing between them as in a crowded tram car. It smells of sweat and sheepskin. The lucky women who have managed to claim space next to the wall hide their faces in their collars and sleep. Others talk about being caught stealing and make predictions regarding treatment and punishment. Ester spots a space at the edge of a bunk, next to someone's felt boot—it can't be more than four inches square—and carefully angles herself onto it. She balances her foot against something she cannot see—it could be the leg of another bunk or it could be someone else's foot—puts her hands in her father's coat pockets, wraps her fingers around the bar of soap her mother slipped in as she was leaving, slouches as much as she can, squeezes her eyes shut against the yellow electrical light, and goes to sleep.

They let her out in the morning, with her bar of soap but without her passport. If the gravity of her new situation was just seeping in as she walked home through the creaky snow in the still-dark morning, when she saw Bella, one sleepless night thinner, paler, and older, she knew their relative stability was gone.

After seeing her daughter taken away, Bella had run to the Polish representative's office to ask for help, only to be told the representative could not interfere in the fate of a Soviet citizen. He also told her it was serious.

He probably knew of other cases in which former Polish

citizens were similarly harassed by the NKVD, and Bella herself knew of at least one. Mikhal Bekker, a Communist and former colleague of Bella's from teaching at the Bund gymnasium, had been deported to Biysk because he had a father who had been arrested—for the crime of owning a business. The NKVD in Biysk had probably approached Mikhal as a potential informer because he had belonged to the Polish Communist Party. Mikhal had the bad sense to tell his mother about having been approached, and his mother had the bad sense to run to his boss—Mikhal was by then working at a factory—and beg him to save her son from the NKVD advances and threats, and the boss had the good sense to denounce him immediately, and Mikhal was sentenced to eight years of hard labor for disclosing a state secret.

So at least Bella and Ester knew not to tell anyone. They also knew they were now Major Gurov's hostages. As Ester was taken down to the cell, Major Gurov screamed that she would see her passport only after she signed. Leaving Biysk, difficult under any circumstances with the ever-harsher travel restrictions going into effect, was impossible without a passport. And in Biysk, he could control what happened to her. He could get her fired, for example. Within about six weeks of that night spent in the detention cell, Ester was summoned to the head of the bottling department at the spirits plant. She was being fired. But why? She worked just as hard as the rest. "I'm sorry, girl, there is nothing I can do," the boss answered. "Orders from above."

Next she got a job as a loader at the lumberyard warehouse. That lasted two months. Then, about a month after she managed to enroll in nursing classes, she saw Major Gurov walking by the window. "You'll see, I'm about to be expelled," she told the woman sitting next to her. "But that's impossible—you are our best student!" She was expelled that very day. She did not spend much longer as an accountant's apprentice before she was told she was unfit for the job. In this case, though, my grandmother, no lover of mathematics, acknowledges that it may have been true.

Gurov's was a slow way of killing them. Every time Ester was fired, she lost her ration card and she and her mother were reduced to Bella's 300-gram-a-day dependent's allowance. That and carrot tea, or hot water, as you like.

NOVEMBER 1943

"He is killing us." Boris's look as Ester makes her pronouncement is undecipherable. Whenever he gets very serious, he looks displeased, as though he could blow up any second. He has a habit of covering his chin and mouth with his right hand—this is to conceal the scar and the dent in his roughly shaved cheek where a piece of jaw is missing—and that makes it even more difficult to understand his facial expression. Ester is forging on because she cannot stop now that she has started. She has decided it is time to tell him: their relationship has gone too far for him to denounce her, and it has gone far enough that he ought to know what has dominated her life for a year now.

Mindful of Mikhal Bekker's story, she has not told anyone. So they do have her in this sense—passport, ration card, and mind. The most she has let herself get away with, before deciding to tell Boris, is writing friends that she is depressed. They have responded with inane cheer.

> *You shouldn't take your troubles to heart. Spit on the asses and on their opinion, look at the world more optimistically, and, just to spite your enemies, live as though nothing had happened. That would be the smartest thing to do, trust old grandpa V.P. I'm sure that if I saw you now, I would slap you around a bit to get the*

depression out of you. The main thing is to give up your foreigner
views and start looking at the world through my eyes. Have we got
a deal? Good.

"Grandpa V.P.," Viktor Pilipenko, the young poet and Party
functionary, wrote that a few months before he died of tuberculo-
sis and about half a year into Ester's ordeal.

Her closest friend from college, Lena Zonina, implored her to
find a literary allusion to explain the source of her depression in a
way that would go unnoticed by the military censors who were
now reading all the mail in the country. Ester wrote that she was
being coerced into the role of Tanya from Maxim Gorky's *The*
Life of Klim Samgin. That character was compelled to inform for
the czar's secret police.

Though they roomed together briefly two years ago, when
Lena's mother was in the hospital, Lena is something of an aberra-
tion among Ester's college friends—a young woman who never
lived in a dormitory but lived in an apartment belonging to her
mother, an apartment that, thanks to her mother's status as a member of the Party elite, they did not have to share with anyone else.
When other students were evacuated, Lena stayed in Moscow
with her mother. Lena wrote back: *Your letter worried me a whole lot,*
and I showed it to my mother. She asked me to tell you that if you are an
honest girl and a member of the Komsomol, then you should stop resist-
ing.

Ester has not written back to Lena in six months. Lena sends
letter after letter, alternately expressing guilt and worry that something has happened to Ester, and Ester has sat down to write to her
on several occasions, but each time a wave of outrage has welled
up. What is worse, right after getting that letter, she raged at
Major Gurov. When he started in again about her duty as a
Komsomol member, she said, "I joined the Komsomol because I

wanted to go into the army to fight Hitler. But now I see that you are not the only one who views the Komsomol in a completely different way than I do. I don't want any part of an organization of snitches. So here is my Komsomol card." Gurov's eyes bulged out then. He rose, pulled out his pistol, and shouted so loudly his voice broke on the high notes: "I ought to shoot you now!" This was the second time he held her overnight.

Major Gurov now has her passport and her Komsomol card. Her best friend seems to think she is a traitor. Her mother thinks she is a hero. Ester is the loneliest person on Earth.

She met Boris Gessen at a friend's house. He is a Moscow Jew, a demobilized soldier, with a wound and medals. He lives with his father, a former journalist from Moscow who was evacuated to the Biysk region, where he now works as the assistant director of a collective farm, the same one where Bella was sent for forced labor. Ester does not find Boris overwhelmingly appealing or attractive, but she accepts his gallant attentions: he travels from the collective farm by train, freezing, to see her, and he brings her potatoes. He deserves to know.

"They come every three or four weeks, and they take me to him."

Boris lifts his head suddenly. "So that's where you were that time?"

There was an evening, early in his courtship, when he came to find Ester out of the house: she was spending the night in jail. Bella fumbled, unable to concoct anything convincing, and Boris left miffed, sure that she was on a date with another man, for he could think of no other reason she could not be fetched when he had come all this way, more than an hour by train, freezing, as always, in the cold space between cars, since he did not have a travel pass. Now he feels relieved, and he smiles his invitation for Ester to confirm and clear the misunderstanding.

"Yes," says Ester uncertainly. Oddly, she realizes she felt guilty. She could tell long ago that Gurov was attracted to her. This, she assumes, is why he regularly gives her biscuits and also perhaps why he has not killed her on any of those days when he has yanked his gun out of its holster and swung it ridiculously over his head, getting redder and redder as he screamed that he would shoot. She realizes she cannot tell Boris why she thinks her tormentor saves her from himself, and that makes a bitter stickiness appear in her throat. She reminds herself that her task is to tell Boris.

"I think we're both sick to death of the routine; every time it's the same thing." She attempts a smile.

Boris nods, his hand covering his chin again. "So, how does it go?"

"He usually begins by saying, 'So, what are you going to say this time? Are you going to be stubborn again?' "

"And you?"

"I say, 'Aren't you tired of this yet? I already told you once and for all.' "

"My God, Ester." She knows Boris suspects her of being crazy—or hopelessly foreign, which is the same thing—and sometimes he reminds her of that in this particularly exasperated tone.

"Then he usually starts screaming and cursing about my mother," she continues. "Then—well, then it depends on his mood. Some days he is very calm and patronizing, explaining that I have 'a civic duty'; other times he shouts and threatens. He pulls out his pistol and screams, 'The safety is off! Here I come!' I don't know, I guess he tries different approaches. Sometimes we have very peaceful discussions, he and I." She added the last sentence to make it clear she is not exaggerating her troubles, but now she tastes that guilty bitterness again.

"What else does he say?"

"That I won't get away from them, that they've got me, that

my mother is a known counterrevolutionary. That there is a war
on, that all decent human beings have to help the Soviet state, that
there are enemies everywhere but I am concealing them because
I am such a 'tightwad.' I tell you, we both keep saying the same
things over and over. And I tell him all the time that as soon as I
see an enemy of the Soviet state I will come and inform him personally, without signing anything. Why are you laughing?"

"You haven't thought of anything better to say?"

"I mean, the topic is always the same," she adds as an unnecessary defensive clarification. "The last few times there has been
another man, of lower rank, who was obviously attracted to me.
As soon as I am brought in, he joins us. I don't know what this
other one's name is, but when he is there Gurov acts much more
civilized than when we are alone. So then he tries to influence me
verbally only."

Now Boris definitely looks angry. "Aren't you afraid?"

"Yes, of course," she answers, and sees she has missed the
point of the question. "What do you mean?"

"Aren't you afraid they will do something to you?"

"Yes, of course, I'm afraid they'll shoot me. Oh, you mean
that? I don't know, it hadn't occurred to me, really."

"Ester, you have to get out of Biysk."

"Good idea, Boris." She regains her footing. "I must say that
has occurred to me."

He gets that expression again. Maybe she should not have
trusted him. Can she really afford a confidence that is contingent
on a romantic relationship? She rises and puts water on to boil.
There is a knock, followed by the squeak of the outer door being
opened by someone who is too impatient or too sure of himself to
wait for an answer. She walks to open the inner door and comes
face-to-face with a sergeant, who surveys the room and gets a
slightly confused look when he sees Boris sitting there in his

uniform, a couple of medals and a yellow badge on his chest. A yellow badge signifies a serious injury. A decorated war veteran commands more respect these days than just about anyone, short of the generalissimo himself. It is clearly difficult for the sergeant to fathom what an upstanding citizen, a hero, could be doing in the company of a defiant unreliable like Ester.

"Come out into the entryway," commands the sergeant.

She follows him, and so does Boris.

"I didn't ask you to come," the sergeant says. "I only asked her."

"We have no secrets from each other," says Boris sternly, as if it were true. "And I want to know why you came."

"What relation are you of hers?" asks the sergeant, stepping back slightly, as though beginning to doubt that he has a right to be here.

"I am her husband," says Boris. "And she is my wife," he adds, as though that further clarified the relationship.

"Husband?" The sergeant's voice is higher than it was a minute ago. "Then wait right here. I'll be back."

The sergeant disappeared out the door, never to return again. Ester and Boris assumed that he reported back to Major Gurov with the news of a husband, a wounded decorated war veteran of the Great Patriotic War, and Gurov decided to stop hounding Ester. Meanwhile, Ester was faced with the sudden possibility of marriage. As soon as the sergeant left, Boris announced that he could not lie to a representative of the Soviet state, and since he just had, they had to rectify the situation by marrying immediately. He was serious, for the most part.

Ester had other options, of course. But Boris was more interesting and better educated than all her other Biysk admirers—mostly very young Jewish mama's boys with no experience in the real world. She tried not to compare him to Isaj: the sooner she killed off any lingering hope of ever seeing him again, the easier it would be to go on. She did not ask herself whether she could love Boris: that would have been too much like comparing him to Isaj. So she tried to evaluate the facts as they were. Boris's was a touching courtship. His intervention in her persecution at the hands of Gurov was nothing short of heroic. His proposal, finally, promised a chance to leave Biysk in the foreseeable future: the Gessens were already making plans to return to Moscow.

But what about Isaj? "I knew he did not survive," says my grandmother whenever I ask her. How? She struggles to remember. She recalls lists posted in the Polish representative's office in Biysk. Lists of Jewish survivors, posted as the cities were liberated. He was not on the list, and neither was Jakub. This is probably an altered memory, if not a false one, since Bialystok was not liberated until the summer of 1944—by which time Ester had already married Boris and followed him back to Moscow. There may have been lists compiled by partisans and Soviet parachutists who got to the area in December 1943; these would have included Jews who escaped the ghetto and death trains and hid with the partisans in the forests. There were a dozen or so such people from the Bialystok ghetto, but Isaj was not among them. About fifty years later Ester learned that Isaj's best friend had managed to escape by jumping off a train headed for the death camps, and that Isaj had already been killed by then. Which means that Isaj was dead by mid-1943, although Ester could not have known it at the time. Yet she says she knew, and this is true: she simply knew. There was no singular moment of realizing the boy she loved was dead. There was no mourning. There was just a heavy, growing, and finally unyielding certainty.

My grandmother Ruzya always says that her friend Ester "has a hero's biography." Foremost in her mind is Ester's refusal to sign that piece of paper that would have made her a snitch. How many people could have faced down the threat of being beaten, jailed, shot? How many did? No one really knows how pervasive informing was in the Stalinist era: unlike East Germany, Russia has not released such records. If they exist, and if they are ever opened, the archives may reveal letters of denunciation from every city quarter, every building, and every other family in the Soviet Union: neighbors informing on neighbors, workers informing on their superiors, brothers informing on sisters, and wives on husbands. Several generations of Soviet children were weaned on the story of martyr Pavlik Morozov, a boy shot by his uncle for informing on his parents, who hoarded wheat during the forced collectivization of the late 1920s. Official Soviet folklore painted this betrayal as martyrdom, a feat any "honest girl and Komsomol member" should strive to imitate.

"I held to this uncompromising position," says my grandmother Ester, "but I should say that they exhausted and tortured me so much that if my mother had not supported this position, I am not sure I could have withstood it all. But my mother supported me in every way."

"But when you thought you were about to be shot, in that moment of panic, how did you keep from saying, 'All right, fine, I'll do it'?"

"No, no, I am telling you, in these moments what held me back was the thought of how could I look my mother in the eye.

How could I look her in the eye knowing that I had signed on with the NKVD, the organization we held responsible for my father's death?"

But here is where it gets tricky. "Did it ever occur to you," I ask, "that if you signed, you might save your mother from being arrested again?"

"No, no, that never occurred to me. And then, after a while, it had developed into such a routine, it wouldn't have been fitting to give in after I'd held out for so long, so I didn't consider it."

If my grandmother had signed, and if she explained her decision by telling me that she had wanted to save her mother from being arrested or that she had realized that her mother would not survive should she herself be jailed or shot, and therefore she had to sign, I would have accepted it without judgment. I would have said that when one is faced with the choice between one's life and one's conscience, one chooses life. But then one would not have a hero's biography.

"Why didn't you consider," I ask, "just signing that stupid piece of paper and then forgetting about it and never giving them any information?"

"They said, 'You just sign, then you won't have to worry, we'll tell you whom to watch.'" Meaning that it would not stop with the signing: she would be tied to the secret police from that point on. "And, you understand, I still considered myself a decent human being and I did not want to be implicated in all that for anything in the world."

There were, of course, people, even among her acquaintances, who thought differently. "I don't want to name names," says my grandmother, "but there was this man, the brother-in-law of a friend of mine, another exiled former Communist, who signed. He was dragged in just like I was, time after time, and he caved in. And he would raise the subject as though in an abstract way and say, 'After all, one could sign and then never write any denunciations. One can stay honest even after signing.' And I think that means—well, I don't know, maybe he really never informed on anyone, but that he signed, I am certain."

That the man brought the subject up "in an abstract way," as she says, probably means he was trying to warn his acquaintances against saying too much in his presence. They probably heeded the advice, but the man was not ostracized. The most remarkable thing about that story is that fifty-five years later my grandmother still would not name him. Maybe she is reluctant to judge, knowing precisely how difficult it was to stand her ground. Maybe she knows that in that situation, where the choice is no choice at all, no action can be condemned. Maybe she suspects that only a twenty-year-old could have possessed the sort of moral certainty that allowed her to stand her ground.

She had, in the end, three options: keep going until Major Gurov succeeded in killing her; marry her savior and enlist his help in escaping from Biysk; or break the "routine" and sacrifice her very concept of right and wrong. Did the Germans, in murdering her fiancé, kill the romantic girl in her? Did the consideration of marrying without love seem insignificant when it made the difference between life and death? In any case, from the distance of fifty-five years, it does not even seem to matter. She was twenty-one years old when she married, a virgin, wearing her father's size forty-five boots: she had long since worn out her only pair of shoes.

PART FOUR

JAKUB

1941–1943

Bialystok, 1941

CHAPTER THIRTEEN

My grandmother Ester does not have a clear recollection of learning of her father's death. Just as with Isaj, it must have been a gradual, seeping sort of knowledge. There were letters she and her mother wrote to a town called Bogoruslan, where a data bank for people who lost one another in the war had been created. In the early days, when the front advanced hundreds of kilometers a week, when evacuations were sudden and haphazard, when some people fled while others were immobilized by fear, tens of thousands were lost. Many of them, it turned out, had the last name Goldberg. So there were letters from the wrong Yakov, Jakub, or Yankel Goldberg searching for his wife, Bella, and letters from the relatives of the wrong Yakov, looking for their cousin Haika or uncle Simon. About fifty letters in all, between 1942, when they first wrote to Bogoruslan, and 1944, when Bella left Biysk for Moscow, certain that Jakub was dead. Later—years and decades later—there would be people who brought bits of information that eventually added up to the story that Ester told.

When I set out to write this book, I looked for documents that would fill out the story. I found more than I planned, mostly in vanity-press books printed in Israel, Australia, New York, and Poland. These are the traces of genocide inflicted on a people wedded to the written word: it seems virtually every survivor of the Bialystok ghetto has written a memoir. Jakub Goldberg was a prominent man in every way, and he figured in all of the memoirs. Some of these were written three or four years after the war; others, three or four decades. There were contradictions, of course. Ultimately, two entirely separate narratives emerged. I shall give both. And then I have my own version.

AUGUST 1, 1941

Jakub Goldberg walks back and forth, up and down the streets leading into the poorer, more crowded Jewish section of Bialystok, which is growing poorer and more crowded by the hour. His mission now is one of vague supervision, of aiding the semblance of order and peace, and every so often he succeeds in shooing or pushing one of the young Polish hoodlums away from the Jews' possessions, arranged haphazardly in open carts and wagons and prams that squeak and stumble on the cobblestones. The street has grown so crowded with people and their objects and their shouts that it is becoming difficult to walk. Still, he is drawing simple satisfaction from walking in and out of what will now be the ghetto, past the people who are, under the supervision of another member of the council, already constructing the wooden walls. He is feeling, perhaps ever so briefly, a free man. All around him there are men—wealthier men and poorer men, men in good suits and men with the lining of their jackets visible where the cloth has worn through, men with beards in Chasidic dress and clean-shaven men in regular European attire. Upon closer inspection, no one looks exactly clean-shaven this morning, but in any case, it is not what differentiates these men from one another that strikes him; it is that they are all the same, the way they fret, the way they rush, the way they expose their hopes of saving their wives, their daughters, their linens, their clocks, their furs, and their furniture.

He has no wife and no daughter. He does not even have his good suit or his warm coat. His wife took those in June, when the Soviets came to arrest them. They told her to pack, to put his clothes separately. "If I have to pack separately, I'm not coming with you," she declared to the NKVD officer in charge of the arrest. Even Jakub was surprised. The officer drew back, as one would from a small dog that has unexpectedly snarled and started nipping at ankles. She did look like a tiny Jewish terrier, his wife. "Fine, pack everything together," the officer granted. Bella packed Jakub's suit and coat, his good shoes, his stockings and hers, all the underwear in the house, her clothes, and the only valuable thing in the entire place: the silverware her brother-in-law had deposited with them before returning to Warsaw to fetch his pregnant wife. They climbed into the car, Bella and Jakub with the suitcase, and the Soviet officer with his soldier, and in a few minutes the car stopped in front of the city jail. The soldier pushed Jakub out before getting out himself, and the car drove off toward the station, taking his wife and his winter coat.

He has no clothes now and no obligations. No wife to save. With any luck, she has long since arrived in Siberia. And if she has not, there is nothing he can know, much less do. No daughter to fret about: she has been in Moscow for a year. One year today, in fact. He no longer has to worry about why she is or is not writing: there have been no letters in over a month, and there will be none, not from one side of the front to the other. He no longer has to pack parcels for the brothers and in-laws (including the father-in-law who disowned him for taking the train on the Sabbath) in the Warsaw Ghetto, now that Jakub is becoming a ghetto resident himself. No debts to pay: those who may have been dogged enough to continue demanding payments have all either been deported to Siberia, back when the Soviets went after the businessmen, or perished in the fire the Nazis set to the synagogue after herding two thousand Jews inside on June 27, or been shot in the Pietrasze Forest a week later. For the first time in thirteen years, if he has a payday, he will not have to start it by sharing with his creditors.

His two closest friends were killed in the forest, along with two hundred other Jewish intellectuals. This, too, is a sort of freedom. He has only strangers to worry about anymore. Do that bearded man's five children have enough bread on the table? Whether they ever did before is irrelevant. Certainly, if the man's children did not go hungry before—and judging from the thin shine of his jacket, they probably did—the last two years under the Soviets have introduced all of them to days without bread and to nights spent in food queues. But now that Efraim Barasz, the engineer who seems to have been appointed head Jew in town, has picked Jakub Goldberg to take charge of rationing for the Judenrat, the ghetto's Jewish council, he will make sure that the Jews, as long as there are any Jews, have bread on their tables.

He was an odd choice. In the prewar *kehilla,* the Jewish community council, in the endless conflicts between the Bundists and the Zionists, Jakub Goldberg raged against the socialists' unceasing attempts to bail out the poor at the community's expense, to force the council to give handouts rather than help. Maybe this was why Barasz chose him: Jakub is not a man of handouts. He is a man of logic and rational decision making, one who will not be influenced by the hungry eyes of children, especially since he no longer has any.

Out of the corner of his eye he spots the boy—Isaj, his daughter's boyfriend, the small and excessively animated character. Jakub should not feel happy to see him. He disliked his conspicuous poverty and the smell he brought into their house, the noxious odor of the leather factory where the boy worked. His overwrought ways annoyed Jakub, whether because his passion came from a different, pathetic world, or because it engulfed his daughter so completely. Where is the boy rushing to now? His family already lives within the new ghetto's limits, so they do not have to move. He is probably on a social mission of imaginary importance, as is always the way with members of the Zionist youth organizations.

He is relieved to have seen the boy. He has wondered about him lately. When he heard that, during the synagogue fire, some young man climbed up to a window inside the sanctuary and knocked out several panes of glass just to be able to scream "murderers" at the Nazis, Jakub's first thought was of Isaj. That screaming boy was immediately shot by the Germans; he fell to the ground but survived by crawling away in the smoke. Or so they said in the streets. No one knew who it had been, though, and Jakub is pleased to have seen Isaj running. This one did not fall from any windows.

AUGUST 3, 1941

He did not expect to see Fridman entering his office at the Judenrat. Surely this textile tycoon—one of the few who managed to avoid deportation to Siberia, for what that sort of luck is worth now—surely he can get by without Jakub Goldberg's hunger rations. Fridman came into the office fuming, such a big cloud of hot air emanating from such a small man, and Jakub told him to take his place in line. He is not sure what made Fridman assume he was entitled to enter without waiting his turn: his riches or the shared fact of their biographies, the four days in NKVD custody a month and a half ago, in another era. Now Fridman reenters, none the more contrite for having spent two hours among the hungry pleaders in the hallway. Jakub sits down behind his desk, signaling the discussion will be formal, an exchange between an official and his constituent, not between two citizens of equal standing, whatever that might now mean.

"To what do I owe the honor?"

"The restaurants you're setting up—"

"The canteen. The canteen I have set up."

"Well, you do not expect us to, surely—"

"Of course not," says Jakub, beginning to see the purpose of this discussion. "Of course, if you have other means of procuring food, as I am sure you do, you will not be forced to eat at the canteen. And cooking facilities. Surely your wife will not be among those setting up fires on the sidewalk. You understand this is a hazard."

"But my business is no more, you know that."

"Then you are, of course, welcome to eat at the canteen. All residents of the ghetto will receive their ration cards. Those working outside the ghetto, and other groups, as outlined in yesterday's Judenrat announcement, will be entitled to additional food allowances."

"But I cannot," Fridman sputters, apparently stymied by Jakub's refusal to grasp the issue at hand. "I cannot eat with them, with my workers, all them—"

"You do not wish to eat with the hoi polloi, then?"

"It is more than just me. I have a letter from the business community."

"Very well," says Jakub, skimming the letter, suddenly inspired. "I see I am going to have to set up a separate, uh, eating facility. Of course, you understand you will have to share in the expense of this undertaking?"

"Of course."

He will. He will set up a separate canteen for the rich, and he will charge them money for the same thin soup and slice of bread that he gives to the poor. He is a free man, Jakub Goldberg, neither indebted nor elected, and he has only so much bread to distribute, and he will not let it go to waste.

NOVEMBER 29, 1942

The twenty-four members of the Judenrat are in their regular meeting, and its agenda, more than anything else, illustrates what they now consider regular and routine. It has been over three weeks since all the other ghettos in the district were liquidated. The victories of their chairman, Efraim Barasz, are evident. First, he managed to convince the Germans that the Bialystok ghetto was still useful to them. Second—and this is, incontrovertibly, a miracle—he secured the return of three hundred young girls who were deported for work on the potato harvest in October. They were taken off a Treblinka-bound train and returned to the ghetto two weeks ago, ending their mothers' squealing demonstrations outside the Judenrat building but overwhelming the ghetto with the fear of death they brought back with them. To make matters worse, the ghetto gates were locked for three weeks, until just the other day, making the daily ghetto-wide bickering all the more desperate. Now the Germans have ordered the ghetto grounds reduced by about a third. Jakub is concerned that his vegetable gardens will be sacrificed. He had high hopes for using the vegetables next year. He had high hopes for next year, period. What will happen first—the Nazis ordering the liquidation or the Jews, fed up, starting to kill one another? Consider the influx of refugees who have entered the ghetto—escapees from the liquidated ghettos, from the Treblinka trains. There are now several thousand. How is Jakub supposed to feed them? How is the Judenrat supposed to hide them, to ensure the security of the rest? Berel Subotnik, another presidium member, asks whether the ghetto police should start denying entry to the escapees.

Rabbi Rozenman, who almost never speaks, rises with evident difficulty. "Our people, throughout history, have done everything possible to save other Jews." His speech is slurred, probably because he has already handed over his gold teeth, and his matted yellowish gray beard muffles the sound. He struggles to enunciate the way an old man in worn-out shoes struggles not to shuffle. "At the very least, Jews did nothing to harm one another. We now know that, in all probability, our ghetto, too, will be liquidated. The Jews should go down helping one another."

Hear, hear. They are unanimous now, and they go on to an easier subject: tax collection. The Germans have demanded another five million rubles from a ghetto they have very nearly milked dry.

"I demand the most severe of penalties for those who evade taxes!" Subotnik is spitting through his thick lips. "Arrest and isolation! And we must post announcements of the penalties imposed!"

"I second that," says Jakub. "I would also like to point out that the poor residents of the ghetto have been responding to the collection, while the rich have been doing everything to shift the burden to the poor." His wife and daughter should hear him now. He is becoming a regular socialist.

FEBRUARY 10, 1943

First there was a suicide. Cwi Wider, a member of the Judenrat, killed himself. It turned out he had been involved in resistance organizing, had been hoping for some sort of uprising. Then, on Monday, the massacre began, and then there was an attempt at an uprising. There were women who shouted obscenities at the Nazis. There was a family that poured boiling water on the Nazis. There was a young man, Itzhak Malmed, who threw a lightbulb filled with acid at a German policeman, blinding him. The German spun around, crazed, and shot, killing his own partner.

The Germans came to the Judenrat building and told them they would kill a hundred Jews they had rounded up if the council did not produce the offender. Barasz dispatched emissaries to all the youth groups, and soon Itzhak gave himself up. As two Germans were setting up the gallows, another pair were beating the young man. He shouted, "I don't regret it! You will pay for your actions!" He continued for a long time. He shrieked in complete sentences, that boy. It must have been a prepared speech. Jakub walked away after they knocked the stool out from under the boy's feet: he had observed several hangings, and this time he wanted to get away before the corpse's intestines began to void.

Instead of returning to the Judenrat building, Jakub went to a cellar that night, one of many cellars into which the ghetto inhabitants tried to disappear. He told himself he was going because the murder was indiscriminate by now and the Judenrat building no longer offered any protection. That may or may not have been true, but it was not the reason. It was the nausea that came when the Judenrat busied itself looking for Malmed, the same feeling that gathered in his throat every time they started doing the math: give up six thousand, save fifty thousand, give up this one boy, save a hundred people. This time the nausea, the painful lightness in his forehead, would not abate, not until he got himself out of the Judenrat building and into the cellar. It was the end of the fourth day of the massacre.

Jakub walked to the basement of the building where he has been renting a room. His people are dying, and that can only mean that he has failed them. If they hate him for it, he expected nothing else. Still, he had to go somewhere and there was no reason to believe he was any less likely to be lynched there than in other basements—and at least there was logic to his choice.

He was not attacked, physically or verbally. He was ignored. The old man who could not stop coughing was suffocated with a pillow. So was a crying baby. But Jakub Goldberg, member of the Judenrat, was ignored in a way that seemed to say "You are not making a sound and therefore not harming us now, and we haven't the strength to punish people for past sins." He stood—the basement's few boxes and barrels suitable for sitting on were occupied—and thought, and enumerated his sins. Sin number one: unlike Cwi, unlike Itzhak, unlike so many of them, he was alive. Sin number two: he had taken part in drawing up the list again, the list of the twelve thousand the Germans demanded this time. He used the same criteria as the first time: there was a new generation of the infirm and mentally unbalanced to sacrifice.

It is Friday morning, and the Germans have not shown up in the ghetto. The murderers had been punctual if not methodical: in the ghetto by seven, out at five. By mid-morning the inhabitants of cellars and attics begin to believe the massacre is over. They come out crawling, then speed up as their numbers increase, until the ghetto seems filled with running, screaming, flailing madmen, each searching for his dead.

Jakub's legs are stiff after a night spent standing up. In any case, he has no reason to run instead of walking. He has no one to look for. This is not true. As he works to distill his motives, he knows he is searching for the boy, his daughter's boyfriend. Looking at the corpses in the streets is no use: the Nazis used dumdum bullets and aimed for the head, so these are anonymous dead, bodies with necks and, sometimes, lower jaws; past that it's bloody pulp, now covered with a thin layer of snow. As the bodies are dragged away to the pile in the cemetery, they leave fading red tracks.

Jakub wanders into the early February dusk. It has been raining for over an hour. The bloodstains on the ground have all but been washed away. Jakub's clothes are soaked, and his face is wet, so he does not know whether he has tears of his own. As he nears the cemetery, he sees a group of Ha-Shomer ha-Zair members gathered around a fresh mass grave. He studies the crowd carefully. His daughter's boy is not among them. Isaj's best friend, Jakub Makowski, is standing a few feet away from the crowd, not slumped exactly but smaller somehow, visibly alone. Isaj is dead. And Jakub Goldberg is a free man.

His legs are much less stiff now, unlike his trousers, with the frozen rainwater, and he knows where he is going and why. His conversation with Daniel Moszkowicz is brief, like a transaction between businessmen who are too weary to detail their obvious mutual benefit. If Moszkowicz's people will help outfit trucks bringing food into the ghetto with hidden compartments, Jakub will ensure that their arms or whatever else they are bringing into the ghetto passes securely. They shake hands, and Jakub walks slowly back to the Judenrat building, the four-story stone structure that used to make them so proud because it housed the Linas Hatsedek, the health service with the fastest ambulance in Poland.

AUGUST 17, 1943

In this hail of bullets, there will be a separate one for him. It began in much the same way as in February, except this time they knew it was the end of the ghetto—and of its inhabitants. People hid in cellars and attics, and the Nazis flushed them out, herding them into Jakub's vegetable garden until they were trampling one another to death. There have been fires and there has been fighting. The resistance learned its lessons from the Warsaw Ghetto, and so did the Germans. The Bialystok fighters were better armed, but the Germans were much better prepared. They forced the confrontation into open spaces, where the fighters could do little other than die with honor. Still, some of them, cut off from the rest, were herded into the transport crowd, which has now been removed to Pietrasze Field—whether for execution or for death camp presorting, he does not know. But for Jakub, the Germans seem to have reserved a separate fate. They have led him out of the Judenrat building for execution. So they know about those dual-cargo trucks. How very fortunate. He dies a free man, and his executioners know this. He is free even of his fiercest secrets, then. Not a bad end, under the circumstances.

The facts, such as they are, are in that narrative. And in this one.

JUNE 23, 1941

"Goldberg!" he hears, followed by a thin laugh somewhere behind the clanking of the locks on the door. An interrogation, finally, he thinks. Good. Let's get this started. He tries to get up and falters. His body is too large to use the tiny metal bed even to launch from. The steel chain-link under the thin mattress sags nearly down to the floor under his weight; his shoulders fold in to accommodate the shape of his iron crib; his feet stick ridiculously up from the sharp edge at the bottom of the metal bed. He reaches down to the floor with his hand to push himself out of the bed trap.

"Yankel!" It is the same voice from the other side of the door, where the lock continues to clank unrhythmically. Since when do Soviet officers call Jews by their Yiddish names? He has grown accustomed to his own official "Yakov" of the last two years. The door finally creaks, then opens with a heavy slam against the outside wall. Feldman, a leftist Zionist arrested four days ago, along with hundreds of other political activists of every sort, stands in the opening, a crooked, grinning smile pushing apart his gray-stubbled cheeks. "You are a free man again, Comrade Goldberg," he says. "The guards have abandoned the jail."

The guards have abandoned the jail, the Soviets have abandoned the town altogether, the people have abandoned the streets. Not since the Germans came into Bialystok nearly two years ago has the place been so empty, the air so thin and gray. Except, that is, for the two thousand men in the streets, the just-sprung inmates, most of them headed toward the poor Jewish quarter while a few others, like Jakub, are walking slowly down other streets to get to their homes. He walks on the pavement, as he always did when he was with his wife. The road is littered with objects that must have fallen off the fleeing Soviet jeeps: a bureau drawer that split upon hitting the ground, a child's stuffed donkey, a paper bag burst to expose tire-flattened onions.

He heard what sounded like an air battle two nights ago and assumed it was the Soviets' exercises. No such luck. There has apparently been fighting in the air, bombs dropped on the town. It looks, from this distance, like a couple of houses must still be smoldering in the Jewish neighborhood. He recalls an old Jewish joke. A man about to be beheaded suddenly turns to his executioner and asks, "What day of the week is it?"—"Monday."—"What a way to start the week." Only Feldman could have called what they are now, on this Monday, "free." Out of one jail and into another. God knows, he has learned enough about what happens to Jews under Germans over the past two years, reading letters from the Warsaw Ghetto. Four days ago he was a man with a wife, a daughter, a home, and hopes, even if they had devolved into avoiding arrest and seeing his daughter again. Now he will go to his empty house, wait for the new jailers to come in, hope for the old ones to return. One's aspirations have a way of shrinking.

SEPTEMBER 21, 1941

The twenty-four members of the Judenrat, gathered in the mercifully dim room in what used to be the Jewish hospital, are composing the first death list. He knew, from what he had heard of Warsaw and Lodz, that this would happen sooner or later. The Germans picked their first ten thousand victims almost at random but, thankfully, without Jewish assistance. Now they want twelve thousand names for a transport to Pruzhany. Presumably, to death.

"Jews, we must refuse to be the tools of their selection." That is Pejsach Kaplan, the editor of the daily *Unzer Lebn*. A thin, dry man with a square face and perpetually burning eyes. A tireless idealist. "I understand we have no choice but to draw up some list, but we should draw it up without making a choice. A lottery would be appropriate."

"This is no time to start shirking our responsibilities." Jakub stands up to speak. "Remember, please, that by creating a death list we are drawing up a list of the fifty thousand who will go on living. This is not a lottery. I can tell you who is more likely to survive, and I can tell you who will die within weeks no matter what we do."

It goes on for hours, and then it is decided: the sick, the hopelessly hungry, the deeply impoverished, the inhumanly crowded, will leave the ghetto. The presidium stays in the hall to go over lists. They are drawing on Jakub's rationing lists, the food and heat distribution charts. They can find only about four thousand hopeless cases. The remainder will have to be selected at random, but the five men cannot bear the apparent cynicism of creating a lottery. The alphabet will have to be their only criterion. The Polish alphabet, as it happens. They take two thousand *A*s and resolve to convince the Germans to halve the requirement. The next day, Chairman Barasz negotiates a miracle by assuring the Germans that the rest of the ghetto population is essential for the functioning of the many factories he is setting up to aid the German war effort. Only a few souls over five thousand go on the transport. Jakub's rolls are relieved of the most hopeless cases, so he can better help the living.

DECEMBER 30, 1941

By the time Jakub arrives at his office on the top floor of the Judenrat building in the morning, the two benches in the corridor opposite his door are occupied. People are sitting on the benches, leaning on the backs of the benches, standing in front of the benches talking with those sitting, discussing rumors of a cut in the necessary workforce, an increase in the numbers—they are saying women will be drafted for labor more and more—another tax collection. Well, yes, the tax collection, he can confirm that one. Some are here to plead their case before the announcement even goes up: there is no way they can give up their fur coats now, they will say, not in the winter. How is he to make them understand that they will never be able to wear those coats around the ghetto without getting beaten or worse? And then the women who absolutely have to have an additional ration for their children, who are starving. All the children are starving. He spots the blonde Grossman girl. She appeared in the ghetto within the last week, out of nowhere, it seemed, confident, careless, a woman who too obviously came on a mission. He knows why she is here: she wants papers showing that the kibbutz run by the *chalutzim* (pioneers)—her young group—is a charity kitchen. If this means they will at least feed themselves and save him twenty-five rations, he will sign anything. If only he could have some assurance they will not try to do something stupid, something that could cost other people's lives. He waves the girl into his office.

He believes this discussion should be formal. He walks behind his desk and pulls up the wooden chair. Why is it that the less freedom you have the smaller is your furniture? This chair must have been made for *cheder* students. His legs bent uncomfortably, his back forced erect, supporting himself on the desk with his forearms, he addresses the girl.

"You know that I know you and your family, and I trust you," he begins. "I shall therefore speak frankly. I have been a Zionist and I remain a Zionist. The pioneer Zionist movements are very precious to me. I think we must help the pioneers maintain themselves. It's true I was never overenthusiastic about the kinds of foolishness you taught my daughter, with all your communist ideas. I am sure, however, that you are good Jews. But all kinds of rumors have reached me to the effect that you are spreading false information and calling on the Jews to act stupidly and irresponsibly, to make war. Is that true? Have you become Communists and partisans? Are you waiting for the Red Army, eh?"

The girl turns red. Beet red, as blondes can. "Who are you to tell me what is true? Here you are, sitting in your imaginary king-dom, distributing food rations to the Jews, thinking you have the power. How can you hate Communism so much that you are blind and deaf to what the Germans have done elsewhere? Do you know about Slonim? Liquidated! I should throw the German rations, the hunger rations for the Jews, at your feet!"

There is no point in arguing with someone who comes with a prepared speech, he realizes. And he cannot refrain from answer-ing. "I understand that is what you have come to do. I can assure you I will find mouths that will be grateful for that food."

"You think you are so important! That you can make or break people by giving them a crust of bread! And you call yourself a Zionist, but you think the pioneers are just children at play. Do you even know what a pioneer is? You never even understood your own daughter!"

"What I understand about my daughter is that she has curly brown hair and swarthy skin. And she couldn't, if the end came, go over to the Aryan side like you will. And if she were here and you were trying to pull her into whatever it is you are thinking up, I swear, I would strangle you with my own two hands." He looks down at his hands on the desk and sees white knuckles and veins purple and thick under the hair. He tries to pull back, forces the back legs of the silly little chair down to the floor. The girl, he realizes, is also trying to step back from the confrontation.

"I don't know what you think we are doing," she says. "We are running a kibbutz. Do I look like a partisan to you?"

"No, no. I trust you, of course: you are the daughter of Nachum Grossman."

He pulls the charity-kitchen papers out of his desk drawer, already stamped and signed, and hands them to the girl, who mumbles a thank-you, either grudging or embarrassed—he cannot tell which.

AUGUST 16, 1943

Jakub stands at the window, holding two pieces of paper, rereading them by the pale early-morning light.

> *Bialystok is becoming* judenrein. *All are required to vacate their houses by 9 in the morning. Each Jew is allowed to take along one small hand-carried bag.*

These are the handbills posted by the Judenrat overnight. Until then, they had been trying to reassure the remaining forty thousand people that the ghetto would go on. There was hope: just a couple of weeks ago there were new orders for goods from the ghetto factories, one request coming from Berlin itself. There was the fall of Mussolini, first rumored, then confirmed, to their gleeful amazement. In fact, though, an entire month has passed since Barasz informed the Judenrat presidium that the Germans were choosing between keeping the Lodz ghetto and the Bialystok one and that he was not optimistic. Two days ago Gestapo footmen came to inspect the gates and walls, just as they had in February. And, just as in February, the Germans withdrew their watches, fixed or not, from the ghetto repairmen. The handbills, then, just confirmed what everyone already knew but no one really believed. Such is the condition of being among the last ghettos to be liquidated: the Jews do not need *judenrein*—"free of Jews"—explained to them.

The other piece of paper is also a handbill.

Fellow Jews! Fearsome days have come upon us. More than the ghetto and the yellow badge, hatred, humiliation and degradation—we now face death! . . . Fight for your lives until your last breath! Die like heroes! . . . Except for our honor we have nothing to lose! . . . Do not flee the ghetto unarmed, for without weapons you will perish. Only after fulfilling your national obligation, go to the forest armed. Weapons can be seized from any German in the ghetto. BE STRONG!

Where do these young people think they live? They have created a separate world in their kibbutz and presume to teach others, out in the real world. The real world is here, in the ghetto, not outside, where Mussolini has fallen and the Red Army is advancing. Here in the real world, Jews with their children and their small bags are beginning to gather in the Judenrat garden, even though two hours still remain until the deadline. What did these youngsters think? That that stooped man with the wispy beard would abandon his daughter and go "seize" arms from the Germans? And have his child watch him die? This little man has no illusions. He knows what awaits him. He has an ambition: to hold his little girl's bony hand all the way to the gas chamber, never to let it go. Could you ever be that strong, you who are so sure of what is right?

There is a bang, the crackling of machine-gun fire, and the sky, within seconds, turns from pale gray to pink. The ghetto is in flames. The sound of gunfire and exploding grenades breaks out everywhere, and people are running, running from every direction. Nazis—German, Ukrainian, and Belarusian—move in from the ghetto fence, forcing the crowd accumulating in the Judenrat garden to contract until it is heaving, moaning, screaming, like a single human body in agony. Gestapo soldiers are running up and down the stairs of the Judenrat building. Someone shouts at Jakub that this is now the Gestapo headquarters. Before he is pushed away from the window, he sees the blonde girl running from the fire toward the crowd in the garden. She runs awkwardly, as chubby girls run, knees knocking, feet far apart, arms flailing out of sync. A pink chintz summer dress under an unseasonably warm coat, torn shoes, blood and filth on her face. And on her face, the expression of utter confusion, the question: "Why are you people going willingly to your deaths? Don't you know the truth?" Jakub feels a pang of compassion for the girl. No one should learn about life by watching people die.

NOVEMBER 3, 1943

He has been lying awake on the bunk for some time when the guards call on the inmates to come out for work. It would be more accurate to say that he has been lying *in* the bunk, for it is a boxlike structure, with boards guarding the sides. It is shaped as though someone had planned to put mattresses on these boards, though certainly no one did. His body has shrunk over the last two years. It seems he is not only thinner but smaller of bone. His flesh has dwindled from lack of food; his bones must have shrunk from lack of air. But he always seems to stay one step behind the accommodations; the bunk in which he now lies might have been made with someone the size of his wife in mind. Angled by boards on every side, he feels like he has been forced into someone else's coffin.

The guard calls them out for work. They line up, as they do every morning, but now one of the guards begins to call out the names of all the thousand or so Jews in this camp, a labor branch of Majdanek. This lengthy procedure completed, several hundred of them are marched through the still-dark winter morning past what he thinks is the main camp. No breakfast today. That is, they will not get their half-liter of the marsh-colored brew they call tea for lack of another word. They stop at the end of the main camp's biggest field, and the rows of men are told to take steps forward and back until they are standing in even rows, about two meters apart. They are given shovels and told they will be digging ditches. They begin to work, slowly, unevenly, silently, their silhouettes gradually turning from black to blue as the light turns an ever fainter gray.

The grass is still green in places, elsewhere a dirty yellow, matted like hair, making it difficult for the dull shovel to cut through it. He stops working for a minute: he has just realized he can, for his punishment could only be getting shot a few hours before his time. The sky is endless, a filthy shade of blue, with contourless clouds that may be smoke. He allows himself a look behind, at the recently built crematorium. No, there is no smoke there. These are real clouds for once, and then there are the lower, black, groaning clouds that are crows. A shiny bluish black, they are almost pleasant to look at: they are the only thing in the entire landscape that does not seem a faded, tired color.

He twists his body, to the extent that he still can, to look back at the fields of the camp. People are being shaped into columns and rows, endless columns and endless rows. He realizes, from the color of these human formations, that the people are naked. A bluish shape farther in the distance must be the other inmates looking on. In a hallucinatory close-up of a sort he has experienced lately, he thinks he has caught a glimpse of the blonde girl. But no, of course not, he cannot see any faces, much less hers.

He saw her face in September, on the day when they led the last nine hundred people out of the mini-ghetto, the single block that had been left the Jews when the ghetto limits were redrawn the second time. He came out then with the rest of the Judenrat,

at the head of the column, fully conscious of where they were going now, with their dignity intact and their consciences clear. He
saw her distinctly among the Poles standing, watching, on the
Aryan side. Her pudgy face was contorted in a square grimace, as
though to say, "I told you so. Is this what you wanted?" *Yes,* he
thought, *this is what I wanted. I wanted to be with my people, safe in
the knowledge that, unlike you and your kind, I never tried to save one of
us over the rest. I tried to save us all. To the extent that it was possible, I
succeeded. We are the last Jews leaving the last surviving ghetto in this
part of Poland. I know that your beloved Red Army is not far from here.
And I would not mind finding myself in one of their jails now. But that is
none of your concern.*

The dull blow of a rifle butt to the shoulder blade turns him
back toward the ditch in the present. He looks down at his shovel.
They are digging very narrow ditches, he and his fellow Jews.
Space has continued to contract to the very end.

These two accounts, then, are based on documents. Fridman and
Feldman are composite characters created to avoid insulting the
memory of real people. But other than that, the facts, such as they
have been recounted and remembered, are there. They are reflected in the documents of the Judenrat and the memoirs of survivors. One survivor remembers my great-grandfather as an
organizer of the resistance effort; another, as a deluded coward. A
third says he was executed in the ghetto; others, that he was shot
in Majdanek. He was not a coward, and he was not deluded. The
rest of the facts would take Ester and Bella, and Ester's children
and grandchildren after them, years to learn, and then to learn to
understand.

Information came in snatches. In December 1944, around the
time Bella's first grandson was born, a woman named Regina

Wojskowska contacted her in Moscow. A ghetto escapee, a partisan who went by the name Lena, she asked Bella to come to a Moscow hospital where she was recovering from an operation on her arm. She said Jakub Goldberg had asked her to let Bella know he had helped the resistance in Bialystok. He had helped smuggle arms. He had not expected to survive, she said. He had told her where his daughter was studying in Moscow and asked her to get in touch. She did not know much more: her group had left the ghetto for the forest before the uprising.

And there was a second woman. The name was Knazew; the year must have been 1946. She traveled to Moscow to be with her older son, who had gone there to study during the Soviet occupation of Bialystok. Her meeting with Bella, it seems, was accidental, though former Bialystokers in Moscow tended to travel in the same circles. Did she know anything about Jakub Goldberg? Yes, she had been his landlady.

The Goldbergs' Bialystok apartment was outside the Jewish neighborhood, so in the ghetto he rented a room from the Knazew family. They were transported to Majdanek at the same time, in September 1943, the Knazews, their ten-year-old daughter, and Jakub Goldberg. Upon arrival at the camp, the males and females were separated. They promised one another that whoever survived would try to find the others' relatives and tell what he or she could. In March 1944, as the Nazis dismantled Majdanek before the Soviet troops arrived, Mrs. Knazew and her daughter, along with some thousands of other survivors deemed unfit for labor, were transferred to Auschwitz. Neither her husband nor Bella's was in the transport.

What else did she tell? That the rats that roamed the barracks in the night liked children's cheeks, which retain fat even when the rest of the body has wasted away. That she was the only woman in her barracks who succeeded in staying awake all night every night guarding her child. But none of that had to do with Jakub Goldberg. What did she know about him? He was a member of the Judenrat. He spoke a lot of his wife and daughter. He was dead.

The woman's survival was a miracle of resilience, but once she was in Moscow with her two children, she could not manage. The Soviet regime considered prisoners of war to be traitors. The woman's concentration-camp tattoo branded her unfit and undeserving. She could not hide it, and she could not keep a job, and after a couple of years she returned to Poland. Neither Bella nor Ester heard from her again.

It was another thirty-five years before another story of Jakub came, brought by a third woman. The blonde girl.

CHAPTER FOURTEEN

JANUARY 1982

In Moscow, you can tell when a telephone call is long-distance: rather than the usual series of rings, it announces itself with a single trill that persists until the phone is picked up. Ester's three matchbox rooms fill with anxiety at the sound, which does not subside when Ester hears Eda's voice. Ester is still in touch with her college roommate, who returned to Poland thirty-five years ago. They write, and they see each other every few years, when Ester goes to Poland as a tourist. But they do not call very often. So this must be important, and it is immediately worrisome.

"What happened?"

"Nothing, nothing. Everyone's fine. But there is a question. I had a phone call from someone in Israel who wants your phone number. Can I give it out?" Eda seems to think this is a dicey proposition. Ever since she returned to Poland, their friendship has been tinted with a certain condescension: Eda thinks of herself as living in the West, in civilization, in freedom, and assumes Ester to be contaminated with all the fears that burden regular Soviet citizens. One of *them,* it goes without saying, would not wish to receive a phone call from Israel. Diplomatic relations between the Soviet Union and Israel, rocky since the 1950s, were severed during the Six-Day War fifteen years ago, and the Soviet Union's virulently pro-Arab foreign-policy stand has gone hand in hand with ever-increasing anti-Semitism inside the country. Contacts with foreigners, though not so dangerous as they were in Stalin's time, are fraught with the risk of attracting the KGB's attention; contacts with Israelis are still more perilous.

"Yes, of course," Ester answers. "What kind of question is that? Of course, give them my phone number. But who is it? Who wants it? Is it someone we know?"

But Eda knows nothing—it may be someone from Bialystok, she thinks, but she is not sure—so they briefly exchange family news of health, household, and work problems. After they hang up, Ester wonders about the future caller, and she grows excited because she has not spoken to someone who lives in Israel in more than twenty years, since a Hebrew theater troupe performed in Moscow.

APRIL 1982

This time it is a local call, but the woman's voice is foreign, almost indecipherable. It asks for Ester Gessen and proceeds, in mangled Polish, to introduce itself: Chaika Grossman, from Bialystok, from Israel, at the Hotel Ukraine.

It is a nearly two-hour journey from the sleeping suburb of concrete-block high-rises where Ester lives to the Hotel Ukraine, a Stalin-era neo-Gothic skyscraper on the bank of the Moscow River. Ester overcomes the bus and the sleet and the subway and the long line at the shop to buy chocolates to bring with her and the long walk to the hotel and the inevitable humiliating examination by the concierge—all in a haze of anticipation. She recalls Chaika Grossman vaguely: they attended the same Hebrew gymnasium in Bialystok, but Chaika was a few years older. She was well respected, though, in Ha-Shomer ha-Zair, to which they both belonged. She was engaged to Meir Orkin, older brother of Malka, Ester's best friend. Meir went to Palestine in the 1930s, but Chaika stayed to organize the Shomerite commune before they went over. Malka stayed behind too, and perished.

They sit in Chaika's room, two women around sixty, both a bit heavy, both in dresses a bit too bright and with voices a bit too loud. Ester assumed, for some reason, that Chaika would have a suite. Chaika assumed they would go to a café. No, Ester says, they would be unable to talk in a café. Chaika wrinkles her face, which is lined heavily, horizontally, in a way that lends itself to frowning smiles. They drink tea from heavy glasses supplied by the maid. Ester sits in the only chair. Chaika arranges herself on the bed like an oversize little girl.

They speak a mixture of Polish, which Chaika has not used in more than thirty years, and Hebrew, which Ester has not spoken in forty. Chaika says she survived the war in Bialystok, took part in the ghetto resistance, joined the partisans in the forest. Ester says her father helped the resistance. Chaika says she moved to Israel in 1948, married Meir. They live on a kibbutz. She is a member of the Knesset, a socialist. She is here with an Israeli delegation invited by the Soviet Committee for the Defense of Peace. Ester frowns, says her socialist views have caved in to life in the Soviet Union. But this is not the point, she says, uncharacteristically sidestepping an argument. She wants to know about Israel, all about Israel. Chaika talks. She tells her the kibbutz is all they once dreamed about, but the country has many problems. She says she has drafted laws on abortion and the status of women and children. They talk into the evening, until Chaika is late for a reception. In Israel everyone is always late, she says, but it is time to go, and Ester rises.

"Listen," Chaika then says. "Aren't you a bit surprised that there are so many people from Bialystok in Moscow, and of all of them I called you?"

"I was just thinking that coming here," Ester says. "Very surprised, yes. Why?"

"Because in 1947 I was working at the Central Committee for the Jews in Warsaw, and we got your telegram."

"My God! To tell you the truth, I forgot all about it. That's so funny."

"It was the only one we got from an individual, and I promised myself I'd find you."

"And a mere thirty-five years later—"

"Here," Chaika says, as Ester pulls on her heavy fur coat. "This is my book about the Bialystok ghetto uprising. I write about your father in it too."

Ester leaves the hotel weighed down by the book, a nearly five-hundred-page brick of a tome, by a sense of bemused envy at someone who is living out their common dream, and by the night, which descends with the heavy dampness of this very cold climate. She will proudly tell her Moscow friends about her courage of thirty-five years ago: when she learned of the UN resolution allowing for the founding of the State of Israel, she sent a telegram of congratulations to the Central Committee for the Jews in Warsaw. Back then it was a reckless act that easily could have cost her her freedom. Now she shows off her reward: the book delivered by a woman who never forgot the telegram, or her, Ester Gessen, daughter of Jakub Goldberg. But the book is overlong and in Hebrew, and she is convinced her language skills are too rusty to make her way through, so the tome just sits there, out of sight of the casual visitor, for the next fifteen years, unread.

AUGUST 1997

In the United States for a holiday masquerading as a tour for my book on the Russian intelligentsia, I go to the recently opened Holocaust Museum in Washington, D.C., and wander into the gift shop on my usual quest for something Jewish for my grandmother Ester. A thick book with an amateurish blue-and-green cover catches my eye, and I can hardly believe my luck: it is an English translation of Chaika Grossman's *The Underground Army: Fighters of the Bialystok Ghetto.* There can be no better gift than this, a chance for my grandmother—whose English these days is better than her Hebrew—to read about her father the resistance hero. I buy the book and, as soon as I am settled for the night in a friend's home, start combing its 426 unindexed pages for my great-grandfather's name.

> *The head of the [Judenrat's economic] department was one of the city's well-known Zionist personalities, Goldberg, the father of a young girl, a member of the ken (Ha-Shomer ha-Zair branch) who had studied in Moscow during the Soviet era and remained there. I knew him, and he knew me. He was not too enthusiastic about Ha-Shomer ha-Zair but he thought its members nice children who, in the course of time, would awaken from their childish dreams. He related to his splendid daughter in the same way. He received me hospitably and I entered without waiting my turn and thought the matter arranged. To my great surprise he began to speak to me seriously.*

So far so good. This is a description of Chaika's coming to see my great-grandfather to receive a charity-kitchen permit for the ghetto kibbutz, which served as a front for a resistance organization. I am pleased the book mentions even my grandmother, and as I turn the page, I anticipate the earnest account of a conversation between allies who come to a common cause from different backgrounds and views. I expect Goldberg to express his support conspiratorially but decisively, and the incredulous narrator to accept it with gratitude. The entire book is written in the explicitly ideological language familiar to me from my Soviet youth, so I expect my great-grandfather to be woven into this heroic narrative in a stilted but definitive way.

Instead, he tells her to give up the silly attempts to start unrest in the ghetto, and she describes him, in this book written about seven years later, the following way.

> *His narrow-mindedness, stubbornness and blind hatred of communism were all leading him astray. He apparently believed that the Germans were not really so bad. . . . He was satisfied, too satisfied . . . that little man . . . to the end he would consider himself one of the elect and forget that it was the Nazis who had chosen him and granted him his imaginary power. He was actually only an emissary, their small and despicable servant. To the end of his days and to the last Jew, he would think that someone could hide himself from the Jewish tragedy and continue to live during the great holocaust.*

Two hundred and fifty pages later, there is this description.

> *It was again a summer day. A wide gate opened on Fabryczna Street, long lines stretched through the gate and beyond. They were Jews, well dressed. They walked slowly, with dignity, without chil-*

dren, almost without any packages. I looked closely: Barasz was marching in the front row, with his wife at his side. His gray head could be seen from afar. Goldberg, and Marcus, the commander of the Jewish police, the whole Judenrat, and after them more hundreds of Jews, all dignitaries: former heads of the factories, leaders of the Judenrat departments, police officers. There was a wire stretched down in the middle of the street. Barasz tripped, and almost fell. He bent over, lifted the wire, and threw it aside. Once again he walked slowly, dignified and erect. The company came closer. Sentries walked along the sides of the street and took care that we did not come too close. The company covered the whole of Fabryczna Street and came to the railway, to the industrial station. Barasz looked around and did not see those standing on the aryan side of the street, watching. He looked ahead as if his eye had been caught by some distant point on the blue horizon. They marched silently. No one wept, no one cried—no one attempted to escape.

And so were led to Majdanek the last of the Jews, who had lived an illusion.

NOVEMBER 1999, BIALYSTOK

I have lunch at New York Bagels across the street from the Cristall Hotel. Leonard Cohen is dancing to the end of love on the stereo; framed posters on the walls feature bagels, the Chrysler Building, and the Statue of Liberty. All of this, like my glossy new hotel, is geared to the homesick Jewish home-seeker of the sort that come here by the tens of thousands from America, Israel, Australia, every summer. The hotel, as it happens, is on one side of the street that used to have the wooden fence dividing it down the middle; the Bagels is on the ghetto side.

I came by train from Warsaw, getting in yesterday after dark. I wanted to see Ester's beloved Bialystok, and I was hoping to find a local historian or, better yet, a contemporary who remembered the ghetto and Jakub and could talk to me. This was something of an unfounded hope. The Bialystok entry in the *Encyclopaedia Judaica* indicates that "after the war there remained 1,085 Jews in Bialystok, of whom 900 were local inhabitants, and the rest from the neighboring villages. Of the ghetto inhabitants, 260 survived, some in the deportation camps, others as members of partisan units. The community presumably dwindled and dissolved." Some presumption. On the train on the way here I read *Jewish Bialystok and Surroundings in Eastern Poland,* written by local journalist Tomasz Wisniewski, one of a score of ethnic Poles throughout this country who have fashioned their fascination with the gap of history into an avocation. He maintains a database of archival mentions of Bialystok Jews. Tomasz's *Jewish Bialystok* says that there are five Jews living in Bialystok now. Professor Adam Dobronski at the Bialystok branch of Warsaw University tells me that, unfortunately, "they have been dying off," and now there are one and a half Jews in the town: one Jew and another one, who is married to a Catholic and does not consider himself Jewish. This is my first trip to a place where the number of Jews is known precisely.

None of the very few survivors of the Bialystok ghetto lives in the town: most of them settled in Israel. The resident Jews, all one and a half of them, are not native Bialystokers, so I do not go to see them. Instead, I walk around a lot. This is a small town, but by no means a backwater. There are something like 280,000 residents, screeching traffic, busy young people, and, even more noticeable, scores of flashy fashion shops serving them. There is no sense of absence, no conspicuous empty space, and the Jewish memorial boards scattered throughout the center of town are overshadowed by store displays. It all reminds me of a line from a Brodsky poem: "Life without us is, darling, thinkable."

I continuously refer to Tomasz's guidebook—the most essential of guidebooks, for it leads the reader through the invisible, from the site of the burned-down synagogue to the city park that was once a Jewish cemetery. His book is also a work of glorified history, the sort that appears in the absence of eyewitnesses. It claims, for example, that Bialystok was exempt from the anti-Semitism and pogroms that swept through Poland in the 1930s. When I meet him, Tomasz also tells me that he believes there is no anti-Semitism in Poland now. Though on each of the occasions when I have visited Poland I have always heard anti-Semitic taunts, I do not argue but ask him, instead, whether he knows if the building on Zlota Street, where my grandmother grew up, still stands. Yes, he says, he has even attended parties there. He draws a map, and I set off.

This is a mystical, slightly nerve-racking pilgrimage, the freezing walk up the long Sienkiewicz Street. In Moscow I live just up the street from the building where my grandmother Ruzya grew up and then raised my mother, and I bike or drive past it regularly, but I have never tried to enter: it seems a regular part of the landscape, as accidental to my family's history as we are to this building's. But the building on Zlota Street fascinates me as a survivor of an annihilated world that is entirely foreign to me.

Guided by Tomasz's map, I find a grayish squat two-story structure of sandstone with the date 1928 inscribed under the gable. I mill around in the fenced-in yard, miraculously unnoticed by the puss-eyed German shepherd, until a young woman and her small daughter enter the gate.

"Do you live here?" I ask.

"Yes."

"I think my grandmother lived in this building before the war."

"You should speak to my aunt, but she is not home now."

"Does she live on the ground floor?"

"Yes." The woman is in her mid-thirties. She has raggedy blond hair and crooked teeth. "Come here tomorrow at noon," she says, then, as I turn to go, suddenly tenses up. "You are not trying to take the place back, are you?"

"No, no, my great-grandfather was just a tenant."

I go back the next day, but before I do, I e-mail my grandmother, who is in the United States visiting her children, and she writes back that this is the wrong building. Danuta Kossakiewicz, the young woman's aunt, tells me the same thing. She is in her sixties, heavyish, dyed blond, and she gives me tea and a jellied-meat dish, and tells me the house I seek was razed nine years ago. She even tracks down one of the former tenants for me to talk to, a certain Kozlowski, but I decide not to venture so far afield: I wanted to see the house, not hear about it. Instead, I walk in what used to be the courtyard where the right house used to stand: if you look carefully, you can see that it is still marked off by larger trees, surrounding the not-quite-empty space of younger, sticklike growth. The building was torn down to make way for apartment blocks, five stories and with panels of poisonous yellow. I walk across the street to my grandmother's Hebrew Gymnasium, a forbidding modern building that now serves as a hospital, and then I go talk to local historians.

There is precious little information I can find in Bialystok, but I do see a photograph of Jakub in Tomasz's files, and Tomasz promises to copy it for me. My grandmother has only two pictures: a group one of the Jewish council and a beach photo, in which her father, skinny and happy, is half turned away from the camera. In the 1950s she had an old Jewish photographer, a specialist in the trade, make a manifold enlargement of her father's face from the group photo. She then had the image transferred to an oval ceramic tile to put on Bella and Jakub's gravestone—a Russian tradition. Jakub has no grave, of course, but he and Bella share a tombstone at a Moscow Jewish cemetery. I look at the picture every September 2: I drive Ester to the cemetery on the anniversary of her mother's death. The image is so blurry that it has never helped me imagine Jakub. I just knew, from listening to my grandmother, that he was handsome and very, very tall. Now I know that he was plain big, at least in the late 1930s: broad-chested, square-headed, proud and confident, judging from the posture.

I accumulate a heap of books and Xeroxes—the printed memories of a Jewish Bialystok and its demise. Refoel Rajzner, a survivor who lived in Australia, wrote that Jakub Goldberg was shot on the second day of the ghetto uprising in August 1943. According to Chaika Grossman as well as that Knazew woman, he was shot in Majdanek during the mass execution of Jews there on November 3, 1943. Rajzner's assertion, probably based on rumors of the sort that feed all closed communities, is almost certainly erroneous.

I learn that Jakub was a member of the Judenrat presidium, in charge of rationing and heat distribution. That he operated two canteens serving identical fare, one for everyone and one for the rich. That he was well respected. Pejsach Kaplan, editor of the Yiddish-language daily *Unzer Lebn,* a man far to the left of my great-grandfather, wrote in his diary: "The council made a Herculean effort to obtain food and distribute it as equitably as possible. Often, some people had to go hungry. But everything humanly possible was done to provide sustenance to the greatest number. The Rationing Department . . . also controlled heating supplies."

I learn that the Judenrat made the Bialystok ghetto population more useful to the Germans than perhaps any other ghetto: twenty different factories operated at one time. That the Judenrat managed to keep the Germans largely out of the day-to-day operations and maintenance of the ghetto. In a large, poorly lit basement room in the city courthouse, amid dust-covered cardboard binders, I find Woldemar Monkiewicz, an old, nearly blind historian, prosecutor, and the chairman of a Bialystok-region committee investigating Hitler-era crimes. "If it weren't for the Judenrat," he says, "it could have been like [in the nearby town of] Tykocin, where all the Jews were exterminated within two months."

I learn that there were about three hundred participants in the ghetto uprising, that they came from competing organizations, and that they did not trust one another. This would explain how someone like Chaika Grossman could be convinced that Jakub Goldberg staunchly opposed resistance efforts while someone like Regina Wojskowska said that he had helped. Monkiewicz, who has been researching Bialystok ghetto history most of his life, thinks the details of underground organizing are probably impossible to reconstruct. "The Communists think they organized the resistance," this former Communist says with obvious disdain. "But the Communists are the ones who survived because they joined the Soviet partisans in the forest before the uprising." And the dead, for the most part, are silent. According to an article written by Monkiewicz, "Jakub Goldberg, a Zionist activist, was among those who cooperated with the Jewish Fighting Union," which "brought weapons and ammunition into the ghetto in the hidden compartments of trucks." He can no longer recall what his sources were for that statement: one interview or another, or someone's handwritten memoir.

In 1944, when Regina Wojskowska told Bella that her Jakub had been a member of the Judenrat *and* helped the resistance, that information did not yet contain an apparent contradiction. History had not been written.

Seventeen years later, in 1961, came the Eichmann trial in Israel, where the attorney general, Gideon Hausner, extolled the heroism of the ghetto fighters, who, he said, "redeemed the honor of our people" with their deaths. Even more important for creating the Judenrat/resistance dichotomy was Hannah Arendt's report on the Eichmann trial. Arendt condemned the Judenrats as the most insidious of the forces that came together to kill the Jews. "Without Jewish help in administrative and police work . . . there would have been either complete chaos or an impossibly severe drain on German manpower," she wrote, adding later in the text: "The whole truth was that if the Jewish people had really been unorganized and leaderless, there would have been chaos and plenty of misery but the total number of victims would hardly have been between four and a half and six million people." The numbers had not yet hardened, but the historical evaluation was taking definite shape: the resisters, hopeless as their cause may have been, were the unquestioned heroes; the Judenrats, the collaborators, very nearly the murderers of their own people.

Arendt allowed that there were different Judenrats, or at least different Judenrat leaders: "They ranged all the way from Chaim Rumkowski, eldest of the Jews in Lodz, called Chaim I, who issued currency notes bearing his signature and postage stamps engraved with his portrait, and who rode around in a broken-down horse-drawn carriage; through [Berlin's] Leo Baeck, scholarly, mild-mannered, highly educated, who believed Jewish policemen would be 'more gentle and helpful' and would 'make the ordeal easier' (whereas in fact they were, of course, more brutal and less corruptible, since so much more was at stake for them); to, finally, a few who committed suicide—like Adam Czerniakow, chairman

of the Warsaw Jewish Council, who was not a rabbi but an unbe-
liever, a Polish-speaking Jewish engineer, but who must still have
remembered the rabbinical saying: 'Let them kill you, but don't
cross the line.' " Half the Jews would have survived had it not
been for the Judenrats' effective organization of their slaughter,
estimated Arendt. That made the Judenrats, in her estimation, responsible for, say, three million deaths.

Arendt's report caused an uproar: one Jewish newspaper
nailed her as a "self-hating Jewess." Still, her portrayal of the
Judenrats stuck. Not all historians agreed, of course. In 1972, New
York historian Isaiah Trunk published *Judenrat,* a six-hundred-
page study. He argued that, in the early years of the ghettos, the
Nazis' ultimate goal of annihilating the Jews was not self-evident
and that even later the hope of saving at least some of the Jews did
not appear unfounded. Nor was the goal of making marginally
tolerable the Jews' last days, months, or years a dishonorable one.
They were not, after all, marched straight from their homes to the
gas chambers. The road to death was a slow crawl from the home
to the ghetto, through the ghetto factories and sometimes labor
camps. All along this journey there was a hope, if not of ultimate
survival, then of reducing the misery. Though hope may not be
the point: that journey, which lasted, in some cases—as in the
Lodz ghetto, for example—as much as five years, was life. Every
day of this life, people ate and relieved themselves and someone
tried to make sure they had something to eat and the plumbing
was working to flush the excrement. (The failure to maintain the
plumbing in working order led to one of the most often cited
horrors of life in the Warsaw ghetto, where the streets were
strewn with shit.) A basic level of dignified organization was also a
question of survival. In 1947, long before the Eichmann trial made
the design of the "final solution" clear, an American sociologist
named Marie Syrkin talked to dozens of survivors. They believed

that the Nazis hoped intolerable living conditions in the ghettos would make the Jews "degenerate to the level of criminals. Those Jews who did not die [of starvation or disease] would rend each other like wild beasts. Perhaps the Nazis expected to be spared the necessity of building special extermination centers. But the Jews did not die fast enough, nor did they degenerate as required." That, in large measure, was the work of the Judenrats.

Judenrat members were engaged in an intolerable but, they thought, essential negotiation with the Nazis, aimed at saving the greatest number of Jews in their ghettos. Some of them, like Bialystok's Barasz, clearly aided the resistance, but as long as there remained, in their minds, a chance of saving at least some of the population, the Judenrats and the resisters worked at cross purposes. Put crudely, it was the difference between working on making life tolerable and working on making death beautiful. Chaika Grossman said as much in a speech she gave shortly after the war: "To live is not a difficult task. You must know . . . how to die." To someone like my great-grandfather, this would have sounded like irresponsible drivel. Historian Raul Hilberg writes that Judenrat members "believed that their service was an obligation, and they were convinced with absolute certainty that they carried the entire burden of caring for the Jewish population. . . . The Jewish leaders were, in short, remarkably similar in their self-perception to rulers all over the world, but their role was not normal and for most of them neither was their fate."

The Judenrats tried to productivize the Jews, making them indispensable to the German war machine; the resisters sabotaged the work—Chaika Grossman describes, for example, that the Bialystok ghetto underground convinced workers to use a special glue in soldiers' boots, causing them to fall apart after a month. From the point of view of historians who reduce the Jews' struggle to the moment and manner of their death, the Judenrats failed miserably;

the resisters failed gloriously. If the resisters died fighting and the Judenrat members died deluded and the rest of the Jews died somehow between these two extremes, then, surely, the Judenrats and the resistance shared no common ground. One of the most striking examples of this historical reductionism can be glimpsed in a footnote in Trunk's book: in describing Barasz's cooperation with the resistance, he is forced to cite the original manuscript of the diary of resistance leader Mordechai Tennenbaum-Tamaroff (who hid his journal in a safe place before the uprising, in which he was killed), because this passage was left out of the published version, presumably because it complicated the story too much.

My grandmother, living as she did in the Soviet Union, remained oblivious to the debate about the role of the Judenrat: such a discussion was impossible in a country that repressed any discussion of concentration camps, domestic or foreign, contemporary or historical. From the stories told by the three women—Regina Wojskowska, Knazew, and Chaika Grossman—she imagined her own history of her father, and told us, proudly, that he was a civic leader, a member of the Judenrat who aided the resistance effort. Having lived in the United States, where the dichotomy between Jewish heroes and Jewish traitors has been established as historical fact, I heard my grandmother selectively editing out the Judenrat in favor of the resistance. Until I found Chaika Grossman's book, that is.

JANUARY 2000, TEL-AVIV

"Your great-grandfather was not a collaborator!" a thin, very dark, and very animated woman is shouting at me at a café in central Tel-Aviv. Yellow and blue and aggressively fashionable, it is an odd place for a meeting for this sort of interview, but I gather that

Sara Brenner, historian of record on the Bialystok ghetto, schedules all of her meetings here because the place is owned by her son and ex-husband. "Not even Chaika Grossman thought so anymore. I went to see her in the late eighties, and she told me that if she had her book to write over again, she would have done it differently. Jakub Goldberg was not a collaborator!" I know. My great-grandfather was a public official, a civic-minded man engaged in that most hopeless of pursuits, the inevitability and futility of which made me want to write this book: the search for a decent compromise.

In Israel, I learn a few more details. That in February 1943, after the first confrontation between the resistance fighters and the Nazis during the second large-scale Nazi "action," Judenrat leader Barasz stopped helping the underground; it is, of course, possible that so did Jakub Goldberg. I also learn that Barasz halted his aid because he believed the underground endangered the lives of the larger ghetto population, which he continued to hope to save almost until the end.

In all, I learn that, while twenty-year-old Ester risked her own life and her mother's to refuse collaborating with the Soviet secret police, her father played a role that caused Ester's former comrades to brand him as a collaborator. While his daughter acted in his name, he probably acted in hers. He hoped to survive to see her and his wife again. She was willing to risk death because she believed Jakub was dead, killed by the NKVD, which was now trying to draft her. She was wrong: for most of her ordeal, her father was still alive; more than that, had the NKVD had time to sentence him and deport him to internal Russia, he might have lived through the war. Had she known, could she have used this as justification to sign on as an informant? Hardly. There is no such thing as a decent compromise.

PART FIVE

SECRETS

1943–1953

Ruzya and Yolochka

Ester and Sasha

CHAPTER FIFTEEN

AUGUST 1943

1. Surname: Solodovnik. 2. Name: Ruzya. 3. Patronymic: Moshevna.
4. Date and place of birth: March 3, 1920, Pereslavl, Ukraine.
5. Ethnicity: Jewish. 6. Party affiliation: Komsomol member.
7. Family status: Widowed.

This is who she is now. Two years ago, when she left Moscow,
she was a history student, a girl in love.

8. Education: Higher.

Somehow amidst the madness of Ashkhabad heat and her husband going off to war and her baby being born she took care of
some final coursework and secured her diploma. She also rejoined
the Komsomol: wartime policies made it easy. All of that, like so
much of the past couple of years, is not even a memory but a faint
knowledge. So this is who she is now: a war widow, a single
mother, a college graduate, a job applicant, very tired.

9. Specialization: History teacher. 10. Foreign languages: German,
English, French.

It almost hurts her to write "history teacher" on this job application form. These are the words with which her diploma, she fears, has condemned her to a life of lying. Ruzya has not applied for a single job teaching history, and she is not applying for one now, but she is afraid that someone—she is not sure who—will tell her she must follow through on the choice she made as a teenager. She would rather do anything than teach history. She cannot tell quite how this happened, but as surely and incredibly as her tiny pea of a daughter has started to walk and say "mama," Ruzya has acquired an understanding, and this understanding means that teaching history in a Soviet school is, always and inevitably, lying. What other options does she have? She can read fluently in three foreign languages, but surely no one is going to pay her for that. And she has to feed her baby, her pale little girl with the huge gray eyes and the black-black hair she inherited not from Samuil, her father, but from her grandfather Moshe. Which is why Ruzya is here, at the Head Directorate of Literature, or Glavlit, applying for a job. She has to be an adult now.

Returning to Moscow was not in itself an adult decision: Samuil's family, the Minkins, wanted to come back now that the front line seemed to be moving steadily westward, and she had simply gone along. In February the Germans were finally turned around at Stalingrad, and six months later, though there were still German troops on Soviet territory, no one seemed to fear any longer that Moscow could fall. Still, not a lot of people were in a hurry to go back to Moscow, but Batsheva and Lev wanted to leave the place where they had learned of their son's death. Ruzya never considered the possibility of staying behind: they were her family now—she had a child with these people. It was not until they were on the train, surrounded for the first time in months by unfamiliar faces, that Ruzya realized she was going back to

Moscow to begin the rest of her life—as a war widow, a single mother, an adult.

She has done all the adult things since she got back to Moscow a couple of weeks ago. As soon as she more or less settled in with Samuil's parents and sister in their two rooms in the communal apartment on the Garden Ring—it seemed to make sense, since her parents were still in the Urals and she was so used to living with the Minkins now—she started thinking about getting work. She had only the vaguest of ideas about how this might be done, so she pretended she was someone who knew how to look for work. That someone looked through her address book for names of people who she thought would have connections.

She waited for a time when not too many people were around the apartment. The telephone sat in the vast entryway to what was once a rich man's flat, on a tall table, tiny but sturdy enough to support the phone in all its black-metal technological heft. To use it, one had to sidle up to the table, perhaps step up on a little footstool placed there by one of the shorter women neighbors, and shout into the receiver for all the apartment to hear. So on an afternoon when all the men were out at work and all the women were out procuring food and anything else that may be procured, she called Asya, a school friend who had married a general many years her senior and—living as she does in the general's luxurious, which is to say large and separate, apartment—fits Ruzya's image of a person who may know important people with access to jobs. Asya works as a translator in the Ministry of the Armed Forces, and Ruzya has taught German to military interpreters—there might be a link, a lead. She shouted that she was Ruzya, that she was back, that her husband had been killed, that she had a child and was looking for work, that maybe she could use her knowledge of languages.

The phone rang a few days later: Asya's mother. She remembered Ruzya well. She might be able to help. Could Ruzya come to see her at her office, at Glavlit, the Head Directorate on Affairs of Literature and Publishing, on Zubovskaya Ploshad?

Ruzya walked here today through a Moscow that frightens her, a city of buildings half destroyed and settled into this state like rotting teeth, of hungry children with screwdrivers sharpened into knives, of residents returning to find that their apartments have been squatted by others or repossessed by the city—a city that knows no end of misery and no compassion. She has to learn to match this city's ways. She should think not about lying to children but about making more money than a schoolteacher can. Maybe then she can make her baby safe.

Asya's mother is a sweetly bossy woman. She sat her down, asked her brusquely whether she knew "what we do here." Ruzya mumbled something vague about safeguarding secrets. The older woman smiled and said, "That's very important work, you know, censorship, especially in wartime." Ruzya agreed.

She took quick reading-comprehension tests in the three languages: a couple of paragraphs from a magazine article in each. Though speaking foreign languages has never been Ruzya's strong suit—the lack of a musical ear has been a handicap—she has always been an unusually perceptive and sensitive reader, developing a feel for a language even before she had accumulated much vocabulary. She must have done well, because Asya's mother has now handed her this application form.

11. Names and addresses of living relatives.

She lists her parents and the twins as living in evacuation in Sukhoy Log in the Urals. In fact her father has written that Boris, one of the twins, ran away nearly a year ago and is apparently serving on a warship in the Black Sea. He is fourteen, and she has such a hard time believing this has happened, and such a vague recollection of the details, that, for the purposes of the application, she puts him back with their parents. Yasha is still serving as a pilot, active duty, at the front. She hands the application form back to the woman, who gestures for Ruzya to keep sitting and leaves the room.

Asya's mother returns not ten minutes later. "They'll be working with your application for a while more, but if everything checks out, as I'm sure it will, you should be reporting for work Monday at the main post office on Myasnitskaya. Your job title will be political editor." She smiles a satisfied, congratulatory smile.

MARCH 1944

She did not know how alone she felt until her father called. They are back from the Urals. With all of her friends still either at the front or wherever they were evacuated, her father's voice is the first sign that something might return from Ruzya's life before the war. She has no patience for the bus or the tram, and so she walks, almost runs, now dragging the child behind her, now picking her up in her arms, back the way she ran two and a half years ago, the day the war began, up the ten-lane-wide Garden Ring, across Gorky Street, barely looking to see if cars are coming, and into the maze of little streets to their building, where her father is already looking up at the sidewalk through the little basement window. He embraces her—drapes his long arms along her back and hangs over her, then draws back and brushes her face with his hands.

"Ruzen'ka, baby." He pulls his eyes reluctantly from her to look at the child. "Yolochka," he states, attaching the name to a little person he has never seen. "I'm your grandpa. Let's go sit down."

They go inside, and she realizes that they must have been

home for a couple of days—the apartment has been cleaned, the furniture moved, some of the stashed-away linens and vases and the clock pulled out of their swaddles in the wardrobe. So he waited until everyone was gone to have her all to himself. She will see the rest of the family later, and there will be joy and tension like there always is, but now he wanted there to be love only. Kissing her father on the head as he sits with her daughter in his lap, she inhales the tobacco smoke caught in his curly hair.

"Well, tell me"—with a nod of the head he directs her to sit—"everything."

"Well, I'm living with the Minkins, but that you know."

He nods.

"I'm working."

"Good. Where?"

"At Glavlit."

"My good girl. What are you doing?"

"I work in the department of incoming literature. I read in three languages, all the newspapers, magazines, books, that come in." His smile is becoming tense. "Not private correspondence, just printed matter."

"And what do you do after you read it?"

"I stamp it. I have three stamps: 'cleared,' 'for internal use,' and 'not cleared.' And sometimes I have to cross something out."

"Do you stamp many things 'cleared'?" her father asks seriously.

"No, well, very rarely, but not so much 'not cleared,' often 'for internal use.'"

"Ruzen'ka, this is very low work. You are the gendarme who shouts, 'Stop him and never let go!'" There is no indignation in his voice, just sadness and, she thinks, surprise.

"Yes. But we have to eat. And if I weren't doing it, someone else would be. And I couldn't teach school, Papa, I couldn't teach history and look those children in the eye."

He smiles with only the corners of his mouth and turns to the child, who has been sitting quietly in his lap, frozen in something like shyness but studying Moshe's large veined hands with deep fascination. "Yolochka. What a pretty round face you have. What big gray eyes. I hear you can talk. Will you talk to Grandpa?"

Moshe never mentioned her job again. Ruzya knew she would never have to face his open disapproval or argue with him about why she had to keep the job. None of this made it any easier to remember, as she did constantly, his sad surprised look and the tender tones of his voice when he called her a gendarme.

Ruzya and Ester returned to Moscow just as they had left it: at almost the same time, under similar circumstances—and still as strangers to each other. Ester also traveled with her husband's parents: Boris himself had gone ahead to make arrangements for their travel. Evacuees were not yet allowed to travel back freely: railroads were still reserved primarily for military traffic, and in any case, travel in the Soviet Union was always heavily regulated. But the elder Gessens were fed up with life on the collective farm, and Arnold, Boris's father, had never been the kind of man who was willing to let bureaucrats, laws, or even war stop him. Boris, who had found his love in Biysk and so was not as eager to leave, still complied with his father's wishes and traveled to Moscow to bribe those who might issue travel permits for his parents, his sister, and his new wife. Being an injured war veteran, Boris was entitled to a travel permit. Getting one was a lengthy procedure, to which he had not bothered to submit in order to travel the short distance from the collective farm to see Ester in Biysk, but he did it now.

Ester, left behind to wait for her permit to arrive from Moscow, was making preparations for her new life—she and Bella were trying, and failing, to scrape up enough money to guarantee Ester some measure of independence. Ester was full of apprehension, which proved well founded. Three months later, she broke the pact she and Bella had made—never to be separated again—and spent five days in a train compartment with the Gessens: it was understood now that Bella would go to Moscow as soon as travel restrictions eased up. Boris's mother, Miriam, who had been raised to be a socialite but grew into the tired housewife of a dictatorial husband, was fascinating and kind company. Boris's sister and father mostly made Ester uncomfortable, though neither of them said a bad word to her. In Moscow, she found Boris already settled in at the Gessens' home—two adjacent rooms in a cramped communal apartment on Gorky Street—comfortable, confident, slightly impatient to take up his role as husband and head of household.

That, of course, he was not. His father, sixty-three-year-old Arnold, a journalist, entrepreneur, and consummate survivor, was a domestic tyrant whom Boris faithfully imitated in situations the older man did not control. Arnold controlled the household finances—a fact he mentioned every time Ester, who did not have a ration card, put something in her mouth. Sick of watching his wife returning her piece of bread to the common plate, Boris declared his small family unit's independence: they would be poor but proud. They could not move out, of course, but they could buy their own food and eat it when they pleased. Inside his little family, though, he demanded to be king, which meant, among other things, having his socks washed by his wife. His wife, taken genuinely by surprise by his expectations, retorted—regularly—

that as long as he neglected to wash his feet, she would refuse to launder his socks.

Not that Ester ever entertained the possibility of becoming Miriam to Boris's Arnold, or of being a housewife at all. Within three months of returning to Moscow she became a full-time student at the university, which was just resuming classes at the Moscow campus. After her first semester, one of her professors convinced Ester to transfer from Romance languages to the classics faculty—the most challenging and prestigious in the philology department. That meant, in essence, starting over, but Ester agreed. Just then she found out that she was, quite soon and quite suddenly, having a baby—my father, born December 25, 1944. She never even considered taking time off from her studies.

FEBRUARY 1945

The way Ester has been fretting all day, it is a good thing that Boris is not the jealous type. His only remark—that one might think she was expecting a lover, not her mother—was made by way of observation. She has to admit she is more excited now than she was a year and a half ago, when she was traveling from Biysk to join Boris in Moscow. Over the course of these eighteen months she has often thought that, had she known she would not see her mother for so long, she might have thought harder about going. Each time she has reminded herself that, by taking her out of Biysk and away from Major Gurov, Boris probably saved her life.

The moment Bella comes in with Boris, who picked her up at the train station, Ester knows something unpleasant has transpired. *A black cat has run between the two of them,* she thinks, in Russian. When did she start thinking in Russian? Even while she is wondering this, she embraces her mother, her tiny, strikingly old mother, bundled up in something gray and complicated and covered with a thin cold layer of snow. Bella stands in the dark hallway looking miffed, thrilled, and expectant, all at once.

"Where is he?" she asks finally.

"You have to wash your hands," Ester answers quickly, and starts pulling off her mother's outer garments, handing them to a silent Boris. The next minute they are in Ester and Boris's room, and Ester picks a tiny bundle out of the crude crib and hands it to Bella. The baby screws up his little face, appearing ready to cry, but then changes his mind and smiles an open, toothless pink smile at his grandmother.

"Oh," says Bella, her voice reaching too high. "He is so— good."

She goo-goos, kisses the baby, goo-goos some more, and then she interrogates Ester.

"Why didn't you tell me sooner you were pregnant?"

"I had no idea. No, this is an incredible story. I mean, I did— I didn't have my you-know-whats and all, so I went to the doctor, and she said there was no chance I was expecting. I believed her, of course, until, oh, sometime in August, when I was standing in line at the bakery and suddenly felt faint, and before I knew what was happening, I'd thrown up right there in the queue. I hadn't eaten anything, mind you, so I knew right away. By then I was four months along. The doctor was still willing to do the operation, since it was her mistake. And I would have done it if it weren't for Miriam, Boris's mother. She very nearly went into hysterics, screaming I could only do it over her dead body. She doesn't have anything against abortion per se, you understand, but such a late one—I may never have been able to have children again."

"Thank God for a wise woman," says Bella. "So she is good to you?"

"Oh, she sympathizes: she's lived with a husband like mine her whole life." Boris stepped out of the room, red and uncomfortable, when Ester started speaking about abortion. The two women are speaking in Polish, but the language is close enough to Russian that he has been able to follow the drift of the conversation.

"On the way from the train station he was telling me about you not laundering his socks. I could have killed him."

"You don't have to. I don't launder his socks."

They laugh, and turn to the baby again. "And are you sure you are going to the university enough—now that you are a classics major, isn't it more demanding?" asks Bella.

"Oh, yes. I mean, I can't go every day or to every lecture, but the nanny really is fine, and thank goodness she is working just for room, board, and temporary Moscow registration."

"We will have to deal with that issue for me, won't we?" the older woman asks, her voice audibly lowered by the realization that, even though she is out of Biysk, she will probably have to deal with the Soviet bureaucracy indefinitely.

Ester picks up the baby, who has grown fussy, and puts him to her breast: she has been a mother for nearly two months, and the motions have grown almost automatic. She looks at her baby, and Bella looks at hers.

"There is nothing quite like this, is there?" the older woman asks.

"No," says Ester.

Boris, who has brought them tea, is wondering what they just said but quickly tells himself to give up trying to understand the quick Polish chatter that, he suspects, he will always have in the background. He is right: just as she promised, Ester will not be separated from Bella again. Within a few days they will begin the arduous process of trying to register Bella to live in their apartment: they will be denied permission because a former foreigner who once faced charges cannot be allowed to live on a street that leads directly to the Kremlin. Soon Bella will find a job teaching Polish to Soviet intelligence officers: she will be trusted with this sensitive task but not with occupying a few square meters in a communal apartment on Gorky Street. They will devise a complicated scheme for getting Bella her papers—she will be registered as living outside of Moscow, at the dacha—but she will never even consider actually not living alongside her daughter. Every evening for the next twenty years Ester will come home and tell her mother everything, blow by blow: her life, her joys, and her worries, in this same hurried, melodic, and mostly incomprehensible language.

CHAPTER SIXTEEN

MAY 9, 1945

The doorbell rings three times, signaling that someone is here to see Ester, Boris, or Bella: every family in the communal apartment has its own code. It is too early in the morning for visitors, but Lena Zonina is here. When Ester returned to Moscow, she resumed her friendship with Lena easily, without much discussion—once Ester was out of Major Gurov's range, she found she could forgive her friend's insensitivity. Lena is all dressed up as though to go dancing—a white blouse, black pleated skirt, and a ribbon in her hair—and she is looking flushed and talking too loud. "Have you heard? On the radio? At six they announced? The war is over!"

"Is that true? I . . . I . . . congratulations! Oh!" Ester feels a little lost: what is the convention for celebrating the passing of a catastrophe? It has been a while since she felt the sense of imminent threat she still remembers from the first months of the war in Poland, and then later, the first year and a half or so of the war in

Russia. The last six months, since the front line moved west of places Ester has lived, the war has become a bit of an abstraction. Somehow she has even stopped worrying about her friends who are still at the front: several former IFLI students, including Eda, who left Ashkhabad for the army after Ester left for Biysk. It did not seem like anything bad could happen to an army that was now unquestionably victorious. Still, the news that it is all over feels overwhelming, as though her body had just become lighter, or the light had grown brighter.

"Let's go out!" Lena Zonina demands, as though in response to Ester's unspoken question. "Everyone is out in the streets!"

Ester pokes her head back into their room, where the baby is still sleeping, and whispers loudly: "The war is over!" Bella's and Boris's heads float to the door for quick kisses, and Ester goes out with Lena, pulling on a light jacket as she bounds down the stairs.

Gorky Street is filling up with people so fast, it seems someone had ordered the floodgates of all the side streets opened all at once. Out of nowhere hundreds and thousands of red carnations float into the hands of revelers, who pass them on to one another like relay batons. Many men and some women are wearing their military uniforms, and these clearly demarcated heroes can barely take a step: passersby gather in groups of five or six and start throwing the soldiers up in the air. Ester and Lena walk about seven blocks to Red Square and turn right toward the American embassy, where the crowd is especially thick. American diplomats have come out into the street, and the crowd is now throwing them up in the air: this is one day when allies are allies, and communicating with foreigners is not a crime.

Ester and Lena shout "hooray" until they are hoarse. They take hold of no fewer than a thousand red carnations, it seems, and they give away every one of them. Their arms get sore from tossing grown men up in the air—along Gorky Street, in front of the

American embassy, in Red Square. They say good-bye at the entrance to Ester's building and make a plan to meet later to go to a party at the university. Ester flies into the apartment, throws the door to their room wide open, about to start telling her mother about the festivities outside, and stops dead: her mother is sitting at the square polished-wood table, her elbows placed wide apart on the lace tablecloth, her face in her hands, her head shuddering slowly and rhythmically. There is no self-indulgence in her crying, and no hysteria: she has years of crying inside her, but she has been given this one day when all emotions are allowed, and she must get it done.

Ester sits down next to her mother and cries too. She cries for Jakub, for Isaj, for her aunts and uncles, for her grandmothers and grandfathers, for her cousins, for her friends, for her dreams, for the last remnants of hope for a miracle. It is finished. There was a war, it is over now, and it took everything away.

Ester makes tea, sets it on the table, says something, and they keep crying. Boris goes to a party at his graduate school. The nanny tends to the baby, quietly. Eventually, it gets dark.

When Ester and Lena stepped out onto Gorky Street, they turned left toward Red Square. If they had turned right, walked half a block and crossed the Garden Ring, then walked left for no more than twenty yards, they would have come to a maze of side streets that even on this brightest and happiest of days were empty and gray. A small slouched figure moved through these streets all day and all night, turning right and right and right again, to keep walking in a circle and stay off the main streets. Ruzya did not look up or ahead, and when the fireworks started she only burrowed deeper into her brown jacket and cried louder: she could not hear herself for the racket. She wanted to see no one, or, rather, she knew that the one person she did want to see she could not. She had read Samuil's letters from the front the night before. The European and American newspapers, which she read for her job, had already announced victory, and it was clear that the Soviet side would follow suit. It seemed like the appropriate moment to take out the white cloth pouch—an old pillowcase—in which she kept the letters and unfold their triangles, laying the sheets flat into a black cardboard binder she had brought from work. It took her three hours to read all that her husband had left her. By the time she was done, she resolved never to do it again.

Ruzya goes home long after Ester, long after dark, which comes late in May. She goes home after she is sure the Minkins are asleep. It is not because she does not want to tell them about the decision she has made to move out to her own parents' apartment: she will tell them tomorrow. But tonight, she wants to be alone. She is alone.

CHAPTER SEVENTEEN

Ruzya has had tears in her eyes since she lay down with the book and turned the light on and then off again when the child would not stop turning and rubbing her eyes. Without getting up, she parted the dusty red curtains and read by the light of the streetlamp. How wonderful that the streetlamps are on again now that the war is over.

This book is like the world, populated with Spaniards and Americans and Gypsies and even American Indians, and she is lucky to see them, as though through a peephole, a tiny window that only a few people share. This is the essence of living, the skill of grasping whatever joy comes your way, like a book across the censor's desk, like the light of the streetlamp through the basement's window, like the visits, every few months, from Colonel Kulikov. He is the dashing man she met two years ago on the train from Ashkhabad back to Moscow. Yolochka, one year old and completely independent, as children are when they first learn to

walk, the skinny girl with gray eyes that took up half her face, in
that little blue dress with lilac flowers, was running from compartment to compartment making friends with the officers—it was all
officers in that car—and Batsheva had said, "It's you they want to
meet." Now the colonel comes every few months. He has a family in Leningrad, and in any case, he would never marry a Jewish
girl, but she loves his visits and his attention and even his tall
colonel's hat. She likes, in a way, that he is so different from the
boy who was her husband: it spares her the comparison between
her dreams and her life, whose joys are so intermittent. But, like
the book says, "It was much better to be gay and it was a sign of
something too. It was like having immortality while you were still
alive."

This book is from a time when war was a distant and glamorous thing. But for all its heroics and all of the author's apparent
sympathy for the Soviet-backed guerrillas, the book could never
have been cleared by her department. Not with the old man saying things like "To kill them teaches nothing. You cannot exter-
minate them because from their seed comes more with greater
hatred. Prison is nothing. Prison only makes hatred." For all their
hardness, the men in the book are human, and their conviction, for
all its simplicity, has limits. They can argue about how serious—
"religious," they say, heretically—their political beliefs should be.
They can argue about killing. Robert Jordan makes her think of
her husband. Samuil, too, was righteous, and he was a volunteer in
the war, but once he wrote a letter about watching a horse die,
and that letter broke her heart, the way he then had to talk himself, there on the page, into wanting to fight. The military censors,
simple souls, did not black that part out the way they blotted out
the names of towns. When she moved back in with her own parents, she left Samuil's letters at his parents' house on the excuse
that they would be safer there, but she remembers the words

and even the way they fit on the page, the graph paper from his notebook.

So many of his letters listed their pleasures together: the walks, the cakes at the bakery on Petrovka, the Mayakovsky poems; he promised her, in one of his letters, that when he came back they would take their son—they always assumed Yolochka would be a boy—and go to all the actors and singers they loved and say, "We didn't hear you all war long. Give us what we didn't hear!" She recognizes this feeling in a passage in the book where Hemingway describes drinking absinthe: "One cup of it took the place of the evening papers, of all the old evenings in cafes, of all the chestnut trees that would be in bloom now in this month, of the great slow horses of the outer boulevards, of book shops, of kiosques, and of galleries. . . ." She has never read an evening paper or spent an evening in a café or seen chestnut trees in bloom, or drunk absinthe, for that matter, but she knows that longing from her husband's letters, and now she knows, from her own life, how happiness comes in tiny bursts. Like a good book.

Robert Jordan and Maria make love outside, in a "robe," which she assumes to be a sleeping bag. She and Samuil also made love for the first time outside, and after that they considered themselves married. That was a life of absolutes. "I loved you when I saw you today and I loved you always but I never saw you before." That is what Maria says to Robert Jordan, and that is how they felt too. Samuil wrote from the service, she remembers: "And we walked away from the crowd. I dragged a bottle from the kitchen. And I knelt on my right leg like a noble knight to hand you your glass. And I already loved you. I loved you very much. And I did not understand yet that I loved you. Did not think." He wrote that on the first anniversary of their first meeting.

Now, at the end of the book, Maria is leaving the dying

Robert Jordan, and, like a teenage girl enthralled with a romance novel, Ruzya wants to scream, "Don't go! Nothing can be worth it." Robert Jordan tallies the time of their love: three and a half days. She and Samuil had eleven months and then another eight months of letters.

The street cleaner's broom scrapes the sidewalk overhead. That means it is seven in the morning, and she can sleep for fifteen minutes before getting up and feeding and dressing Yolochka, to drop her off at nursery school and be at work by eight, when the day's pile of newspapers and magazines and books will already be on her desk. She slips the book under her pillow and goes to sleep with her hand on its newspaper-wrapped spine—a basic precaution to avoid letting it be known that the censors are taking books in and out of the building, and to avoid damage to the cheesy black-and-red dustcover. She dreams briefly of Spaniards and Americans and a Gypsy, and she wakes up with a crick in her neck and a sense of responsibility to remember the book so she can tell her friends, and also the sense that she is terribly lucky to be alive and to know foreign languages and to have a job that gives her great books to read, if only for a night.

She will always think that *For Whom the Bell Tolls* is Hemingway's best book. But she will warn people that reading it can be "pure suffering."

People returned to Moscow. The generation that came back from four years of battle found most of itself missing. The Soviet Union lost twenty-seven million people in the war, most of them born in the 1920s. Those were the ones who were killed; several million more returned from German prisoner-of-war camps only to be consigned to Soviet labor camps for "treason": everyone who allowed himself to be taken prisoner was deemed a traitor. The Jews in the postwar Soviet Union saw even more empty spaces around them than most other people: by some estimates, every other Soviet Jew was dead.

But those who did return came back unspeakably hungry for life. Beaten and crippled and hardened, they still dreamed, as Samuil had, of "hearing everything we didn't hear" during the war and reading all they did not read and seeing all they did not see. But the space available for the life of the mind and spirit, a space already small before the war, was now collapsing in on itself, until what was allowed was a tiny dot in the wasteland of the banned.

Two months after the war ended, the State Jewish Theater, a remarkable Moscow institution led by the actor Solomon Mikhoels, reopened to a packed hall, with *Freylekhs,* a feverishly festive play about a wedding. Mikhoels was possibly the country's best-known Jew. "When the theaters open again," he is said to have promised, "we will have to begin with something noisy and joyous, to shake people up. Enough of this darkness." He was performing for Europe's sole remaining Jewish community. Ester was in one of the first audiences of *Freylekhs.* She had been something of a feature at the theater before the war. The first time she went, invited by Semyon Krasilshik, one of her "mentors," she translated for him from Yiddish—softly at first, so as not to disturb the other viewers, then louder as other people moved closer and asked her to speak up: the new generation of Soviet Jews did not speak the language of their parents. She went frequently from then on, and regulars recognized her as the interpreter. Now she was back, and so were a few of her regular listeners, all of them transfixed by the frantic happiness on stage.

Mikhoels had chosen a show to answer the survivors' desperate love of life. But, had he wanted to stage a play that was a memorial rather than a celebration, it most likely would have been banned, the way the Jewish Anti-Fascist Committee's *Black Book,* a monumental effort documenting the Nazi murder of Soviet Jews, was banned, the way more and more Jewish literature was banned, the way the Jewish Theater would soon be shut down—and Mikhoels himself killed.

How does one begin to understand why something is banned—or, as Ruzya had to do, when something ought to be banned? As a novice censor at Glavlit, Ruzya studied memos like this one explaining why a U.S.-published biography of Albert Einstein could not be allowed:

> *1) The author of the introduction recommends studying the works of contemporary reactionary philosophers John Dewey, G. Santayana, G. Mupa, Bertrand Russell and others. In several places in the introduction the author calls such backwards personalities as Bertrand Russell, J. Dewey and others "great thinkers."*

> *3) In the chapter called "Einstein's Social Philosophy," the author relays Einstein's thinking: Einstein believes that the world is facing a crisis and that humanity is in danger of a catastrophe. The only salvation lies in organizing the intellectual and spiritual forces of the world into one moral force, something like the "conscience of the world." Morality is the highest value of all, such is Einstein's credo. Never do anything that contradicts your conscience, even if the state demands it. . . .*

So morality fell outside the law because it might contradict state policy. And memory fell outside the law, too, because it could contradict the official version of history. For these reasons, as well as the obvious analogy with Stalinist concentration camps, the *Black Book* was banned. For the most part, thought itself fell outside the law. So the censor, whether she was reading "incoming printed matter" or outgoing reportage, occupied one of the small spots of cosmopolitanism in the country. Glavlit, the Head Directorate on Affairs of Literature and Publishing, founded in 1922, now employed 233 people in its Moscow offices and in management positions elsewhere and about five thousand more throughout the Soviet Union. This group was one of the Soviet Union's tiny islands where a sort of enlightenment was, bizarrely, cultivated. Glavlit records contain the text of a speech by the head of the directorate, Konstantin Omelchenko, in which he stressed the importance of a well-rounded, continuing education for the censors. "The censor should be familiar with the history of censorship," said Omelchenko, a man Ruzya would come to know well. "We should think about choosing four or five of the most cultured and experienced staff members and assign them to prepare, over the course of two months, lectures on the history of censorship. . . . Foreign languages must be studied. . . . The censor should exert a generalizing influence. We have to analyze the processes that occur in literature. No one knows literature as well as the censor does."

Of course not. Because virtually no one had access to the sort of literature that the censors could read. Take *For Whom the Bell Tolls* and tally up the reasons it could not have been allowed: the author was ideologically unreliable—neither a Soviet sympathizer nor safely dead, which meant he could make a comment about the Soviet Union at any moment; the book showed the Spanish communists as terrorists; the book included questioning of acceptable violence against the class enemy; the book contained sex scenes. Any one of these factors was sufficient to put the book on the banned list.

The books available to the general Soviet public were a literature of elisions, and in a sense this was as it should be: literature reflected life. The central feature of Soviet life was unspoken. This feature was fear. For Ruzya's generation fear turned into a habit. Before they finished high school, Ruzya's gang had learned to shout praise for the Soviet Union into the ceiling vent—a gesture that was probably of little practical use but helped stave off the fear. As soon as telephones were installed in their apartments, they developed the habit of placing pillows over them to disable them as bugging devices. This went along with the habit of writing the most sensitive information on scraps of paper and then ripping them into shreds. Ruzya had the habit of saying, when conversation veered into risky territory, "Comrades! We live on the ground floor, and the window is open." In other words, do not forget to be afraid that you may be overheard.

The fear began in the late 1920s or early 1930s, when they were still children. They became increasingly aware of it as they grew into adults. The fear of being denounced and arrested did not abate even during the war: soldiers were regularly plucked out of their platoons for saying a wrong word.

After the war, the fear grew more specific. On January 13, 1948, Solomon Mikhoels, the actor, was killed, signaling to the Jews of this generation that they were now the punitive machine's main target. The targeting of Jews began earlier, of course. When? Some people think it started in 1946, with print attacks on Yiddish-language writers whose work was apparently found to contain "expressions of Jewish nationalism." That same year, prominent novelist Nikolay Tikhonov published an article called "In Defense of Pushkin" in the newspaper *Sovetskaya kultura*. Tikhonov accused a literary critic named Isak Nusinov, whom he called "a vagabond without a passport," of trying "vampirically" to "Westernize" the great Russian poet. Various other substitutes for "wandering Jew" made the newspaper rounds until the name for the state's new enemy was firmly established: "rootless cosmopolitans." The state never called anything by its real name, and this provided its loyal citizens with additional motivation: they were always striving to show they understood their orders. This was how Bella came to be fired from her job teaching Polish to Soviet intelligence officers: certainly they could not be taught by a "rootless cosmopolitan."

One of the most concise definitions of the new enemy appeared later, in the lead article of a 1949 issue of *Voprosy istorii* (*The Issues of History*), the scholarly journal that would have been Ruzya's bible had she found work as a history teacher: "The rootless cosmopolitans . . . falsify and misrepresent the worldwide historical role of the Russian people in the construction of socialist society and the victory over the enemy of humanity—over German fascism—in the Great Patriotic War."

Russian, in Russian, is an exclusive term: it means ethnic Russians only. So, translated into practice, this passage meant that any historian who neglected to sing the praises of the heroic ethnic Russians, regardless of the time period and even the place discussed, was a likely traitor. Usually these traitors had Jewish surnames; though, on rare occasions, a person with a different name was thrown in for good measure (as were some ethnic Russians who happened to have Jewish-sounding last names).

Before the war, internationalist rhetoric had ruled in the Soviet Union and the concept of Russian ethnicity was taboo. But then Stalin signaled that this was changing. During a Kremlin reception to honor Red Army commanders on May 24, 1945, he made a toast: "I would like to raise my glass to the health of our Soviet people and, first and foremost, the Russian people." Here, as the official transcript indicates, Stalin was interrupted by "active and long-lasting applause and the shouts of 'hooray!' " He continued: "I drink first to the health of the Russian people because they are the most outstanding nation of all the nations that make up the Soviet Union. I raise my glass to the health of the Russian people because it earned in this war general recognition as the leading force of the Soviet Union among all the peoples of our country. I raise my glass to the health of the Russian people not only because it is the leading people but also because it has a clear mind, a stalwart character and patience." That Stalin himself belonged to an ethnic minority—he was half Georgian and half Ossetian—had no tempering influence on the new policies of xenophobia.

That speech signaled the official beginning of the process, speedy and thorough, of excising Jews from the history of the war. Newspaper articles referred to Jews who sat out the war in Central Asia with such venom and frequency that the assertion became commonplace within weeks. In reality, virtually all able-bodied Jewish men served in the wartime Red Army and about two hundred thousand of them died in its ranks. Jews had the largest proportion, of any Soviet ethnic group, of Heroes of the Soviet Union—the highest military honor awarded. This may have been a measure of their relative desperation more than anything else, but this part of Jewish history, too—the death of about a million Soviet Jews at the hands of the Nazis, and the deadly threat the rest faced—was systematically obliterated on orders from the top, even as it was occurring. "Hitler wanted to turn the Jews into a target," wrote the writer Ilya Ehrenburg in his regular call-to-arms column in 1942. "The Jews of Russia showed him that a target can shoot. . . . Once upon a time the Jews dreamed of a promised land. Now the Jew's promised land is the front line of defense." The following year Ehrenburg was told to tone down the Jewish references.

Stalin's antagonism toward the Jews probably predated any sign he gave of it in public. One Hitler-era memoir recounts Ribbentrop's report on his negotiations with Soviet officials:

"Stalin made it clear that he is waiting only for the moment when the USSR will have enough educated people of its own to finally put an end to Jewish dominance." This statement did not become public in Russia until the mid-1990s. But at some point in the 1940s—as early as 1943 for some, perhaps around the time of Mikhoels's murder in 1948 for most, and certainly before the arrests of a group of Jewish doctors in 1953 for all—every Jewish man and woman living in the Soviet Union came to realize that they were targeted by the regime, to feel that hopeless fear in every bone.

For most of the Jews of the wartime generation, this fear eventually pushed out the hunger for life with which they had come home, leaving only the desperate wish to survive, a cornered animal's bloodshot hope.

FEBRUARY 1946

Ruzya's eyes are red, as they always are in the afternoons, after hours of reading. It is freezing, as it always is on Saturdays, when the office cleaning lady refuses to work, even though she does come in when she is supposed to and leave when she is supposed to. She is in her fifties, graying, short and somehow crooked, and she speaks—grumbles, rather, about the mess they make, the mud they drag in—with a strong shtetl accent, and nothing, no amount of ridicule, some of it anti-Semitic and some generically anti-religious, all of it unmistakably mean-spirited, can force her to put firewood in the little black-metal stove on the Sabbath. The war has been over for nine months and in some ways Moscow is really back to normal, but central heating in the main post office still has not been repaired, so on weekdays the "political editors" sweat in the stifling heat from the woodstove, and on Saturdays they try to work the stove themselves, but it requires attention and each of them has more work than a human being can possibly do, so the stove goes out and the coats go on, and still they freeze. Ruzya marvels at the cleaning lady's resolve, at her showing up every Saturday to freeze with them, but she has never said anything, because anything she says will somehow be a comment on the woman's Jewishness, or on Ruzya's.

She is not the only Jew among the editors: there is Zhenia Galperin, a skinny one-armed polyglot. As the story goes, years ago, before the war, he was trampled in a tram so crowded that his arm had to be amputated. Somehow this accident, or maybe the amount of time he needed to recuperate, moved Zhenia to study foreign languages, one after another. Then he wound up at Glavlit, and until recently he was even living in some room—more like a janitor's closet—off this endless hallway. He must have lost his apartment while he was evacuated—this happened to many people who failed to keep their documents current and could not fight the squatters. Or it may have been some sort of a family conflict—no one really knows. But Zhenia is so valuable to Glavlit that he is allowed to live here; once Ruzya spotted his one spare shirt and a pair of foot-wraps hung to dry in the janitor's closet. Zhenia is allowed such transgressions because he can read in a dozen languages fast, and he rarely makes mistakes.

They all make mistakes, of course, all the dozen or so "political editors." There is no way to read every word in the stacks that pile up on their desks, and so they skim, with varying skill, but it is so easy to skip over that one line that will soon be caught by the frightened director of some small library where the book or the magazine lands. Ruzya overlooked *The Letters of Georges Bizet,* and soon enough it was back at the Glavlit offices, with passages circled: "Paris has fallen too low even for corruption. We have no more revolutions, only the parodies of revolutions." Blasphemy.

She had paid little attention to the book, figuring that something written a century ago could hardly be anti-Soviet and she should spend more time on the contemporary books. She had, as she recalls, a parcel from "the Brother" on her desk that day, and that always made her uneasy, even anxious.

These packages from France come every couple of weeks, books—mostly scientific books on biology but also fiction—and scientific journals, full of diagrams and indecipherable terms, the bane of her existence. They are addressed to a man somewhere in the Arkhangel'sk region, beyond the Arctic Circle. She commented on them once, and Zhenia relayed the legend: the sender was a Russian nobleman, an artist who emigrated to Paris right after the revolution; the addressee was his brother, a biologist, who stayed in Russia and was exiled to the Arctic years ago. The books and magazines were usually shipped off to restricted-access libraries, and only a rare volume, once every few months or so, was cleared and sent to the Arkhangel'sk region.

Everyone in the department knows this story, and no one, she thinks, wants to handle these parcels. So much better to censor the books shipped by impersonal publishers to anonymous libraries. Though two more women—her former classmates—have been hired since the war ended and the inflow increased, Ruzya is still the newest French-reading member of the department, so she has Brother duty. And there is a pile of books for him on her desk again today.

The door opens, letting in a blast of prickly, frozen air from the corridor. It is a secretary from the larger room next door, where the supporting staff open and sort incoming packages and transfer the censors' marks to copies before shipping the materials to their assigned destinations. She picks up the stack of read materials from Ruzya's desk and says, "The department director has asked you to stop in at three." A tension spreads quickly through the room, the censors lifting their heads to scan the secretary's and Ruzya's faces for signs of worry. Then everyone is looking back down at the publications on their desks; two of the censors are twisting tooth-marked round pencils in their fingers; Zhenia, Ruzya can tell from the way he is squinting, is scanning the magazine on his desk for some innocuously funny line to read out to his colleagues. She looks at her watch: she has another fifteen minutes, enough for the *Daily Worker*.

The head of the department is a colorless middle-aged woman who has been understanding and helpful to Ruzya. Everyone else here works nine to five, but Ruzya, as a single mother, is allowed to work from eight to four. All in all, Glavlit's Department of Incoming Printed Matter is a very humane place to work, which does not, of course, mean that there might not have been a report, a denunciation, some kind of trouble, and that makes Ruzya's knock a bit uncertain. She knocks again, too loud now, then enters and tries to search the woman's face, which is bland and blank as usual.

"Please sit down," the woman says, and puts aside a drab-brown folder. It must be someone else's personnel file, Ruzya registers, but then she does not know whether this is a good sign or a bad one. "There is a transfer request for you."

Ruzya clears her throat, and it comes out embarrassingly high-pitched. *Transfer* is a vague term.

"The department for work with foreign correspondents is being moved out of the Ministry of Foreign Affairs and into Glavlit," the woman says. "They will be giving Glavlit some of their people, and a few more will come from the services, but they need our help, and they've asked for multilingual personnel. All of the Foreign Ministry people read only one foreign language. I have recommended you. The pay is half again what you get here now."

"Thank you."

"So you are agreeing?"

"Yes, of course, I would like it very much." She really would like it very much. She already likes it very much, because she is tired of her current job—true—but more than that, because she was chosen for the only thing that makes her truly proud: her language aptitude. She has been chosen for a promotion! She, a Jewish girl!

"You'll have to go to the head office on Monday for a language test. They will be setting up at the Central Telegraph."

"Thank you."

She will soon learn that this is a real promotion, a step up to tangible privilege. On days when she has to submit written reports to Omelchenko, the head of Glavlit, she will be driven to his office and then home. She will have a direct line to Stalin's secretariat. Best of all, when a correspondent from a new country is accredited, she will be crash-taught his language.

The way her father says "congratulations" makes her want to disappear.

NOVEMBER 30, 1947

The Central Telegraph building, with its catholic architectural aspirations, its digital clock and its multicolored half-globe on the facade, and its location just two blocks up Gorky Street from Red Square, is one of Moscow's most assertive landmarks. Its facade is that of a stunted Gothic temple updated with flashy modern touches. But this facade is one of those lies that, for the attentive observer, makes Moscow a city of easy metaphors. The facade is designed for a building an eighth the size of the Central Telegraph. In fact, the building takes up an entire city block and possesses a multitude of separate entrances, some easier and some more difficult to spot, each with a separate system of stairways and corridors. Entrance ten, an unremarkable side-street door, leads to the telegraph hall for foreign correspondents. In a room adjacent to the hall, shielded by a curtained door, the censors do their work openly but invisibly. Foreign correspondents have to file their stories from this hall, and they have to submit them to the censor first: such are the terms of their stay in the Soviet Union.

Ruzya is wrapping up the night shift, translating the reports by American correspondents—only the Americans file at night. It has not been a difficult night: for once, the big Soviet story of the day, Ambassador Andrei Gromyko's initiative in passing the UN resolution in favor of a Jewish state, is written out of New York. Moscow-based correspondents have filed simple regurgitations of the official Soviet media reports—the easiest work for the censor. Here all she has to do is compare the English-language copy to the Russian text and, provided there is no commentary, stamp her copy "cleared," then ring the bell for the secretary, who fetches the dispatches and sends them on before handing their copies back to the reporters. Only once did she have to translate a small passage and call it in to Stalin's secretariat on the direct phone, the black one without a number pad. It was something about the possibility of Soviet Jews now moving to Palestine, and being purely speculative, it was, of course, not cleared.

She has already prepared the morning report, a digest of the journalists' dispatches. As usual, it begins with United Press's Walter Cronkite, at once the most concise and least imaginative of the reporters, so she translates his brief item almost in its entirety, then adds a few details mentioned by the others, then the passage that was not cleared—and she is done for the day. This is certainly not as interesting as when she has a long *New York Times* essay to translate—these often lose large chunks when she is censoring, but she translates the unadulterated copy, and this is always a challenge, the most creative part of the job. But the short report means it won't take long to dictate it to the typist, then she is out the door and in the car, which will make an ostentatious U-turn on Gorky Street and rush her down the Garden Ring to present the report to Omelchenko. By then it will be daylight but still an hour or so before the city's homemakers come out to raid the stores, so she should be able to find something in the food shops before going home to sleep. Shopping has become an especially depressing chore in the months that have passed since the rationing and money reform, with most food-distribution centers closing and prices rising by a factor of three. Compiling today's report is such mechanical work that she is already thinking through her shopping as she writes it, and, as she anticipates the wave of exhaustion that will cover her in the store, she starts to hurry and rings for the typist.

The door opens immediately, and for a moment she tries to fathom how the typist transported herself so quickly, but, of course, it is Zadorozhniy, one of the two people on the day shift today. Of all the people she dislikes in this department—and, if pressed to talk about it, which she never is, thankfully, she would have to admit that she dislikes all the people in this department—Zadorozhniy makes her the most uncomfortable. Here he is, smiling at her as he takes off his tall military-type hat and carefully hangs his soft British-style coat. Possibly the only difference between the ones from the Foreign Ministry and the ones from the Interior Ministry is that the former are snappier dressers. Otherwise, they are equally uncultured and comparably unpleasant.

Zadorozhniy hangs his brown silk scarf over his coat and smooths it lovingly before turning his large figure toward her again. "So, good morning and congratulations!" he booms.

"Hello."

"A national holiday for you, eh?"

She looks silently at the door, making it clear, she hopes, that she is just waiting for the typist so she can complete her work.

"Finally, a state of your own!"

The typist enters with a few sheets of paper, says her greetings, and sits down at the typewriter. Ruzya starts dictating, hoping she can pace herself so that she does not have to pause. But as slow as Ruzya tries to be, the typist cannot keep up and glances up in slightly pathetic surprise. Ruzya stops.

"So, you must be packing your bags to go to your new motherland!" Zadorozhniy laughs at his own vision.

Ruzya thinks she notices the corners of the typist's mouth struggle with a smile that wants to break through. She dictates another two sentences.

"I see your friends the Americans are just as excited about this." Zadorozhniy demonstrates that he is paying attention to the dictation. "You'll all have a great time living in the desert together!"

What a relief that the report was short, that she is already pulling on her coat even as she rushes out the door toward the car. A year ago the car seemed so glamorous. To think: she was driven around by a personal driver! Not *her* personal driver, but still. Now it signifies only relief, and the pleasant calm of a visit to Omelchenko. He is such an unusual man, the head of Glavlit, so—well, for lack of a better word, he is so *cultured*. He is very literate, and sometimes he finds small errors in her text, like when he pointed out that *commentary* is a masculine noun, but he is always gracious about pointing out mistakes. In her department everyone says that this handsome, imposing sixty-year-old widower is courting her. This is absurd, of course, but she can sense that he is attracted to her, and she feels safe.

The same morning that saw Ruzya, exhausted and dejected, step out of one of the back doors of the Central Telegraph building and disappear into a shiny black car, brings Ester, animated, flushed, and slightly disheveled, running in through the front entrance. She is holding the morning's *Izvestia* in her hand.

The words in the paper are plain. As though Jewish homelands were created every day. Ester wonders if there has been a mistake, for surely life could not so casually go on if the dream of all dreams has been fulfilled. And if it is true, what is she to do with this information? For what to Ruzya is at once an abstraction and a threat—the news has already turned the tension in the office up another notch—to Ester is a thrilling, astonishing promise. She was reared to wait for this event but never to expect it, and she certainly never believed in the possibility of Erez Israel after all of those with whom she had dreamed and hoped were killed.

So who will share her joy? True, almost everyone she knows well is Jewish. Still, her mother was always only a reluctant participant in the dream, and any mention of Israel's existence now will make her grieve for her husband. Ester's husband, like her friend Lena Zonina and her acquaintances at the university, are Soviet Jews, a separate breed whose disregard and even distaste for all things Jewish she will never understand. She knows what they will say: the era of nation-states is over; any state must base its culture on a spirit of internationalism. They say this even though that spirit is less and less in evidence in the Soviet Union these days, and there are ominous signs that when all of them graduate the university in six months' time their job options will be as limited as their ethnic origins are clear. There is no immediate personal cause for celebration in the creation of Israel. Ester cannot leave this country. There was a brief window of opportunity a year ago, when former Polish citizens were allowed to go back, but she hardly considered it: there was nothing left in Poland to call her back and, at that time, no other place in the world she could call home. Besides, Soviet-born spouses could not go along, and she figured Boris would not let her take Sasha. Not that she particularly wanted to leave Boris anyway.

This recent history reels through Ester's mind as she arrives at the Central Telegraph, which is no more than a twenty-minute walk from home. Why is she here? Because festive occasions call for congratulations. She has no one to congratulate at home, but surely there are people alive still who can share her thrilled amazement? Where would these people be? In Erez Israel, sure, but she does not know anyone there. She once knew a lot of Jews in Poland. She knows—she is not sure how or where she snatched this bit of information—that there is a Jewish committee in Warsaw. She recalls the Soviet-style name: the Central Committee for the Jews in Poland. They are her people; they will know what she feels.

She marches up to the polished wood counter, grabs the red-painted pen, and, dipping its point into the well of purple ink, writes out the telegram: CONGRATULATIONS NATIONAL HOLIDAY STOP LASHANAH HABA'AH B'YERUSHALAYIM STOP ESTER GESSEN. "Next year in Jerusalem." She pauses. There is a chance, always, that someone she knows will read the telegram. Is that not why she is sending it? She adds: HYPHEN GOLDBERG. She elbows her way to the telegram window before she can think better of her actions, as she well knows she should: the risk she is taking is great. She imagines the NKVD coming to arrest her and Arnold looking at Boris in reproach, as though to say, "I told you marrying someone so emotional and willful was a bad idea." But she has already put down the coins that will pay for her words to travel to Warsaw.

Where Chaika Grossman, the blonde girl from the Bialystok

Hebrew Gymnasium and the ghetto resistance, will pick it out from a sea of impersonal telegrams sent by Komsomol committees and figurehead international friendship organizations and recognize "Ester Gessen-Goldberg" as the wonderful Estusha Goldberg from Bialystok Ha-Shomer ha-Zair and remember it for the rest of her life.

Chapter Eighteen

January 14, 1948

The morning papers are brought in the still-black night, as usual, and the top one—*Pravda*—has a few melting, prickly snowflakes on it. Ruzya already knows what is going to be in the papers: there was a TASS—Telegraph Agency of the Soviet Union—announcement yesterday, and more fact whispered as rumor and rumor declared as fact than she could absorb. And still first she looks to the obituary, as though something could be gleaned from it. "One of the greatest actors of all time," *Pravda* says of Mikhoels. "The image of this great, admirable Soviet artist will rest forever in our hearts." None of the papers has a word about the circumstances of his death. "Has died," "death has ripped out of our ranks," "left this life," "life has stopped"—such are the terms for murder. Even the official version—a car accident—is but a whisper. But Batsheva, Samuil's mother, is no whisperer. Last night, when Ruzya went to the Minkins' to pick up Yolochka, Batsheva announced: "He was murdered." She said it with a certainty that made Ruzya reach for Yolochka with both hands, as though to snatch her away from the knowledge. Batsheva saw.

A single image haunts every memoir's description of Mikhoels's funeral: a nameless thin man, standing on the roof of a low two-story building to one side of the theater courtyard where Mikhoels's body lay in state, playing the fiddle in the brutal cold, well into the night. I suspect the image may be inspired by the role for which Mikhoels would be best remembered—Tevye in Sholom Aleichem's *Tevye the Milkman,* later popularized in the West as *Fiddler on the Roof.* In any case, Ester, who went to the funeral with Bella and several fellow students, does not remember the musician. Ruzya did not go. As a principled cosmopolitan she felt no strong pull to such ethnocentric occasions, and in this era of "anti-cosmopolitanism," which really meant anti-Semitism, it was best to stay away no matter how one felt. She had seen Mikhoels in the theater only once, as Tevye. Decades later she still remembered his performance, which had reduced the audience to tears.

Both within the country and abroad, Mikhoels had come to symbolize all of Soviet Jewry. In 1942, moved by a creative fit of desperation, the Soviet authorities formed the Jewish Anti-Fascist Committee (JAC), whose main purpose was to mobilize American Jews to aid the Soviet war effort. Contrary to Stalin's statement at the end of the war, when he gave ethnic Russians exclusive credit for the victory, Soviet Jews proved very useful to him during the war. Virtually all prominent Jews who had survived the purges of the 1930s were called upon to join the JAC board; they included foreign minister Molotov's wife, Polina Zhemchuzhina, film director Sergei Eizenshtein, and violinist David Oistrakh. In 1943 Mikhoels, poet and secret-police informant Isaak Fefer, and writer Ilya Ehrenburg were dispatched on a public-relations mission to the United States.

The trio's first line of attack was damage control related to the then-recent disappearance of Polish Bund leaders Henryk Ehrlich and Viktor Alter, executed by the NKVD on the credibility-defying charges of collaborating with the Nazis. In addition, they had to cover up the Soviet government's abandonment of about a million and a half Ukrainian, Belorusian, and Russian Jews to the Nazis, by advancing the fiction that the Soviet Union had evacuated a million of them (this particular lie survives in some Western books about the Soviet Union to this day). Some members of the Soviet Jewish propaganda team may have been more deluded than others, but on most occasions, it seems, they were consciously lying. They worked wonders: rallies at which they spoke drew tens of thousands; estimates of the amount of money they collected vary from a million and a half to sixteen million dollars. They managed to convince the American Jewish Joint Distribution Committee—"the Joint"—to renew its relief work in the USSR: the Joint had broken off relations with the Soviet Union in 1938, when the purges reduced its Soviet staff from three thousand to one hundred. Finally, they clearly contributed a great deal to making Americans supportive of the idea of a second front.

The JAC kept on after the war, an incongruous organization in the midst of the anti-cosmopolitan campaign and on the threshold of the Cold War. But, if its continued existence had served to reassure some, then Mikhoels's death took away almost any doubt that Soviet Jews were a people under siege. In a message to the secretary of state, a U.S. embassy official reported that the actor's death "has roused a remarkably large crop of rumors in the USSR." Ruzya, of course, had no doubt that the most frightening of the rumors—that Mikhoels was murdered by the secret police—was true. Ester, who was still months away from feeling the full extent of the anti-cosmopolitan campaign, did not doubt the official version. Even if she had, she probably would have gone to the funeral anyway, disregarding the voice of caution.

JUNE 1948

"We should chat," Konstantin Omelchenko says after he signs Ruzya's morning report and gives it to his secretary to make the Rotaprint-machine copies for the twenty people who receive it. "You are not in a hurry, are you?"

"No, Konstanin Kirillovich."

"Very well. This has to do with the annual attestation coming up."

She feels her feet go rubbery and a sensation of weightlessness spread almost up to her knees. The attestation is Glavlit's annual torture, an exam on the List, which is just that—a list of all the facts and objects, some grouped, some listed separately, that the censors cannot allow to be disclosed. There are probably more than a thousand points on the List, and, were the examining experts to make it their goal to fail someone, it could always be done. Ruzya does very well on the List—she is young, and she has a linguist's trained memory, but if Omelchenko is bringing it up, there must be trouble.

"You generally do very well on the List, and I have no doubt that there will be no trouble this year." Omelchenko's words eerily echo her thoughts.

"Yes," she manages.

"But the censor's job, as you know, is not a mechanical application of the List, but an ideologically important post."

She thinks she hears a tinny, false note in Omelchenko's words, a carefully coded sign of insincerity, but louder than that she hears the threat: so many acquaintances have lost their jobs lately, and their jobs were not nearly so sensitive as hers. "Yes," she says.

"So, I'll get right to business." He smiles.

He smiles. She is not fired. She smiles.

"You need to put in an application to join the Party." He smiles again, a kindly smile in which she reads the gallant hint that, though it would be rude to mention this, she turned twenty-eight in March, which makes her three months too old now to remain a Komsomol member, and anyway, he only wants to help, for surely she understands how unusual it is for someone in such a responsible position not to be a Party member.

Does it matter that she has always wanted to stay out of the Party—well, if not always, then at least since that day in 1937 when the school Komsomol organizer asked her to become an informer? Does anything matter anymore? Just a few weeks ago, her friends Max and Lusya Akivis, along with another half dozen of their friends, were expelled from Moscow University's mathematics faculty on the eve of their graduation exams. One of their crowd, a most devoted Komsomol member, had asked the university Komsomol secretary to explain why the authorities seemed to be targeting the Jews. So the whole circle of friends—including Max, who was already a candidate to join the Party—was kicked out for, as their documents indicated, "actions that demean the honor of Soviet students." The catalyst for the girl's question had been a set of verse letters written by Ehrenburg and his close friend, the poet Margarita Aliger, which had been circulating in handwritten copies among people who trusted one another. "Not sparing our lives, we took paths deserving of legend, to hear what—that they, the Jews, defended the rear in Tashkent!" says the woman's side of the correspondence. "We are to blame because we are the Jews," responds Ehrenburg. Because it had all started with the poems, Max and his friends decided to try to ask Ehrenburg to intervene. "You are luckier than you can know," the famous writer told them. "Lie low, sit quiet, ask no questions, and wait for the times to change."

"Yes, a great honor," mumbles Ruzya. "I want to file an application."

She thought it was a disgrace, a distinct new step in her dishonorable cooperation with the system, but after that conversation with Omelchenko, Ruzya never doubted she had to join the Party to save herself and her child. The procedure for joining was straightforward enough: one filed an application and became a candidate, then submitted two recommendations from colleagues who were Party members, then one's candidacy was considered at the next workplace Party meeting. If one did not become a member within a year of being granted candidate status, one was disqualified.

It would have been straightforward if only this had been a time when colleagues would write a recommendation for a Jew without worrying about the potential personal repercussions. "But you were late once," one of the other censors said. "But you have used your position to bring your daughter to see our dentist," another recalled. "That was not an honest action worthy of a Communist." Now, this was a transparent hint. The dentist at the Central Telegraph's clinic, which only employees were allowed to use, was a Jewish woman—and bringing a Jewish child to see her just might turn out to be part of a Jewish conspiracy.

When Ruzya's candidacy year expired, someone—perhaps Omelchenko—bent the rules so she would not be disqualified, which would have brought automatic dismissal from her job. She became a perennial candidate and thus a potential problem for the Glavlit Party organization. To cover themselves on the record—to distance themselves from her irregular status, which was itself a violation—her Party-member colleagues made criticism of her work a fixture of all workplace Party meetings.

She never felt relieved for not being accepted into the Party. In fact, she bawled her eyes out every time she was rejected.

In a letter to the Central Committee culture chief Mikhail Suslov in June 1951, Omelchenko boasted that, since taking charge at Glavlit after the war, he had reduced the percentage of non-Party members among the censors from 5.4 to 1.6. With the total number of censors on staff hovering around sixty, that 1.6 percent would have been my grandmother.

It is worth noting that Omelchenko's boast was written in re-sponse to a denunciation of him by one of his censors and that this denunciation was apparently related to a scandal surrounding a Jewish Glavlit staffer who had been arrested. Following his arrest, two staff members were taken to task for having once recom-mended him for induction to the Party. Someone clearly thought Omelchenko should be the one held responsible.

It is also worth noting, as my grandmother does nearly every time the subject of Glavlit comes up, that "Omelchenko was a very decent man," a "good man." What does that mean? "There were no ugly scenes at Glavlit, as there were at so many other places." At times such as these the standards of human decency are lowered.

What would have been an ugly scene? In March 1949 the his-tory and economics departments of the Soviet Academy of Sciences held day-and-a-half-long meetings aimed at cleansing their ranks of "rootless cosmopolitans." Isaac Mintz, one of the leading Soviet rewriters of history, who happened, unfortunately for him, to be Jewish, was now accused of "cultivating an admiration for German historiography in 1928" and engineering "the cosmopolitization of Soviet history" together with his three Jewish students. During a break, when the preliminary results of the meeting were reported to the Central Committee, an order to add more names to the pariah list was issued. So in the afternoon session another ten or so historians were found to have sinned. Across the hall from the historians, the economists were attacking an old Bolshevik, Yevgeniy Varga, who also had the bad luck to have been born Jewish. He was now accused of miscalculating the Germans' oil reserves on the eve of the war. One drunk speaker shouted that "the blood of Russian soldiers is on Varga's hands!" Varga's only son had died in the war.

At around the same time the Moscow section of the Soviet Writers' Union held a meeting at which the Jewish poet Aleksandr Kushnerov was scheduled to denounce the JAC and agents of cosmopolitanism in the union ranks. Kushnerov proved not up to the task: when he was literally dragged to the podium, he burst into tears, unable to utter a word. He died too soon afterward to be arrested, but his wife was consigned to the Gulag.

November 17, 1948

A friend is the bearer of a good rumor, a rare treat these days: the Jewish Anti-Fascist Committee has a job opening for a Hebrew translator; Ester should be qualified. She has to agree this is a dream job.

That, admittedly, is an adjustment if not an exaggeration. Half a year ago she was planning on the academic career for which she had been groomed ever since the university resumed functioning in 1944 and Professor Piotrovsky strong-armed her into switching to the classics department to specialize in comparative linguistics. At the time, she was heavily pregnant and none too enthusiastic about doubling her workload, but the professor persisted. She excelled in her new field. Her thesis on Plato's dialogues should have served as her ticket to graduate school. But Piotrovsky warned her a few days before her thesis defense that something might go wrong. Her defense turned into one of those "ugly scenes," with the committee split evenly between the old classics professors, with little to lose, proposing a mark of "excellent," and the young ones, in favor of "good." Finally, a young instructor who knew nothing of the thesis was yanked from her lecture to cast a tiebreaking vote in favor of "good," and that was the end of graduate-school dreams.

Well, not exactly. There was a glimmer of hope a month or so later, when one of the department's old men, Professor Radtsik, alerted Ester to a graduate-school vacancy in classics at the City Pedagogical Institute. A less prestigious institution than the university, this one should have welcomed a graduate with all "excellent's" on her exams, even if she had merely a "good" thesis. She got "excellent" on all four of her entrance exams and considered herself, briefly, a graduate student—until she was summoned by the rector, one Shegolev. The middle-aged burly man wasted no time on formalities, ignoring even her "hello," and spitting out what sounded like a rehearsed statement: "Comrade Gessen, I want to tell you that I am the boss at this school, and I make the decisions about whom I want to have as graduate students. I don't need you here, and I am not admitting you to graduate school. I would advise you against filing complaints, which will do you no good. Good-bye."

She realized she was lucky to have been admitted as an undergraduate before the war, before all this began: her professors, who did not have to take the blame for having admitted her, had been free to teach her. So until she graduated she had been shielded in a sense from the anti-cosmopolitan campaign and, like most people who live in a place and time of great danger, she had secretly suspected she personally was immune to the worst of it.

Unlike her friend from the Bialystok gymnasium, Baruch Kaplan, a chemistry star who must have applied to nine different graduate schools, Ester quickly accepted the futility of further efforts and started looking for a job. She had to. Bella, suddenly discovered to be a "cosmopolitan," had lost her own job teaching Polish to future intelligence officers, and Boris, who defended his engineering dissertation just as she was finishing her thesis, was working as an assistant professor for a pittance.

Six months have passed since she began looking—a long time to try to live on one person's inadequate earnings—and she is seriously starting to worry that if she does not find a job soon, the four residents of this room in this communal apartment, Ester, Bella, Boris, and four-year-old Sasha, will starve.

As it is, they have not been eating well, and it shows. A few months ago a pediatrician paid a house call to Sasha, who seemed to be running a fever. Bella tried to draw the elderly Jewish doctor's attention to the boy's looks, an object of family pride: "Look, Doctor, his eyes show two thousand years of Jewish sorrow." "At this age," the pediatrician responded, "Jewish sorrow can stem only from malnutrition."

The jobs she did not get: a Latin instructor at a teachers' college; a cataloger of war-trophy books at the Lenin Library; a librarian at the Library of Foreign Literature; a librarian anywhere; anything at all. Most of the interviews had gone well, except for two or three occasions when she was asked how she was related to the Gessen who had served in the prerevolutionary parliament.

He was a cousin of her father-in-law, she assumed, though the elder Gessen had never entertained such queries. In any case, she generally said, "We are no relation: that politician converted to Christianity, and our side of the family did not." If the elder Gessen, who is sure she or her similarly careless mother will one day get them all arrested, knew she answered this way, he would have a fit, and he would have a point. Then again, the outcome was always the same, regardless of the pleasantnesses of the interview: when she returned to see the personnel officer who had reviewed her application—the form always asked about ethnicity right after establishing name, surname, patronymic, and date of birth—she invariably heard that there had been a misunderstanding, there was no vacancy after all, they were sorry (or not), nothing to be done.

So the JAC job sounds like a dream because they could hardly be looking for a non-Jew—and, anyway, where would they find one who knew Hebrew, the study of which has been banned in the Soviet Union for thirty years?

NOVEMBER 18, 1948

It was such a good interview that it hardly felt like one. She half expected to see the JAC dignitaries—at least the famous poet Isaak Fefer, who took over after Mikhoels's death—but the fairly grand, if dusty, two-story building on Kropotkin Street was half empty. Still, a manager greeted her enthusiastically, administered a simple test—interpreting as she read from an Israeli newspaper, a task whose only difficulty was the excitement: she had never seen an Israeli newspaper before. Then he had her fill out an application and, without any personnel department interview or other fuss, offered her a job with a mind-boggling salary of one hundred

and fifty rubles, which would more than double the family's income. And that, for translating Israeli papers. If there is no God, at
least there is luck and possibly justice. Her new life will begin on
Monday, in four days. Meanwhile, the room on Gorky Street is
the site of gleeful wine-drinking, and no one, temporarily, is worried whether Sasha can fall asleep with only a curtain shielding
him from the cheer.

The Central Committee order instructing the Interior Ministry to
shut down the JAC, but "not to arrest anyone yet," was signed
two days later, on Saturday, November 20, 1948.

NOVEMBER 22, 1948

She recognizes the uniform worn by the young man standing
guard in front of the two-story building, his bayoneted rifle held
ceremoniously across his chest: he is NKVD. She knows what the
seal on the door means. Still, she asks, and the soldier responds
obligingly and predictably: "The Committee is no more." It is
back to the job hunt, and there is no hope.

Owing to the demented precision of the most powerful conspiracy theorist on Earth, the major events of Stalin's war on the
Jews took place on the same date in different years.

On January 13, 1948, Mikhoels was murdered.

On January 13, 1949, the wave of arrests of JAC board mem-
bers began with the detention of fifty-nine-year-old historian
Iosif Yuzefovich and fifty-seven-year-old medical doctor Boris
Shimeliovich. The JAC itself had been shut down in November
1948 on orders from the Soviet of Ministers; Fefer, the poet David
Gofshtein, the actor Veniamin Zuskin, who headed the Jewish

Theater after Mikhoels's death, and Molotov's wife, Polina Zhemchuzhina, had all been arrested in the fall; before the end of January 1949, the remaining high-profile JAC activists were detained. Zhemchuzhina would disappear; the rest of the JAC detainees would become the accused in perhaps the most convoluted of all Stalinist trials. All were interrogated and tortured into the spring, and all confessed to having engaged in espionage—posthumously implicating Mikhoels as well. Before a trial could begin, though, they reneged on their confessions, and the investigation had to be reopened. Instead of the show trial that was probably meant to have taken place in 1949, they were finally tried in a closed session from May to July 1952. Thirteen—that is, all but two of the accused—were executed on August 12, 1952. Historians have come to call it "Stalin's last execution."

But since the JAC trial had to be held in secret—because the accused refused to cooperate—the chronology of the Jewish purges was the stuff of between-the-lines hints and whispered news of yet another Jewish writer or Jewish doctor or simply Jewish acquaintance arrested. Every Jew in the Soviet Union wrote her own history of the last years of Stalinist terror; every Jew had her own day when she felt she was personally a target, when she lost sleep and hope, and when she first thought her life might be worth more than her principles.

DECEMBER 22, 1948

How many ways are there to arrest a person? They can come in the middle of the night, take the elevator or the stairs, conduct a search or not, and lead you away to a car or a bread truck. They can find you at home, at the dacha, or in the hospital. They can bring you back and take you away again. Or they can even just telephone.

When the call came for Ester, she realized that she was someone for whom just a telephone call would be sufficient. Why would they bother sending a car for someone who could hardly get away—any attempt to escape would leave her son and her mother as hostages. The person on the phone told her to report to the building at Dzerzhinsky Square at ten in the morning. That leaves her about twenty hours for the good-byes and the packing: a sweater, a change of underwear, a bar of soap, a cupful of sugar carefully wrapped in paper, and some dried bread in the same sort of packaging. She and Bella take turns crying and comforting each other. In the intervals, Ester worries about the future. Yes, Boris promises he will take care of Sasha. No, of course he will not abandon her mother. He turns his back to her and busies himself with Ester's bag, crumpling the paper loudly.

Ester knows she brought this upon herself with that telegram to Warsaw two years ago, but she will not mention it for fear of her father-in-law's wrath, which would for once be well founded. The Gessens are in and out of their adjacent room, her father-in-law frowning, her mother-in-law crying, her sister-in-law pestering the child until he, too, is on the verge of tears. There will be no sleep tonight, only the constant shuffling of fear.

After this most sleepless of nights, Ester does not even think about the absurdity of her actions: she is actually delivering herself to prison. She moves in a fog, aided by the vagueness of Moscow light on a winter morning, and she is on the metro, then out of it at the other end of Gorky Street and walking uphill to the unconscionably large secret-police building squatting behind him. She wanders among the brass number plaques until she finds the right entrance and pushes the heavy oak door, almost falling in to hand her passport and her bag over to a young man wearing the same uniform as the soldier in front of the JAC a month ago.

This soldier ruffles in her bag and raises a cracked-lip smile: "Girl, these sorts of bags belong next door!" He chuckles. "That's all right, though, I'll keep it safe for you here—you can pick it up when you go out."

Ester reminds herself that this means nothing. A friend of a friend was jailed, interrogated for days or weeks, refused to sign a confession, and then the investigator told him there had been a mistake and he would be released; he accompanied Yasha to the door of his apartment but caught his hand just as Yasha was about to ring the doorbell. "Just one more little thing," he said. "Sign these." And when Yasha did not sign the confession again, he was taken back to jail.

The young man is talking on one of those faceless telephones that connect directly to one of the important offices.

"Someone will be here in a minute to take you to Major Ivanova." He smiles again, hanging up.

Major Ivanova, up three floors in the elevator, then down the hall, down a quarter-flight of stairs, then another long corridor— Ester will never find her way out of here, even if she is free to go—is a woman of about forty whose most memorable feature is her uniform, its skirt precisely knee-length and its jacket a bit too tight in the chest.

"Hello," she says. "Sit down."

Ester sits down, hugging her elbows, partly for fear that this is not what it looks like, partly for fear that it is just a business conversation—though God only knows what the business could be. She is certainly not hugging herself because she feels cold—she is dressed warmly and hideously: for jail.

"We have a proposition for you," Ivanova begins with a sentence noxiously reminiscent of Major Gurov. "We would like to offer you a job. Tea?"

"No, thank you."

"You mean 'no, thank you' to tea, I hope. Tell me if you change your mind. We would like to offer you a job as a Hebrew translator."

"I'm sorry?"

"You see, with the formation of the State of Israel, we have a lot of this sort of work. And no one to do it. Your name came up in connection with the case of the Jewish Anti-Fascist Committee."

"Oh!" This is the first thing all morning that has made sense.

"Now, before you say anything, I want to tell you about the job. You will have a flexible schedule: there really isn't enough to keep you here all day long, and there is no point in just sitting around, you understand? So you will come to work in the mornings and leave as soon as you are done. The salary is two hundred a month—that's better than you would have had at the Jewish committee, as I understand it. We'll start you out as a lieutenant, and if all goes well, you'll make captain before you retire. We have retirement benefits—oh, but it's too early for you to be interested in that. Now you talk."

"I'd like to think about it and give you an answer tomorrow."

"All right."

"I'll come at the same time tomorrow, yes? Now, if I may, I would like to get home."

"Oh, I understand." Major Ivanova laughs. "Your family must have been scared when we asked you to come."

"They are still scared. I want to go home and tell them I am all right."

"Well, then, until tomorrow." Major Ivanova smiles again,

indicating that they are allies who have risen above petty fears of arrest.

———————

Has anyone ever been so incredulously happy upon opening a door as Bella is when she sees her daughter? Possibly not. And does the news of Major Ivanova's courtship cause agony? Not exactly. That is, there is a moment of silence—as there always is when the secret police enters the room, in whatever fashion—but not a prolonged moment, because Miriam, Ester's mother-in-law, shouts, "My God, we won't be able to say anything at home anymore!" And everyone laughs.

There is no further discussion because the choice is clear: it is better to have a job than to have your child's doctor tell you he is malnourished. Jobs that do not compromise one's integrity have become extinct; this one may not be too compromising, and they all hope not too many of their friends will shy away from socializing with an NKVD lieutenant. A mixture of relief and dread settles into the two rooms as their six adult residents ponder the probability of a new isolation. This time, the silence is broken by the phone.

Major Ivanova cannot bear the suspense, and Ester says yes.

DECEMBER 24, 1948

Ester has filled out more than her share of job applications in the past months, but the one Major Ivanova has handed her is unlike any she has seen. It is an entire notebook, ready to be filed—she would rather not think where. The first page warns of criminal penalties for forgery; the following page asks, like all Soviet job applications, for name, surname, patronymic, date and place of birth, and ethnicity; and the rest—the twenty or so pages that follow—ask for a complete listing of relatives living abroad, including third cousins however many times removed. All job applications ask for relatives abroad, but usually they are limited to immediate family, and here Ester has rarely stumbled: what immediate family did not come to the Soviet Union are dead.

Realizing this is as futile as every other job application she has filled out—but ever so much more time-consuming—Ester shuts the notebook and addresses the major.

"There is no point in my filling this out," she says as definitively as she can manage. "I have relatives in every foreign country. My mother had nine siblings, and my father, seventeen."

Major Ivanova laughs her best-friend laugh again. "Darling, anyone else we might consider for this job has just as many relatives in just as many places. It's just, the other people who speak that language are forty years older than you."

Ester has to laugh, too, and she has to fill out the application.

Two and a half hours later, Major Ivanova marches out of the room with the notebook-application, and in a few minutes, she is back, triumphant: "Congratulations! You have been hired. Now all you have to do is pass the medical exam."

What an odd feeling it is to be so wanted.

"I want you to go to the clinic immediately," Major Ivanova continues, looking Ester up and down. Ester is wearing her good dress today, but this stare makes her feel somehow inadequate. "If you have anything wrong with you, you had better tell me now so I can get it cleared ahead of time. Because, you know, our medical exam is very strict—and we are very, very interested in you."

"I am healthy as a horse," Ester answers with all the indifferent confidence she can muster.

DECEMBER 25, 1948

The NKVD clinic, as it happens, is on Zhdanov Street, a few doors down from the Committee for Higher Schooling, the site of Ester's 1940 triumph over anti-Semitism. There are times to quote clichés even to oneself, and this is a time to recall Marx's "history repeating itself." For the spectacle of Ester Gessen arriving for a medical exam at the NKVD clinic, where no Jew has set foot in years, would be worthy of the Jewish theater around the corner—had this very organization not engineered its dissolution just days ago. There is not a nurse in the building who cannot find an excuse to ask "And what is your job going to be?"

"I'm sorry," she answers proudly, "but that is a state secret."

There are no secrets here, though. Shuttled from office to office, she is made to strip again and again, and men and women in white coats poke, stare, and hammer at her body. "Healthy as a horse" is their shared verdict on this fragile, swarthy woman, until she comes into the last office, the ophthalmologist's. It is when he tells her to cover her right eye with the little paddle that she remembers the eye exam for the driver's courses that discovered she is virtually blind in her left one.

"But it's not like I'm getting hired to be a sniper!" she objects.

"It's not like you are getting hired to be anything at all," the duty doctor responds with a treacly smile. And signs the wrong line on her work-readiness certificate, which Ester now has to deliver to Ivanova.

Who is livid. "But I told you!" she shouts at Ester. "I warned you!"

"But it's not on purpose," Ester mumbles. "You must understand that if I decided to go through all this humiliation, I wanted the result to be positive!"

Major Ivanova knits her brows in puzzlement over the word

humiliation, and then she is shouting into the phone, at the head of the clinic: "But I told you!" she screams. "I warned you! But you understand that if I decided to go to all this trouble, I wanted the result to be positive!"

She hangs up in exasperation: "He says there is nothing he can do now, that he should have known in advance. Listen, he told me your records will be archived in six months and then they can examine you again and do it right. Can you please come back in six months?"

"Yes."

"I want you to promise me you will come back in six months."

"I promise."

"You promised! I want you working here."

There is more threat than desire in that statement.

———

In the evening they celebrate Sasha's fourth birthday with the food and wine they bought in anticipation of their new riches. "But maybe it's a sign," Ester says into the tension. "Maybe it's better I don't work for the NKVD. We'll manage—somehow." They drink to that.

MARCH 1949

"It seems *Internatsional'naya literatura,* the journal, is splitting into two," says Bella after she hangs up the phone; an old translation contact of hers just called. "They'll have 'foreign literature' and 'Soviet literature,' or something like that—anyway, one of them will have a Polish-language edition, and they need native speakers to work as translators. Why don't we both try?" And so it is that both women start translating for the journal and Ester gets a staff job that she will hold for over forty years and that will cause her to say, when Major Ivanova phones in June, "I'm not looking for work anymore," and that will cause Major Ivanova to sound more like a woman scorned than an NKVD officer affronted.

Chapter Nineteen

The tram stop near the Belorussky Rail Station is crowded on a Sunday morning, thick with people rushing to and from a nearby peasant market, weighed down with bags of every shape, shuffling in their felt boots. At exactly ten o'clock two young women arrive at the station from different directions and find each other in the crowd. Both walk briskly, trying to keep warm: neither is wearing an overcoat. They are dressed in bulky sweaters, knit hats, and narrow slacks tucked into hideous men's shoes, black ones with flat thin soles that flare out to the square toes. They are, it is obvious to anyone, going cross-country skiing.

They make an odd pair. One is short but big-boned, with large, strong hands that she is constantly trying to hide. Sometimes she looks like she is trying to hide all of herself: though her conversation is worldly and peppered with jokes, she has an air of abiding shyness about her, as if she always wishes to defer to someone more confident. This is Ruzya. Her companion looks like a woman who accepts everything as her due: tall, slender, with a mane of dark brown curly hair and the glamorous, if outdated, looks of a 1920s film star. Her speech is loud and a little odd—overly melodic—and she laughs often and with abandon, showing off a gleaming set of perfect teeth unique in a country that has been ravaged by war, famine, and epidemics for four decades. This is Ester.

A quick peck on the cheek, and they board the tram, a splendid, though well-worn, contraption of wood and copper, with a touch of leather. They exchange their usual news: Yolochka, Ruzya's seven-year-old daughter, has immersed herself in reading and refuses to go outside; Sasha, Ester's five-year-old son, has run into a problem in the courtyard, the epicenter of his social life—but Ester promises to tell Ruzya about it in more detail later. Sixteen years from now Sasha and Yolka will marry, and a year later I will be born—an absurdly cinematic culmination of these women's friendship, struck up just a few months ago, when they met at a mutual friend's home. Theirs was a bond instant and self-evident; cemented, over the last seven or eight weekends, with these skiing trips.

The tram takes them to the end of a wide avenue and continues along its narrow track, which is now barely visible under the snow. In another two decades this area will become the city's prestigious outer center, with nine- and twelve-story brick apartment buildings boasting ambitious design and famous occupants, but for now it is Moscow's far reaches, where low wooden structures—some rural houses, some barracks—huddle close to the track. It is a composition in two colors: white snow beneath a muddy white sky, and black houses and people in small black clumps that get off the tram and separate into tiny black dots as each seeks its own half-hidden path through the waist-high snow. Ester and Ruzya walk to one of the rural-style houses, crooked and evidently creaky under a small mountain of snow frozen on its sloping roof. This house belongs to the father of their friend Lusya. She, her husband, Max, and a half-dozen other Jewish mathematics students were recently expelled from Moscow University for discussing the wave of anti-Semitic terror sweeping the country. Max will ultimately go on to a prominent academic career in the Soviet Union and in Israel, but now and for a number of years to come he and Lusya live off odd jobs and stay with Lusya's father in this old wooden house, where Ester and Ruzya keep their skis.

They extract them now from among the brooms and shovels stacked in the entryway, and they are off: the ski track begins just behind the wooden house and runs for miles into the forest. The skiers are well matched: Ruzya has an athlete's low posture and drive, while the tall Ester has a naturally long stride. They ski for about an hour, silent and concentrated, side by side when the track splits in two but mostly one behind the other, the woman in front never turning around but aware of the swoosh of her companion's skis. The black-and-white landscape gives way to an evergreen forest, then turns stark again as the pine trees cede to bare oaks and aspens. Finally, after climbing a hill not very steep but exhaustingly long, the two women stop, flushed and out of breath, and they rest by talking.

"So," Ruzya prompts her friend. "You were going to tell me about Sasha's problems in the yard?" She knows that whatever it was, it could not be told on the tram, where any one of the silent and apparently indifferent passengers could be a pair of ears perked and a pen poised: a potential informer. She guesses that it has something to do with being Jewish—the most volatile, the deadliest, subject these days.

"Yes, can you imagine?" Her friend often begins her stories this way and manages to sustain the pitch throughout—a quality Ruzya decided she adored as soon as she met Ester. "He went out to play the other day, and the boys in the courtyard were playing some sort of game, and the biggest bully they've got there, Shura is the name, told Sasha, 'You can't play because you're Jewish.' Sasha didn't breathe a word to me, of course, but then he comes home ecstatic yesterday: apparently he went out, they were playing and Shura wasn't there, so they let him into the game. Then this Shura character comes out, and one of the boys shouts at him, 'So what if Sasha is Jewish? You are even worse!'

"And my son is happy about this? I think I have to start talking to him about his heritage."

"Oh, I think you should be careful with this." Ruzya half smiles, half frowns, knowing her sincere words of caution will only rile her friend further.

"Certainly, when I was growing up in Bialystok, despite the anti-Semitism in Poland at the time—I tell you, it was not unlike what we're experiencing here today—still, I knew to take pride in my Jewishness. If someone had said something like that to me—"

"Well, I am a product of a different society, of course, but, you know, I am convinced that this is nothing to be proud of, per se," Ruzya objects, but immediately interrupts herself to encourage what she is certain will be a delicious excursion into a world she can barely imagine: "But what did your parents say to you when you heard slurs in the street?"

That they have ventured so far into the forest, where the ski tracks almost disappear, that they stand atop a hill so they can see much farther than they can hear—that, in other words, the secrecy of their conversation is very nearly assured—is instinct rather than plan. And now it is habit too. They have been coming to this forest every weekend since late autumn, when the layer of snow was barely thick enough for skiing, and they have talked for hours, long past the point of getting cold, on this hilltop and other hilltops.

"We told each other our lives," my grandmother Ruzya will say fifty years later.

They have vastly different ways of presenting their stories. Ester has polished most of hers to perfection, with a beginning, a middle, an end, and a punch line. She takes pleasure in the telling, and she has little doubt her audience will enjoy the listening. Should something interrupt her, she will pick up confidently where she left off. She respects stories, and she likes her own. Tempting as it is to ascribe a part of the difference in style to the two women's professions—Ester the magazine editor with a confident nose for a good story, and Ruzya the censor with the black excision pencil ever poised—it is more likely a difference in personalities. In any case, Ruzya tells her stories almost reluctantly, uncertain they deserve the attention, and she is ever ready to stop, abridge, or even retract.

Ruzya is twenty-nine and Ester twenty-seven, but the stories they tell in the first months of their friendship are the tales of a different era and different lives: before the war, before the deaths, before they grew, abruptly, into burdened, disillusioned, and sometimes conflicted adults. Their stories are populated with people who are now dead, and they unfolded in places that are now gone. The distance between now and then is the reason both for Ruzya's reticence and for Ester's mastery of presentation. And it is another reason to ski far and deep into the woods before launching into the stories.

For both of my grandmothers, friends are the main—possibly the only—constant in their lives. Empires collapsed, entire countries disappeared, cities changed beyond recognition, the boys they loved died, the men who replaced them left the women lonely—but they had friends. *Friendship,* in Russian, is an exalted concept, possibly the most overburdened word in an overtaxed language. Should you ever encounter a Russian, prepare to see her wince at your casual reference to someone as "a friend," or worse, as "a friend of mine"—a hint at a numerosity the Russian word for *friend* precludes. My grandmother Ruzya says, "I know there was not a single informant in our circle of friends."

"How do you know?"

"We are all here, aren't we?"

My grandmother Ester tells me that though her marriage was, for the most part, a disaster, she remembers her twenties as a happy time because my grandfather was not the jealous type, and this meant she spent all of her free hours with friends. When I ask her to tell me about her friends from that period she lists Baruch Kaplan, her classmate from Bialystok; and the Akivises, Max and Lusya, at whose house she and Ruzya kept their skis—all of whom now live in Israel—and a number of other people, most of whom have also emigrated, or died. She rarely mentions Ruzya, with whom she spoke on the phone almost daily, with whom she went skiing every weekend and to the theater, when means and obligations allowed, practically every other day, and who is still never far away—perhaps because her relationship with Ruzya has for so long now straddled the line between friendship and family.

So how to define friendship, as it was understood by women living in the Soviet Union in the middle of the twentieth century? It was probably most like family: a bond that, once established, was believed permanent. If a break occurred, it was momentous and painful. Such was my grandmothers' friendship, so self-evident that both women find it difficult to trace its beginnings.

They met during that time when Russia's various Jewish communities had closed in on themselves in fear, when few strangers would have been able to trust one another. When they met at their mutual friend's house, they chose each other instantly. My grandmother Ruzya can recall the source of the attraction: "She was the life of the party. She laughed. She told stories. She held everyone's attention comfortably. And she laughed." I think she can still hear that laughter and feel the joy of seeing joy. I imagine the twenty-six-year-old Ester, effortlessly elegant, half lying on a couch, curly hair tossed back, laughing. I imagine Ruzya, shy, unnoticed at first, observing Ester and remembering what Hemingway said about "the gay ones": it was "like having immortality while you were still alive."

I imagine Ester unaware at first that a stranger has joined in the conversation. They talk about theater, a new production they all have seen within the last month, and Ruzya makes a comment that takes a minute to be heard: she speaks softly, so the categorical nature of her opinion surprises. Something about the lead actor's genius saving the entire effort, what with its uninspired staging and clunky direction. I imagine Ester disagreeing vehemently—precisely what she herself liked was the production, the director's effort, and she hardly thinks the lead actor would have been worth watching were it not for the entourage. I imagine them testing each other a little, bringing up other plays, surveying each other's cultural terrain, and immediately starting to build connections between their territories, making a quick pact to bridge over their differences for the sake of the spirit that is bringing them together.

My grandmother Ester does not remember their first meeting and the beginnings of their friendship at all. It is as though it had always been there, or had at least always been meant to be. I can say with some certainty that, beginning the winter following their meeting, they spent their weekends cross-country skiing together, telling each other their lives. Some of these skiing excursions grew to include husbands and boyfriends and children and friends. By then Ester and Ruzya had filled each other in on all the essential milestones and had grown to assume each other's presence in their lives, as they have for more than half a century.

Of course, they have proceeded to argue continuously, just as they did that first evening. They are different as women, as Jews, and as citizens. They argue about topics both know intimately, like books read and reread, and topics they have barely encountered, like feminism. During my first visit to Moscow in March 1991, when I was reporting on the Soviet Union's fledgling women's movement, I stayed at my grandmother Ester's apartment. I conducted most of my interviews there as well: the city had virtually no public places where people could meet, and most of my subjects lived in cramped settings that precluded entertaining a foreign journalist, which I was at the time. My grandmother Ruzya happened to be visiting when a young graduate student came to tell me about her discovery of feminism. The grandmothers elicited the briefest of summaries from her over tea, then turned to each other.

"I find all this misguided," declared Ruzya. "It is clear that men and women have different talents and proclivities—for example, men are more gifted in mathematics and exact sciences."

"What are you saying!" Ester exclaimed, as each of them generally does when one of them says something the other finds outrageous to the point of absurdity. "Women have simply systematically been kept out of certain fields."

The graduate student stared. "And you've never even read any feminist theory?" she half asked, with the awed condescension of youth toward age.

"Young lady," Ester responded. "In my seventy years on this Earth I have taken some time to think." And with that she turned back to her friend.

Perhaps it is the constant difference of opinion on everything that keeps them interested in each other: even after all these years, they cannot predict each other's reaction to anything. Each listens for the other's opinion so she can argue her dissent. And they laugh at each other's familiar ways. Ruzya giggles over regular instances of Ester's tactlessness: she can ask people about estranged spouses or make disparaging comments about current ones, and this is generally the least of it. Ester snickers at examples of Ruzya's shy indecisiveness and never fails to be surprised by Ruzya's reluctance to make a simple phone call to a literary agent or to take on a job she fears may exceed her expertise. And they wonder at each other's strengths—Ester's eternal fearlessness, Ruzya's boundless energy (like when, at the age of eighty-one, Ruzya undertakes and carries out an apartment move all by herself).

They feel so different in their lives that I have been tempted to write the story of their relationship as tragic, with the attraction so strong and the meeting point never found. But that would be as absurd as looking for tragedy in the love of two sisters who preserved the closest of bonds for their entire lives. Consider the evidence. If I am looking for one of them, I can call the other—and I will be told she has gone to have an ultrasound and will probably be back by two in the afternoon. They trust each other completely, which is to say, with their lives.

JUNE 1951

Ester feels distinctly guilty. Not that she should. In her marriage to Boris, there have been more years when she suggested a divorce than years when she did not. Her suggestions were gentle at first, then ever more firm. He holds fast to his "no." They both know this is the end of the discussion, because they have one room in a communal apartment, indivisible, and she has a son and a mother and no place else to take them. And she should not feel guilty, because she knows in her heart as well as in her mind that she did her best while Boris did not. Even his mother, who has put up with her own domestic despot for over thirty years, looks on with sympathy. Still, Ester feels guilty—perhaps because she knows that her own good faith was not inspired by love while Boris's petty tyranny was somehow tied to powerful emotion. Or, perhaps, she feels guilty simply because what she is about to do, though undertaken daily by married women the world over, is not a done thing. She, for one, has never done this before.

The source of her guilt is one Alexander G, he of the non-Slavic surname but Slavic roots. He is reasonably tall, fairly handsome, and has been entirely focused on her ever since she arrived at this resort two weeks ago. He is married, as is she, but the rules of resort romances allow their liaison to proceed quickly and unambiguously, unhampered even by her nagging feelings of guilt.

In a fortnight they have exchanged personal histories, including information about their spouses and children: etiquette dictates that these sorts of affairs initially masquerade as friendships, making deceit or even discretion unnecessary. She has told him about Sasha and about Boris, and about how they met after he was released from the hospital, with that yellow ribbon on his chest and half a jaw missing. Alexander is a college instructor. He has a son, seven—Sasha's age—and he was not in the military during the war. "I never tried to avoid the service," he tells her. "I did not hide, but I did not try to get there either. And it worked out that I didn't go to war: I got an exemption." This strikes Ester as odd, if not necessarily false: she does not know any men her age who did not fight.

Tonight is the night. Tonight there is hardly any talking, because they dance. They move closer and closer in the dance, with
that jittery excitement that comes despite mutual knowledge of
what will happen next. They leave the dance hall hand in hand
and kiss on the porch. Then they walk down a tree-lined alley
slowly, deliberately, in a tiny final tribute to discretion. He carries
her flat black purse. They talk. Ester steers the conversation toward "the Jewish question." Though she has no doubt that
Alexander is aware of her ethnic origins, she feels compelled to
test his attitude one more time before she does something she
might regret much more than simply betraying her husband—
sleep with an anti-Semite. She has no reason to believe that
Alexander is anti-Semitic, but in this age every non-Jew is suspect. She mentions that she had difficulty finding work after college—an uncharacteristic understatement—because she is Jewish.

"Well," Alexander says in a tone that strikes her as smugly
gentle. "I am no anti-Semite, but you must admit that Jews are
not a particularly reliable group in a time like this. I mean, I am no
anti-Semite, but if there were another war, surely your son would
hide out while mine would serve."

She stops dead to face him and removes her purse from his
hand. "That must be because during the war that we did have,
you hid out while my husband became a cripple." She moves her
purse from her right hand to her left and with a closed fist hits
him, striking, quite by coincidence, the exact spot that is missing
in Boris's face. Then she turns around and walks away.

She can hear Alexander spitting behind her. It may be curses
or it may be teeth, for all she knows and cares. Her hand hurts that
much.

We—my brother, my father, whoever else might hear one of these stories of my grandmother Ester's—are invariably awed. Sometimes these incidents showcase her fearlessness—like when, at the age of seventy, she sought confrontation with a deranged megaphone-equipped anti-Semite in a Moscow street. But this is not what awes us. It is the immediacy of her reaction, the true absence of the tempering anti-Semite inside. People who grew up in the Soviet Union are not like that; we have a tiny nagging need to hide our Jewishness or apologize for it, or at least apologize for not hiding it. My grandmother Ruzya has always, with alarming regularity, lost companionship over anti-Semitism, but not because of the immediacy of her reactions—because of the very opposite. After pushing the perennial topic off as long as she could because it pains her cosmopolitan heart to discuss it, but also because she wishes, just a little bit but for as long as she can remember, that she were not Jewish, she will finally discover an acquaintance's views on Jews and realize that they are unacceptable. My grandmother Ester could never lose a friend over the Jewish Question because for her it is an integral part of testing someone's intellectual and human credentials before forming a friendship—even if, as in the case of Alexander G, the exacting nature of this test might cost her a much-needed distraction.

So she returned to Boris still, in essence, a faithful wife. She had no need of sympathy: she was unhappy as a wife but perfectly content as a person. By that point she had a job she liked, a child she loved, and friends whom she trusted. Her house was always full of people: they lived on Gorky Street, in the very center of the city, a place virtually everyone passed through several times a week, walking past her building, able to look up and see if there was a light on in the apartment on the fourth floor—and this in a time when few people had phones, so calling to arrange a visit was rarely an option. She no longer thought of her life as difficult. Her mother was home and could always watch the child, her friends were interesting, and so were the many events around town, and Ester felt she was living life to the fullest—in no small part because of the nagging suspicion that all this would end soon, when she and Boris and Bella and little Sasha and all their friends would be loaded into cattle cars again.

CHAPTER TWENTY

JANUARY 19, 1953

For nearly a week now, Ruzya has been translating Harrison Salisbury's *New York Times* articles in their uncensored entirety for her morning reports, and for a week now she has been feeling nauseated. She loves translating Salisbury: he is a good and intelligent writer, and his writing makes her a better translator. But the chill in his words becomes hers. Salisbury, who has been here for four years, knows the best way of getting his copy cleared quickly is by reporting only what has appeared in the Soviet press—but the way he chooses his quotes makes them sound even more ominous, if that is possible. Three years ago, for example, she killed an article of his that was virtually a direct translation of an *Izvestia* item, dated January 13, 1950, announcing the reestablishment of the death penalty (which had been nominally abolished in 1947), for "traitors, spies and subversives." Salisbury was the only foreign correspondent who realized, and made transparent in his retelling, that this was a clear warning of more show trials to come.

Six days ago, on January 13, the Soviet press announced the arrests of nine Jewish doctors who have ostensibly confessed to poisoning Central Committee members Andrei Zhdanov and Aleksandr Shcherbakov in 1948. Ruzya knows that many other Jewish doctors in the city have been arrested over the last couple of years, but the way the papers are covering the latest nine makes it clear that this is the final act of the drama that began with Mikhoels's murder five years ago. This clearly is going to be a grand-scale show trial. The newspapers are detailing the doctors' alleged crimes and printing endless letters from the public demanding punishment for the Jews. The public, fed a steady diet of anti-Semitic propaganda for the last five years, has truly been whipped into a frenzy. If a show trial commences, which it clearly will, all Jews will be in danger. There is talk, in Jewish circles, of having to ask to be saved—perhaps to be evacuated, as people were during the war.

The day before yesterday, Ruzya was awed by Salisbury's masterly composition: she had translated and called in an entire passage that had made her shiver, but it was cleared by Stalin's secretariat. Reporting on the media's continuing coverage of the arrests, Salisbury had written:

> The alleged connection of the arrested doctors with Zionists was not emphasized. It has not been found necessary to say anything in the press about the religious origin of some of what the press calls "fiends in human form."
>
> What might be considered an indirect reply to the chorus voiced abroad that the Soviet charges have an anti-Semitic as well as an anti-Zionist basis was published in the leading editorial of Pravda today. Its subject was cultural exchange with other countries. In one of the first paragraphs, however, Pravda denounced what it called "zoological racism of the Hitlerites." Pravda charged that reac-

*tionary forces in the world today were seeking to use the "Fascist
idea of zoological racism" to trample upon the national achievements of peoples.*

*In contrast, Pravda pictured the Soviet Union as a land where
the greatest respect was shown to its own people and those abroad.
Pravda said the Soviet Union paid special consideration to the cultural achievements of all peoples, in contrast to "man-hating" capi-
talists.*

Ruzya had assumed that at least the speculative opening lines
of the second paragraph and the *however* in the following sentence
would be deleted—but no, apparently this publicity for the *Pravda*
editorial was appreciated at the top. Today Salisbury reached all
the way to *Ukrainian Pravda* to make his point with quotes. Which
Ruzya will dutifully dictate to the typist, who is just now entering
the room with that smile on her face that has been there for a
week and that makes Ruzya want to run away.

" 'Speaking of the perpetrators of these crimes,' " Ruzya dictates, tensing her facial muscles in preparation for a passage that
she must now recite without flinching, " 'the newspaper said that
the "profound hatred of the people is aroused by all these Kahns
and Yaroshetskys, Greensteins, Pers, Kaplans and Polyakovs." ' "

"I'm going to tell you a joke," the typist announces in a tone
that will entertain no objection. "A phone call: 'May I speak to
Rabinovich?'—'He's not home.'—'Is he at work?'—'No.'—'Is he
on a business trip?'—'No.'—'Did I understand you correctly?'—
'So, yes.' " The typist's laugh does not invite participation.
Fortunately, Ruzya has already heard the joke, which has been
making the rounds for a couple of years in far more convincing
renditions of a Yiddish accent than the typist was just able to produce. In fact, the typist's effort was merely a weak imitation of
Ruzya's own stereotypically flawed *r*. Before she can stop herself,

Ruzya scans the next paragraph for *r*'s, which are, of course, plentiful, then clears her throat and resumes the dictation.

" '*Ukrainian Pravda* declared that a loss to the state in'—open quote—"millions of dollars"—close quote—'had occurred through the depredations of these criminal gangs.' "

"So, I hear you are all going to be deported," says the typist suddenly. Her tone suggests a statement so obvious it needs no context.

Ruzya stares at the typist's back, at the brown knit cardigan and the ponytail slung over it. She tries very, very hard to focus on the ponytail, because what she sees in front of her eyes is the image, brown like the typist's hair but so much sharper, from the nightmare she has been having for many days: she is in a cattle car, holding Yolochka, who keeps begging for a drink of water. But Ruzya has no water. As the typist turns, seemingly surprised by the pause in the dictation, her face comes into focus and Ruzya manages to dictate the next sentence, about popular demand for the death penalty for the "fiends."

The deportation talk that pervaded Moscow in the early months of 1953 could hardly be called idle rumor, so numerous were the precedents. Starting in 1944, six different ethnic groups had been packed in their entirety into cattle cars and moved to remote areas of the Soviet Union, ostensibly for their disloyalty: the Chechens, the Ingush, the Kabardines, and the Karachayevs from the Northern Caucusus; the Tartars from the Crimea; and the ethnic Germans from the banks of the Volga. Naturally, if Jews were now found to be a nation of criminals carrying out murders on behalf of a worldwide Zionist conspiracy with the American Jewish Joint Distribution Committee at its center and the murdered Mikhoels as its main agent, they would also be deported.

The deportation, everyone assumed, would follow the show trial of the doctors.

Meanwhile, the "ugly scenes" continued, with increasing frequency and on an expanding scale. On January 17, Konstantin Omelchenko, the cultured head of Glavlit, was reproached by the Central Committee for not going far enough in writing his directive on removing books by the newfound enemies of the state from libraries: the way his order was written, apparently, only medical texts by the accused doctors and theater-related works by Mikhoels, as well as a book that portrayed some of the doctors as war heroes, would have been removed—when the order should have covered all books written by or containing any mention of the "fiends."

In March, leaders of the Writers' Union wrote a letter to the Central Committee entitled "On Measures Undertaken by the Secretariat of the Writers' Union to Unburden the Writers' Organization of Useless Ballast." The letter identified one hundred and fifty writers—one in seven Moscow section members—to be dumped. The letter was signed by Writers' Union chairman Aleksandr Fadeyev and his two deputies, Aleksey Surkov and Konstantin Simonov. At least two of the men—Fadeyev and Simonov—were married to Jewish women. Fadeyev would commit suicide in 1956 in what the Russian literary world has consistently interpreted as an act of atonement. The other two survived with their reputations intact: the fact that they signed the letter was not generally known. Various members of my own family lived in the same apartment complex as the Simonovs for years; there were social connections and even a romantic entanglement, and all of us perceived the association as a proud one.

Of all the wretched letters written during the early months of 1953, one that was not published for over forty years held the greatest significance. In February, an ostracized historian and a

journalist made the rounds of Moscow's few remaining prominent Jews, pressuring them to sign an open letter decrying the rise
of anti-Semitism in response to the "Doctors' Plot" and asking
Stalin to move the Jews to Siberia for their own protection. The
letter, which was slated for publication in *Pravda,* would have
launched the deportation process. Something—perhaps the writer
Ilya Ehrenburg's refusal to sign—held up the publication for a
week or two, by which time Stalin had died and the "anti-
cosmopolitan" machine abruptly stopped. The process halted, but
no Russian Jew emerged from what one writer called "the
shameful years" both alive and uncompromised. As a prominent
poet is said to have remarked about Ehrenburg, "He was cowardly; whoever was not, was killed."

My two grandmothers survived. My two grandmothers compromised. They made similar decisions for similar reasons: Ruzya became a censor while Ester agreed to work at the NKVD. That
their stories are ultimately so different was a function of circumstance more than intention. Ester failed the medical exam and ultimately had nothing to atone for. Ruzya happened to be very
good at her job.

Hers was not a mechanical job. The censors thought that they
were working with clear guidelines and a transparent set of standards, but the foreign correspondents found the censorship to be
frustratingly, mind-bogglingly changeable. A line that was cut
from one correspondent's copy might pass in another's—especially if submitted during a different shift. The correspondents
whiled away endless hours, possibly as many as they spent in the
Central Telegraph hall waiting for their copy to be cleared, wondering about their censors—their personalities, tastes, and reason-
ing. "Who the censors are, how they are chosen, whether men or

women—these questions have been subjects of endless, and some-times bitter, speculation among correspondents, waiting into the night as dinners get cold and faraway editors get hot," wrote Daniel Schorr in a *New York Times Magazine* article published in 1958, shortly after he returned from working as a CBS correspon-dent in Moscow. "It is believed that most of the censors are men, judging from the heavy hand (literally, as well as figuratively) with which they wield the black pencil."

In 1997 I met Schorr and told him that the censor who man-gled the Americans' copy most often was a diminutive young Jewish woman, and I suggested that, since he still traveled the world, he might meet my grandmother one day. Schorr was dis-mayed to hear that she is Jewish, and taken aback at the prospect of meeting her. "After hating that guy for forty years, I don't think I can face a sweet little lady," he explained. "Tell her hello, and tell her that the rest of the message is deleted."

I passed on the message nervously, but my grandmother greeted it with her most contagious laugh.

Meanwhile, in a short piece he wrote for National Public Radio, Schorr said that hearing about my grandmother was like learning who his "masked executioner" had been. This I chose not to pass on. He was talking about a land and a time when mil-lions of people were executed—the only thing my grandmother butchered was copy.

Then I got hold of a long-out-of-print memoir by Harrison Salisbury, Ruzya's all-time favorite charge. Salisbury was different: for several of the chilliest years of my grandmother's tenure—the early 1950s—he was the only foreign newspaperman in Moscow: the rest were wire-service scribes, whose jobs did not require them to analyze the news. Unlike many of his colleagues, who stayed in Moscow because they were married to Russian women who could not leave, Salisbury, a bachelor, was not one of Stalin's

SECRETS, 1943–1953   275

hostages. Nor did his political beliefs necessitate the sort of compromises that skewed some other Moscow correspondents' dispatches. Salisbury had no special expertise on Russia when he arrived—he never really mastered the language—but he stayed for a long time, and he had a talent for noticing simple things. He was also possessed of a dogged determination to work the censorship system, sometimes hounding Glavlit with complaints, other times substituting his intuitive guesses for analysis in his stories—to see the censor's reaction and gauge his own accuracy that way.

"What does a censor do with a cable which he or she passes verbatim after one hour and forty-five minutes—sit staring at it for one hour and forty-five minutes?" the huffy correspondent wrote in a letter to Omelchenko in February 1953. "Or does he or she sit drinking tea and reading light literature until the spirit moves him or her to do a small amount of work? Yours in some asperity, Harrison E. Salisbury." The answer was neither, of course. In all likelihood, an hour and forty-five minutes was how long it took Ruzya to read the piece, translate one or two paragraphs that gave her pause, call them in to Stalin's secretariat, and get them cleared.

But most of what Salisbury wrote was not cleared. In January 1950, for example, the censor killed thirteen—or about half—of Salisbury's stories outright, and severely mangled the remainder. The reporter vacillated between badgering his editors at the *New York Times* to include a "cleared by Soviet censor" disclaimer with his articles (they never did) and trying to use the censorship system to obtain information. "I was impressed by the nuances that could be adduced by careful phrasing and rephrasing of my submissions to the censors," he later wrote. In February 1950 Salisbury guessed that the Soviet Union wanted to indicate a willingness to enter into negotiations with the United States on some key issues, including atomic control. Unable to obtain confirmation in a conventional manner, he wrote a speculative story and waited for the censor's reaction. The censor's approval, which came after thirty hours, served as his confirmation. He proceeded to write four more dispatches on the subject, which were held up by Glavlit for five days before being cleared, presumably by Stalin himself. Salisbury even received a phone call from the Central Telegraph inviting him to come in and transmit the series.

For a journalist in Moscow, isolated and denied the usual tools of reporting—Salisbury was allowed neither to travel nor to have any contact with ordinary Soviet citizens—to be able to tell his readers anything new, as Salisbury occasionally managed to do, was a reporting coup. Not until a decade and a half later did he learn that his success very nearly cost him his life. The Soviet secret police were becoming increasingly harsh in dealings with foreign correspondents. In January 1949 NBC's Bob Magidoff was accused of being a spy and thrown out of the country. A few weeks later Anna Louise Strong, an American reporter exceedingly sympathetic to the Soviet regime, was arrested on espionage charges and held for a week before being expelled from the country. The Russian staff of the *Moscow Daily News,* an English-language paper on which she had worked, stayed behind—in jail; the paper itself was shut down.

Around this time Salisbury, who had first worked in the Soviet Union during World War II, arrived for his second stint in Russia, and soon demonstrated an uncannily good understanding of his assignment. Whether he was writing stories that the Soviet authorities wanted published—as was the case with Stalin's unspoken diplomatic initiatives—or banging his head against the wall writing pieces that would never see print, every time Salisbury's intuition or his powers of observation yielded an unusually accurate guess, it affirmed someone's suspicion that the journalist employed a well-placed source or sources. When a search for the leak proved fruitless, a discussion on eliminating Salisbury apparently ensued. As a Soviet defector would tell him many years later, there was a plan to give Salisbury a drug that would paralyze him and, if it did not kill him right away, necessitate his immediate evacuation; but some glitch in the plan granted the journalist a last-minute reprieve.

So here was the chain of events: Salisbury wandered the streets of Moscow, collecting tiny snippets of information where he could get them, and wrote his pieces. Ruzya translated them, often in their entirety, and killed them after calling them in to Stalin's secretariat. Then she included them in the digests submitted to Omelchenko. Omelchenko's secretary ran off the twenty or so copies that landed on various desks within the NKVD and Interior Ministry systems. The officers behind those desks read the journalist's dispatches, were duly impressed, and made a plan to cripple him—or worse. Is there such a thing as an innocent cog in a killing machine?

In all fairness, unenviable as Salisbury's position was, he probably faced lesser risks than any Soviet citizen—including the censor herself. But Salisbury's writing would not have been half as good nor his perceptions half as sharp had he not allowed the Moscow of the early 1950s to chill him to the bone. As he recalled, when he read the announcement of the "Doctors' Plot" on January 13, 1953, he instantly imagined the way the web would spread to envelop—to kill—many in Stalin's inner circle, who would be accused of being agents of Zionism and world imperialism, drafted perhaps by George Kennan, the recently expelled U.S. ambassador to Moscow, who was aided in his dirty deed by, say, an American journalist who lent him his dacha: Harrison Salisbury. So this was why my grandmother Ruzya still remembers Salisbury's articles as the most torturously enjoyable part of her job: they were good journalism because they were about her, their main reader; they were terrifying because they were true. The censor and the reporter lived the same fear.

DECEMBER 1, 1999

"I knew," says my grandmother Ruzya. "I was absolutely conscious that my work, to put it bluntly—that my work had a bad smell. But I held on to it quite consciously. More than that, I loved my job, because, in essence, I was a translator. I was a translator who had to produce very exact translations because I answered for them with my head, and my translations were immediately delivered by car or transmitted over a direct line all the way up as high as Stalin, you understand, and, basically, it was there that the decisions were made, while I just implemented them, so to speak. But nonetheless, of course, I never thought then and I continue not to think that the role I played is to my credit. I was compelled to do it because it was the period of that horrible anti-cosmopolitan campaign, so this was, you understand, a forced measure, of course, but at the same time it testified neither to the strength of my character nor to my courage nor to a desire to resist, you understand, it meant only that I acquiesced to the circumstances that life had forced on me. That's all. Which is why I think that I do not look good in your book. Unlike your other grandmother, who has a hero's biography."

Ruzya holds to this opinion even when I remind her that Ester agreed to work for the NKVD. That job—translation and nothing but translation—would not have been shameful, she maintains. In any case, ultimately, Ester did not work for the NKVD, and so we remember only Biysk, where she refused to become an informer. And so Ruzya, as though forgetting that when she was sixteen she, too, refused a similar proposal, maintains that she is the one who compromised and my other grandmother, the hero, did not. Admiration untouched by jealousy is in that nod to jointly crafted family legend, which distributes the roles so neatly. Life happens to be more complicated.

PART SIX

STALIN'S FUNERAL

1953–1959

Ester and Sergei at the resort where they met.

Chapter Twenty-one

MARCH 6, 1953, 7 A.M.

In the blue blackness of early morning Bella's shouts ring out like cries for help, and Sasha is fully awake and ready to rush to her aid before he realizes she is screaming for joy.

"Dead!" she shouts. "He is dead!" she repeats, and turns the radio volume up as she leaves the kitchen to spread the word through the apartment, which she has already awakened with her screams.

Sasha stops in the hallway in front of his parents' room to pull up his pajama bottoms and let his mother and his grandmother, rushing toward each other like long-lost lovers, meet in the doorway. His father sits up in bed looking on, frowning.

MARCH 6, 1953, 8 A.M.

Yolochka carries a sense of special knowledge with her today, and now that she has caught up to one of her classmates, also walking to school, she anticipates an opportunity to boast of it. The other girl looks like she has been crying, and she makes no effort to conceal her red eyes and nose the way an eleven-year-old normally would: there is something terribly adult in the way she is trying to project her grief.

"Comrade Stalin died," she stage-whispers to Yolochka, skipping greetings that would seem lighthearted and inappropriate today.

"I know." Yolochka seizes the opportunity. "They came to get my mother for work in the middle of the night, and I woke up and asked what happened. My mother said, 'Nothing happened. Stalin died.' "

The girl, stricken, stares at Yolochka. "What do you mean, 'Nothing happened'?" She starts to cry and breaks off from Yolochka, rushing toward the school, toward the company of other children and adults who would better understand her singular, terrifying loss.

At the school, children and adults alike are inconsolable and disoriented. Nothing, it is clear, is or can be the same anymore. Even the most difficult and serious of classes would seem frivolous in the face of grief. So children cry sitting at their desks while teachers force back tears to announce that school will let out early today. There will be no school tomorrow, they assume; indeed, it is hard to believe there will be school ever again.

Some girls seem overcome, wailing, flailing, shocking their classmates and teachers and deepening their sense that the world either has or is about to hurtle out of control. Yolochka wonders whether she, too, needs to cry. She tries to summon tears by thinking of the moment she learned of Stalin's death, but her mother's words—"Nothing happened"—make her feel calm, even sleepy. She can feel nothing of the emotions raging about her, but even she knows she cannot sit at her desk reading. She tries to sit idly instead, and she succeeds for a few long, torturous minutes, before she opens her textbook. The printed lines reassure her, but she tries her best to hold back from reading. Her hands find a soft-leaded black pencil, and she starts doodling in her textbook. She draws a thick black frame around a picture of Stalin in the book—the sort of frame the newspapers always place around the faces of dead people. Then carefully, in large, thickly drawn block letters, she writes HOLIDAY. She ascribes no joy to this word: she just means that there are no classes today.

MARCH 7, 1953, 9 A.M.

At first Ruzya mistakes it for quiet. It is not; it is the absence of the usual frenetic Gorky Street current, the Brownian motion of people and cars, each with its own separate urgency. Today this part of Gorky Street is closed off to civilian cars and to pedestrians who lack special passes—Ruzya has one because the Central Telegraph building, where she works, is located in the lower part of this street. There are still a fair number of people around, but even the way they walk seems different today, perhaps because their thoughts are united by a single focus: the body, lying in state barely three blocks away, in the Hall of Columns, the ostentatious, chandelier-flooded building across from the Kremlin. It is Stalin's final stepping-stone on his way to the mausoleum in Red Square, where even now stonecutters are engraving his name next to Lenin's over the entrance. And there is the quiet, which is not quiet at all but the distance of noise, which is coming to this deadened street from the cordons, formed by trucks whose drivers are constantly gunning their engines to keep from freezing, and from Bolshaya Dmitrovka, the street just below Gorky, where hundreds of thousands are marching, pushing, trampling, clawing, and crawling to see the dead man, to bow their heads before the ruler one last time.

It has been a long, hard, wonderful day. It began more than twenty-four hours ago, with the messenger ringing her bell and stating the news right there on the threshold. It was not the first time she was fetched in the middle of the night when she was resting after a day shift: lesser stories, or the whims of American reporters, had often required her presence at the Central Telegraph. Sometimes she found it annoying, other times she was glad to be yanked out of her mother's house with its endless quibbles and quarrels. But this time she felt a warmth, a happiness, spread steadily through her being as she awoke and dressed and steered her mind toward the story she knew she was about to read over and over. An initial communiqué on Stalin's ailment had come out two days earlier, signaling that someone on high thought things quite hopeless. In fact, she thought at the time that he might already be dead. In any case, she was not surprised when the news came to her doorstep, and she was certain of how she felt about it.

The driver delivered her to the Central Telegraph building around the same time that correspondents began to arrive, apparently prepared to sit vigil for as long as it took; she knew they had been frantic and sleepless for two days. Salisbury had apparently been moved to write something, anything, during the wait: there were two stories on her desk, one about the ways Moscow correspondents have of begging Stalin by letter for information handouts and the other about Stalin's early attempts at poetry. There was a lengthy quote in this story, full of blooming flowers, flying

larks, and seventeen-year-old patriotism. Ruzya read the two stories and pushed them aside with a smile: these were not standard
regurgitative fare, so they could not be cleared at her level, and
she was certain there would be no one on hand to wave them
through from the top. More writing for her eyes only.

At 4 A.M. exactly, TASS, the government news agency, cabled
the news. Salisbury was first off the mark, with a story already
written. Within minutes, she heard shouting and banging from
the correspondents' waiting room, then an odd screeching pop—
and then a silence that she assumed to be of the shocked variety.
The secretary walked in, her face already tear-streaked and her
hair somehow disheveled. From what Ruzya could gather from
the young woman's disjointed, sobbing report, the correspondents had very nearly stormed the counter and the room's two
phone booths, but the switchboard operator had long since received instructions to put no international calls through. The correspondents had lost all fear and sense of decorum, and a
technician had put a stop to the pandemonium by removing the
back of the switchboard and yanking out the main cable.

By this time one of the secret-police handlers, who must have
arrived just before Ruzya did, informed her that nothing was to
be cleared. Nothing, of course, meant nothing, not even dispatches that repeated the TASS cable word for word—there was a
small stream of those coming from correspondents willing to try
anything to get something out under their names. So Ruzya did
nothing. She did not fiddle; she did not read; she did not attempt
to occupy herself with some neglected organizing task. She sat
back and dreamed. It was the oddest kind of daydream, coming as
it did in the middle of the night, and conjuring only what she
knew to be the absolute truth. He was dead. The monster, the
tyrant, the murderer, dead, dead, dead. In a different setting she
might have danced for joy. Here she let herself luxuriate in a

knowledge that needed no elaboration to be possibly the best news she had ever heard.

Just before eight o'clock she was told to start working. Twenty-four hours of the same story followed. Even as she grew tired, Ruzya made the pleasurable mental note that reporting the death of Stalin was quickly becoming routine. Before she left work, she was handed a pass that allowed her to walk on Gorky Street. She called home from the pay phone just outside the Central Telegraph; Yolochka said she would have no school today but that the teacher had told Ruzya to come in and see her urgently.

Out on Gorky Street, the roar of engines and the hum of the distant crowd are disconcerting, but her joy refuses to abate. Ruzya heads for the large Yeliseyevskiy food store on the other side of the street: while everyone else is in a paroxysm of mourning, or at least agitation, Ruzya intends to celebrate by shopping for food. She buys all the things she cannot find when the usual crowds fill the stores: salmon caviar, beef tongue, and smoked sturgeon.

In a few days, after Moscow goes back, tentatively, to its routine ways, Ruzya will go to see Yolochka's teacher, who will take Yolochka's desecrated textbook from some hiding place in her desk and tell Ruzya to talk to her daughter and buy her a new textbook. She will mean that surely this kind of thing—implying, in effect, that Stalin's death was a joyous holiday—could land the mother in jail and her child in a special orphanage for the off-spring of "enemies of the people." Ruzya will thank her and smile, taking the book. The teacher will take this smile as a sign of gratitude and an acknowledgment of Ruzya's uncommonly good luck. It will in fact be the fear lifting.

MARCH 7, 1953, 3 P.M.

Ester can see the cold even before she feels it as she nears the glass doors of her office building. The people outside—there must be thousands in Pushkin Square—have telltale red ears, and the men have a white coating over their five o'clock shadows. She tries to pull her coat closed over her belly and steels herself for the cold and the crowd outside. She does not remember being so protective of her body when she was carrying Sasha. Nor does she remember being so tired, so weighed down and so clumsy, waddling on her swollen feet, or so impatient to get to the finish line. By her count, she is eight months pregnant, and this time she is counting the days.

She had always thought she would have a large family. Her father had seventeen brothers and sisters, and her mother had nine, and those aunts and uncles produced lots of cousins, so Ester's parents' three-person unit always seemed like an oddity in the family (or, for that matter, in the town). Even as she half-consciously reaped the benefits of being an only child—her mother's undivided love, her father's unconditional devotion—she made plans to live her life differently. But it must have been very soon after Sasha was born that she knew she wanted no more children with Boris. This was not a heartrending realization—after all, she had not wasted time trying to convince herself she loved him—more a sense of disappointment that seemed to have been there, and growing, from the day she agreed to marry him. It grew until she was certain she wanted a divorce; he was just as certain he did not. She worked on him and on devising the means to leave someone who refused to be left, trying to figure out a way around the naked fact that she and Bella and Sasha had no place to go. She tried to have an affair and failed. The disappointment grew. And then, not that long ago, no more than a year, she realized that if she were going to have more children, it would have to be with Boris. She got pregnant almost right away, proving that she was, after all, still in control of her life.

She steps out onto the sidewalk, intending to walk along its inner edge until she can get to Gorky Street, just half a block away, and find a way to get across to the other side, where her apartment building stands. She touches the wall of the building with her right arm as she walks, like a blind person; this creates a buffer zone between her and the wall, against which she is afraid of being pushed. The crowd is so thick it seems jammed in places, where the force pushing down toward Bolshaya Dmitrovka Street has met resistance, or perhaps where someone failed to walk fast enough or—she wonders if this might be the case—fell down. Not that she is surprised so many people are willing to risk bruises or worse to see the monster in state, but an awful kind of irritation is rising through her as she pushes against the tide of these people, humiliated and duped by the man even in death.

As she nears the corner of Gorky Street, she has to push away from the wall and walk into the sidewalk. She immediately feels that walking is more difficult. She puts her arms out, hands in front of her belly, but the tide is pushing against her. She turns right and left, and too late she thinks of turning around to join the tide: she cannot. *I am going to be trampled,* she realizes. A gloved hand, with a thick covering of black hair between the glove and the sleeve, comes over and between the shoulders of two of the people about to trample her and grabs her forearm. She pushes back instinctively, forcing the hand away from her belly, and the hand yanks hard and again, and pulls, refusing to yield, until Ester is wedged somehow between those two shoulders. She closes her eyes for a second, feels herself twirling, and then a tall unshaven man in a square black cap is shouting at her: "What are you doing here?"

"I work here."

"Go home, you idiot!" The man has not let go of her hand, and now he is pulling her along Gorky Street, away from the crowd. "Go home!"

"I am!" she shouts back, and adds, "Thank you."

Sasha was reasonably happy to have to stay home with his grand-mother today, but the full meaning of staying home really seeped in only a couple of hours ago. His mother had told him as he was going to sleep the night before that he could not, under any circumstances, go outside. He slept late. He read after breakfast, a thick brown book about microbes, which failed to keep his attention. He switched to his favorite, *The Three Musketeers,* but after a couple of hours he began to feel restless. He listened to the radio, a sequence of speeches and morbid pronouncements. He started in on his grandmother. He just wanted to go take a look, just one look at whatever he was not supposed to see out there on the street. Finally Bella relented, and now he is waiting downstairs as she makes her slow way. She has told him he will have to hold her hand constantly, and they will only just go outside the courtyard onto Gorky Street and turn back. Just a peek: she has taken him literally, as she usually does.

As they walk through the yard and into the huge stone archway, the howl gets louder and clearer. When they are out on the sidewalk, Bella giving him the agreed-upon minute before they have to turn back, the noise is unbearable. The awful minute seems to last forever. The black cars and olive green trucks moving through this part of the street are blowing their horns. A bigger noise is coming from a distance: the city's factories are blowing their horns. The city is screaming. This is the sound of fear.

The despot engendered as much fear in death as he had in life. The announcement of his passing hypnotized the country, spreading ever wider the mass hysteria that had characterized the past decades. Hundreds, possibly thousands, were trampled in the streets leading to the Hall of Columns. Their bloodied bodies were carried endlessly, it seemed, past Ruzya's basement windows. There appear to have been a number of trampling incidents: in courtyards off Dmitrovka; in Pushkin Square, where the stranger saved Ester; and in Trubnaya Ploshad, a square at the foot of two steep hills, which saw people, some of them already dead, rolling down to a stop in the square, which had turned into a round pool of blood. This despite the fact that Moscow had been closed off, as were some of the central streets, in order to limit the number of people trying to get to the body. The number of desperate mourners doomed all attempts at crowd control, inept as they were.

Like a family that has lost a violent and all-powerful father, households across the Soviet Union went into deep, obsessive mourning—even though hundreds of thousands of these families had lost someone to the Gulag. Former prisoners describe the grief that descended on camps whose occupants had been put there by Stalin. The intelligent, the insightful, the educated, succumbed. The Soviet Union's most admired dissident, Andrei Sakharov, then still a loyal servant of the regime, recalled falling into an altered state in the days following Stalin's death. "In those days I veered far off the path, as they say," he wrote. "In a letter to [my wife] Klava—intended for her eyes only, naturally—I wrote, 'I am under the impression of a great man's death. Thinking about his humanity.' . . . Very soon I came to blush when recalling those words. How to explain their appearance? I still cannot understand it fully. I already knew a lot about the terrible crimes—arrests of the innocent, torture, hunger, violence. I could not have thought of those responsible with any emotion other than outrage and disgust. Of course, I was far from knowing everything and connecting what I knew into one cohesive picture. And somewhere in my subconscious there was the idea, impressed on me by the propaganda machine, that major historical events make cruelty unavoidable. Additionally, I was certainly affected by the general atmosphere of mourning, the emotional awareness of everyone's susceptibility to death. In short, it appears, I was more impressionable than I would have liked to think."

There were very, very few people in the entire country who felt consciously happy in the days of early March 1953. Ester and Ruzya were among them. Being Jewish certainly helped: it meant that for the preceding two months, following the arrests of the Jewish doctors, they had felt perched at the edge of a precipice. In Ester's case, her non-Communist upbringing played a key role: unlike her peers, she had never had to liberate herself from the Stalinist ideology they had swallowed as children. In Ruzya's case, the ten years she spent inside the censorship agency, with plenty of time to think about the nature of the bans and the banned, had cemented her difference from the mourning masses. Whatever small part of her may still have believed when she was a schoolgirl, or during her brief life with Samuil the believer, had long since died. Now she felt only one thing: glee.

When the messenger rang the doorbell in the early morning of March 6, Ruzya's mother came out into the hallway, wrapped in a sleepy gray shawl. "Comrade Stalin has died, and Comrade Solodovnik must report for work," the man at the threshold announced, and Eva burst into tears. *My mother is an idiot,* Ruzya noted to herself with a cruel midnight clarity. Two days later she went to the theater with a good friend from school. "How terrible that he is dead," the friend said, for no one talked of anything else then. Ruzya exploded. "What are you saying?" she said. "Dead is a tyrant, the executioner of hundreds of thousands." She did not know then that his victims numbered in the millions, but she had her friend convinced in three minutes flat. But she had to trust her friend to make the arguments: it would be another three years before it was safe to engage in this kind of discussion in public.

Ester and Ruzya—three years into their fast friendship by this point—may have bonded even more through their shared joy, but what each felt was different. Ester was profoundly optimistic, nearly convinced that death itself was a form of revenge and certain that justice was now within reach. Ruzya's joy was a form of detachment, a way of separating herself from her weeping colleagues and sobbing mother. This very detachment is part of what makes her remarkable. The distinguishing characteristic of her generation—the trait that made them the Komsomol's most devout members, Stalin's most loyal soldiers, and much later, in the case of a very few, the dissident movement's founders and guiding lights—was its ongoing profound engagement with the country. Sakharov, in trying to decipher why he was so moved by Stalin's death, finally concluded that the main reason was that he "felt a part of the same mission that, it seemed to me, Stalin had undertaken: creating the might of the country so that it may live in peace following a terrible war."

In 1936, at the dawn of the Great Terror, André Gide wrote in his book *Return from the USSR* (where it was banned for its fairly harsh criticisms of Soviet life), "I do not think there is any place other than the USSR where one can feel with such force that one belongs to humanity. Despite the language barrier, I have never felt myself to be more of a comrade and a brother."

But after ten years of working to safeguard the country's secrets and its image, Ruzya did not feel she was part of a community of "brothers"—with the qualified exceptions of one of her own three brothers, Boba and the high-school gang, and Ester. Even they, though, were separated from her by the secrets she carried around. Several members of the gang, like many others of their generation, would later go through the wrenching process of finally disengaging from a society and a regime that had fooled them, imprisoned them, humiliated and sacrificed them. In the 1970s their peers would invent the term *internal émigré*—a sort of double entendre that perfectly described the state of having escaped the country by finding refuge inside one's own head. Ruzya achieved this state much earlier than most, while she was working at Glavlit, staying sane and sure, thanks to no one but herself and one or two perceptive foreigners she would never meet. Detachment was her best defense—and a radical position to have staked out in the forties and fifties.

So while Ester celebrated, all but dancing with Bella in the narrow hallway of their apartment, Ruzya felt a more private, calm kind of joy, rooted in the certainty that now things would not get worse. For a woman who had been stalked by a nightmare about cattle cars, this was a happy time.

APRIL 4, 1953, 3 A.M.

"Unlawfully arrested by the former minister of state security of the USSR without any legal basis." Ruzya rereads the phrase in the morning's *Pravda* to make sure she understands it correctly. Yes, it says the Kremlin doctors were "unlawfully arrested without any legal basis." That their confessions were obtained through "unacceptable means." That the state is releasing them! That their "accomplices" are also being released! And that Dr. Lydia Timashuk, the woman who originally denounced the doctors and went on to star in the case, is being stripped of her Order of Lenin—because, it says, it was "incorrectly awarded."

"That bitch, that animal, that lowlife!" Ruzya whispers her Timashuk litany, but the last insult comes out kind of crumpled, uninspired, because the woman, Ruzya realizes, is no one now, and she does not warrant this kind of attention. Less than a month after Stalin's death, the case against the doctors is over. And it is all Ruzya can do not to shout out or drum a victory beat on her desk—do something, anything, that is never done. She has sat alone in this room through so many nights and so many news stories, but this is the first time she has been one-on-one with good news. She is on the night shift, so it will be at least an hour or two before the first of the correspondents come in and she can find a reflection of her joy in the notes they pass from the other side of the wall. She picks up the phone and dials Batsheva's number: her mother-in-law, she knows without thinking about it, is the person who would most love to know.

A sleepy, creaky voice answers on the sixth ring. It is Ida, the tiny old lady whose room is closest to the tall table with the heavy black telephone. *What am I doing,* Ruzya gasps as she quickly puts two fingers down on the telephone hook. *It's three o'clock in the morning!*

APRIL 4, 1953, 5 P.M.

A huge woman moves down Gorky Street in a drunken waddle. Days from giving birth and on her way home from work, Ester is sober, of course: she is simply unhinged by the day's news. The release of the doctors—thirteen of the original fifteen arrested; two have already died—seems to her much more than justice partially restored to a few. It feels like manna from heaven, joy to the world, a miracle. She walks down the too-wide sidewalk scanning the faces of other pedestrians, and when she spots the dark kinky hair and the prominent noses of Jews, she offers a tentative smile that, in most cases, leads directly to a hug. Her momentary acquaintances end up embracing her belly more than her self, but this strikes her as appropriate: she is bringing her child into a world that just might be livable.

Though they will spend an hour and a half on the phone tonight, right now Ruzya and Ester do not embrace; they are moving in opposite directions on sidewalks on different sides of Gorky Street, and they do not see each other across the eight-lane road. After working a double shift, Ruzya is going to Batsheva's to pick up Yolochka. In her rush, she answers the smiles she encounters with a perfunctory wave. Not that she is oblivious to the meaning of the stories she has been reading all day, but all that work and all that emotion have left her drained and withdrawn into a haze. It is only when she finally arrives at Batsheva's and the older woman runs up to embrace her in the hallway that Ruzya realizes the source of all that friendliness was the good news of the day: it does, after all, affect not just her little family unit but all the hundreds of thousands of Jews in this country.

As the older woman's bulk moves out of the way, Ruzya spots the tiny Ida behind her. "It was you who called last night, wasn't it?" the old lady asks.

"Yes." Ruzya prepares to apologize, but Ida cuts her off.

"You could have told me. I would only have been grateful."

Within weeks of the end of the Doctors' Plot accusations and, with it, the anti-cosmopolitan campaign, Ruzya was inducted into the Communist Party, quickly and without fanfare. Someone in the Glavlit Party organization restarted the process that had been stalled for five years; someone else quickly wrote her recommendation; the whole event had the feel of an inconsequential transaction.

Chapter Twenty-two

MAY 1956

At 7:45 in the morning Ruzya is getting ready to leave work. Not physically ready, mind you—even though leaving early or arriving late for work no longer carries a criminal penalty, as it did in Stalin's time, she still would not risk her job for anything—but mentally ready, slowly detaching and relaxing. The Americans are done for the night, which, from their perspective, followed an uneventful day. Though foreign correspondents are not nearly so isolated as they were just two years ago, most of them still do not have a sense of the city, do not know that it is buzzing with an event of monumental proportions. An Italian film festival opened in Moscow yesterday. In a city of millions, only a few hundred will be able to attend each day—and these will be only the carefully selected, the well connected, the preternaturally lucky—but everyone is talking about it. Some pass around lists of films with brief synopses and musical, otherworldly names: Mario Matolli, Federico Fellini, Renato Castellani, Sophia Loren. Each star, each director, sounds like a genius and a beauty. Ruzya wonders briefly whether the Italian correspondents realized the magnitude of the event on which they surely reported yesterday, during the day shift. No, of course they did not. They could not know.

It is another ten minutes to the end of her shift when the secretary walks in with an envelope. A late dispatch? An early one? In an envelope?

"The Italian correspondents brought this for you," the secretary mumbles, and disappears back behind the door.

The envelope is unsealed—to save the secretary the trouble of steaming it open. There is a small piece of thin cardboard—a ticket to the morning show at the festival. There is no note.

No, of course she cannot go. The Italian correspondents have no doubt planned it so that they would be sitting on either side of her. Everyone wants to see the censor, and the censor cannot be seen. But the movie has to be seen. What are the stakes, after all? She is no longer afraid of the cattle cars. If the secretary reports her, if she is caught at the movie theater, if the Italians brag of their invention, she could lose her job. This is a great price to pay for seeing a movie. Is it too great?

In the two hours before the morning show begins, Ruzya walks to the movie theater, taking a circuitous route, stopping at several food stores, pausing to think on the Big Stone Bridge over the Moscow River, where she plans her steps in detail. She will wait in the large foyer until the film is about to begin and will slip into her seat once the lights go down. She will slip out before they go back on. She will not take off her beret. She will look at the screen and never to the sides.

She does exactly as she has planned. She never forgets the curious correspondents at her sides; she does not loosen her coat or take off her hat, even as she starts to sweat; and she gets up and leaves without looking back at the film's last frames.

She will always remember that movie—Federico Fellini's *La Strada*—as the best film she ever saw. For days and weeks she will remember the moment when she left the theater, as Anthony Quinn, the crude circus performer Zampanò, who let his one true love get away, walks off into the sea.

She recalls and rehearses the story of Zampanò's life as she makes her way home and, once there, while she gets ready for bed and goes to sleep. She will tell it to Yolochka tonight, when they go for their walk. How tense these walks make her. She invented them as an antidote to Yolochka's reading. Her daughter reads everywhere, all the time: in class, holding her book half under the desk; at home after she goes to bed, huddling under her blanket with a flashlight; in the reading room at the library, where she goes after school and stays till closing. She is regularly caught reading and punished for it: her teachers summon Ruzya to school; her grandmother Eva takes away Yolochka's flashlight; Ruzya herself goes to libraries and demands that her reading-room membership be revoked. Yolochka just finds another library to join, locking Ruzya into a hopeless chase. Soon she is also going to reading groups and young writers' groups. Ruzya has wasted hours trying to explain that this dusty habit of reading all day is unhealthy, that she is resorting to desperate measures only to make sure her little girl gets some fresh air.

Ruzya felt sure Yolochka would develop some terrible disease that afflicted sedentary children and this would mean that she, her mother, had failed. The nightly walks were her attempt at compromise: if Yolochka insisted on going to the library every day, then she would have to accompany her mother on a walk every night. Yolochka submitted in wounded silence at first, and Ruzya struggled to find topics or stories that would make their wanderings along the crooked, dimly lit streets enjoyable. But what could she, with her top-secret job and precious little free time, tell her well-read daughter? She talked about the theater, mostly, the shows she attended with friends; her thirteen-year-old listened sullenly, dropping occasional comments that made Ruzya suspect she did not know theater as well as her daughter did. Then one day Yolochka suggested she could recite some poetry to her mother, and Ruzya heard poems she had never known—by Alexander Blok, Marina Tsvetaeva, Anna Akhmatova. Yolochka seemed to have memorized entire books; she recited them every time now when they went outside, sometimes shifting between poets in such a way that they seemed to be talking to one another, other times literally going through an entire poetry collection from memory.

Ruzya will sleep until about seven in the evening. Then she will dress and have breakfast and wait for Yolochka, who will be home from the library for their date at eight. They will go outside, and Ruzya will tell her daughter that she went to the movies this morning—yes, in the morning, yes, alone; you would not believe what I saw: a Fellini film at the Italian festival; yes, the one the whole city is talking about. Then she will tell her everything: what it looks like, how it is shot, and, most important, the story line. And, of course, how good the actors are. She will be offering something of value to her daughter, who will take away to her friends some much-sought-after information from the fascinating, inaccessible Italian film festival.

MARCH 8, 1956

A wispy boy in a short jacket stands in the doorway, shifting from foot to foot. Ruzya takes the roses—they are short-stemmed and, it seems, countless, the bouquet coming apart in her arms, looking like it will separate into so many flowers she will never be able to put it back together—and thanks the boy, not even attempting to look like she ever expected to take delivery of a bunch of red roses. A note on a small, official-looking card informs her that "from now, whatever happens, you will always receive a bouquet of roses on International Women's Day."

Inside four months she will marry the author of that note, the tall, elegant, square-jawed Semyon Zenin, a writer and a talker. He showed up barely a week ago, announcing himself with a businesslike phone call: he claimed he wanted to take German lessons. He had been referred by a friend of hers—no big surprise, since all her friends knew she was in perpetual need of additional income. But this friend, as it turned out, was playing matchmaker from the start. She prepared for a first lesson, but he took her to a restaurant instead, and he talked. Later she will learn that friends say, "Zenin with two shots of vodka inside him is not yet a talker, and Zenin with four shots inside him is no longer a talker." He ordered precisely three shots, drank the vodka fast, and talked all night; she was hooked.

It has been fourteen years since she was widowed. And oh, there have been men. Her first postwar romance, that desolate affair with the married colonel, dragged on for years, but ultimately she thawed enough to love. There was Alexander, a boy eight years younger than she, who climbed in through her bedroom window at night and proclaimed undying love for two years. But his mother, an aging Austrian Jew obsessed with the idea of returning home—she would eventually succeed in 1961, after nearly thirty years' efforts—would not hear of taking on an older woman with a child, and so Alexander ultimately retreated. There has been love and conflict and drama that she has sworn not to tell her granddaughter about, at least not until after this book has been published. But now here is Semyon, fourteen years older than she, a man, not a boy, a survivor whose wounds do not embarrass him: he turns them into stories.

Unlike Ruzya, he had an adult life before the war. A Jew, and a believer like Samuil—incredibly, this one, too, admires secret-police founder Dzerzhinsky, and, incredibly, this holds a certain nostalgic charm for her—Semyon became a member of the Komsomol in the 1920s and an "ideology worker" in the 1930s. He was an editor at *Izvestia,* the country's second-largest newspaper, under the direction of Nikolai Bukharin, Stalin's once-ally and occasional critic. *Izvestia* of the mid-thirties was one of the last bastions of revolutionary romanticism, though by then one had to be highly discerning to read any criticism between the lines of Bukharin's articles. Bukharin's staff included several old Bolsheviks—participants in the revolution, a breed already endangered by Stalinist purges. The topic at which the editors hammered away most tirelessly was the inevitability of a war with Germany and the intrinsically evil nature of Hitler's regime. Bukharin himself wrote of its "beastly bullying, oppression, violence and war." A paranoically insightful reader may have perceived parallels between Hitler's Germany and Stalin's Russia, but Semyon, even from his vantage point inside the editorial offices, did not see this.

Bukharin was arrested in February 1937. He would star in the grandest of Stalin's show trials, in which he and eighteen others were convicted of numerous acts of terror and espionage. Every night, it seemed, the police came for someone who worked for *Izvestia,* until the offices were decimated. Every night Semyon waited for them. They never came for him. A year went by. Every day in March 1938 Semyon did his bit to get the reports on the trial ready for the morning paper; every day moved the trial closer to its inevitable conclusion, until, in the wee hours of March 13, all nineteen defendants were sentenced to death. Two days later they were shot. More arrests followed. Once again Semyon waited for his turn, and still it did not come. Why? Semyon knew himself not to be a snitch. He could not explain his luck, and he lost his mind.

Ultimately, Semyon had to be confined. Disconnected and disoriented, he watched from inside the psychiatric ward as Stalin proclaimed friendship with Hitler's Germany and moved to divide Poland between the two countries. Semyon agreed with his doctors that he could not go back into the world outside: it no longer made any sense. Until, that is, Germany attacked the Soviet Union. It was the first event that seemed to belong in the world as Semyon knew it. He set about writing petitions to be allowed to volunteer for the front, and sometime later, after all the sane and healthy men had been used up and the military opened up to the insane, the infirm, and the very young, Semyon's petitions were granted.

He remade himself as a soldier. He dug in outside of Moscow; he held fast while the Red Army was on the defensive; and he marched forward as it began to attack, moving westward and turning into a marauding, raping mob. After four years, he still was not sure he was equipped to return to the confusing world of peacetime Russia, and so he stayed in the war, working to set up the new order in Soviet-occupied Vienna.

Accomplished, healed, finally sure of himself, he went back to Moscow, anticipating something of a hero's welcome—only to find that the country was now divided into the Jews and the non-Jews, and he was once again on the wrong side of the divide. He had no one here—that much he had prepared himself for—and he was no one but an unemployed and unemployable Jew with a history of mental illness, questionable political affiliations, and some pretty funny ideas about the way the world ought to work.

He tugged at every string he found until someone got him a low-level job at a film studio. He climbed up the ladder there slowly, hanging on by his fingernails to each successive step. Life gradually began taking shape when he found a wife, a younger Russian woman—and lost all semblance of order again when he discovered, by absurd accident, that his wife was setting him up to be arrested as a "rootless cosmopolitan." Apparently it was the apartment she was after, and Semyon cut his losses, leaving the apartment with her in it.

So here he is now, a man who truly is a rootless cosmopolitan, a man thrice reinvented and somewhat the worse for wear, living in a medium-size square room off Gorky Street. Will she marry him? He says he will bring her roses every year on Women's Day. She will. He will not.

MARCH 1956

A handwritten notice glued to the wall in their shared office announced an extraordinary meeting of the department's Party organization. So now the entire department—eight people, including the two typists, all of them, including Ruzya, Party members—are gathered for the meeting. Ruzya has a hopeful inkling of what this is about. Some of the correspondents' dispatches in the last few days have contained fishing references to a secret Khrushchev speech at the Party congress now under way—references apparently intended to gauge the censors' reaction. Ruzya has been checking the stories against the official text of Khrushchev's opening report—a mostly dull speech that contained an intriguing mention of Stalin's and his cohorts' overreaching while in power, but also praised Stalin for conquering "the enemies of the people." Rumor of the existence of a second speech seeped out a week or so after this text was released, and Ruzya has the idea that the meeting they have been called to is related to the secret speech and will therefore be worth remembering so she can retell it to her friends who are not in the Party: she is thinking, of course, of Ester. She clears her throat and prepares to listen. Her colleagues project a uniform look of strained enthusiasm, as though they expected to have to struggle to stay awake over the next couple of hours.

The secretary of their Party organization, a pudgy bespectacled man Ruzya has rarely seen, removes a thick stack of typing paper from his fat brown briefcase. "The speech of Comrade Nikita Sergeyevich Khrushchev at the Twentieth Party Congress will be read aloud in its entirety today," he announces. There is more shifting in the room; a couple of people cough preventively, as before a performance at the philharmonic.

There will be dead, stunned silence in the next hours as the reader relentlessly, with short breaks only to take drinks of water or turn the page, traces three decades of terror and betrayal. He reads letters and reports received by Stalin—alternately dry and impassioned accounts of torture and treachery. A spine broken during interrogation. A former ally pleading for intervention from the very man who has ordered him killed. And then there is more. Stalin is blamed for the Soviet Union's failure to prepare for the Nazi invasion. And he was wrong—a criminal—to deport several ethnic groups to Siberia at the end of the war. And the Doctors' Plot was a lie and a crime engineered by Stalin himself, as was virtually everything that happened in this country between 1924 and 1953. Ruzya feels herself shudder: for years she has said this, if not in so many words, and she has thought it for much longer. But to hear the truth being broadcast in the colorless voice of a Party functionary to a roomful of people who would have reported you for saying something like this just a few hours ago—this is thrilling and sickening at once. She gives no thought to why the information is finally being released. She does not care what has moved Khrushchev to break open the past: his conscience or his desire to shore up his own power. That this is happening at all—she feels like the walls of this building should be shaking in outraged disbelief. She wants to get out of this room, with its thick, astonished tension, and she wants to stay to soak in every word. Of course, this is not a choice: she cannot break Party discipline and she cannot leave even when the meeting runs on past its announced time, past all sorts of working hours, and the image of Yolochka cooped up in some dusty reading room starts to gnaw at Ruzya.

The streets are long empty by the time the reading finishes and the department's Communists file out of the building in an orderly fashion, a few silent, a couple straining to chat about summer camp for children or tomorrow's weather. No one dares talk about what they just heard. Elsewhere in Moscow, the readings of Khrushchev's secret speech to Party members are proceeding in their different ways. Some organizations hold long discussions. The Party members in the Writers' Union hold a three-day meeting with confessions and mea culpas, tears and rants, and even suggestions for changing the way things are done—suggestions that, in another couple of years, will sound naively dangerous. No such floodgates have been opened at Glavlit, where everyone will continue to fear everyone else and where Khrushchev's speech, like any other document originating with the authorities, will, in every professionally censorious brain, be processed into a set of guidelines on how best to tread the Party line. Ruzya walks alone, clasping her hands together through the pockets of her coat, as though to hold the joy close, to make sure she transports it whole until it can be shared.

The three years between Stalin's death and Khrushchev's speech had changed Ruzya's job in ways she had never dared dream. Her job description and the mechanics of her job remained essentially the same: she was still required to quash anything that did not simply paraphrase Soviet newspaper articles. But the sense of inhabiting a gradually imploding space lifted as soon as the Doctors' Plot was debunked, and from that point on her world began to expand. The correspondent corps, which had become skeletal by the early 1950s, grew quickly. Journalists began to arrive—from Poland, Italy, Hungary, Sweden, Romania, the world. All of them had to be censored. So the censors began to cram languages. At first all six of the department's "political editors" were herded into a room in Glavlit's main building (it would have been more logical, of course, to hold the sessions at the Central Telegraph, but there seemed no way to clear the teachers for entry), but only two of the censors proved capable of learning languages by shorthand. So Ruzya and Margarita, a dowdy middle-aged woman Ruzya tried but never managed to like, were left to study together. It was exhilarating, even if Hungarian never did stick. For the first time since she joined Glavlit in 1943, Ruzya felt like she could just simply like her job—not because it gave her financial security or the occasional rides in a chauffeured Volga, but because she enjoyed what she was doing. Some days she even thought that the undeniably positive aspects of her work—she and her colleagues did, after all, help keep Soviet military secrets secure—might outweigh the negative. It was an easy delusion to entertain: she was learning so much more and banning so much less than before. But there would come a day, in 1956, when she had to admit that hers was, as her father had put it, "a gendarme's job"—when she felt it with a clarity that was perhaps more terrible than ever before.

Though the text of Khrushchev's speech was classified, its

message got out—through closed readings at Party meetings like the one Ruzya attended, through summaries that went out to the Party organizations in Soviet satellite states, and through at least one leak of the complete text—and the seemingly immovable structures of Soviet power began to shake. In the Soviet Union itself, the leadership quickly backtracked, sending out the message that public discussion had to stay within narrow bounds. But in Hungary, at that point perhaps the most Stalinist of all Warsaw Pact regimes, unrest broke out. On October 23 the students took to the streets. They had the public behind them. The Communist state caved. A multiparty government was established, headed by excommunicated Communist Imre Nagy.

Soviet troops moved in. It took three weeks to put down the popular revolt. Imre Nagy and dozens of other leaders of the uprising were summarily executed.

Ruzya's language lessons focused on newspaper texts. Struggling as she did with Hungarian, she made a valiant effort to read that country's newspapers—supplied helpfully by the Glavlit language instructor—throughout 1956. Through the haze of language she saw a revolution as righteous and romantic as the ideal she had been taught in the 1920s. Starting at the end of October, she read Polish writer Wiktor Woroszylsky's daily dispatches from Budapest in the Warsaw papers: cleaned up by the Polish censors though they were, they still bore witness to the death of the revolution.

She did not really have much to do with censoring this particular tragedy. Most of the important reporting was done, naturally, from Budapest. At the height of the crisis the Soviet authorities expelled Welles Hangen, one of the two *New York Times* correspondents in Moscow, effectively preempting any attempts to try to write about the conflict from Russia; no one really tried. Maybe this is why it all became so clear to Ruzya in the fall of

1956. The big story of the day, the news that worried her most, was not hers to censor. She was not struggling to deduce what was and was not allowable in the coverage of Hungary; she was simply using her position, privileged by the access to information, to observe. Nor was she a participant or a potential victim of the events this time, as she had been throughout the anti-cosmopolitan campaign. But every day the Hungarian and Polish newspapers told her how the system she served was taking freedom away from a country that had risked everything to gain it. It was not Stalin doing this, or even his successor, Khrushchev: it was, she now saw, the system. She worked for this system. She hated herself for the job she did.

She loved the job.

NOVEMBER 1956

There is some tense milling around in the narrow hallway before the general Glavlit Party meeting. Ruzya peeks into the meeting hall. It is already nearly full: this is a general meeting of all Party members on staff, and their presence is mandatory. The usual faceless little men are seated at the long table onstage, with their deep-red tablecloth, their thick water glasses, and their crystal pitcher as a centerpiece. The usual shuffle of papers, creaking of chairs, sounds of stifled irritation at the last-minute stage arrangements. One of those crumpled gray men rises, walks over to the light-wood podium set stage-right, turns on the little light, stands a moment as though trying to remember what brought him here, then moves his reading glasses up his nose and places some paper on the surface in front of him. It is another couple of minutes until the meeting begins, and Ruzya does not want to go in a second sooner than she has to. She turns back into the hallway.

Against the two-tone brown oil paint of the walls, everyone's face looks pallid and desolate. Seva Yakovlev, a Japanese-language specialist Ruzya knows from her incoming-media days, catches up with her.

"Watch out," he says. "You are on the agenda in Part Two."

"Right," she says, and she looks down at the brown linoleum that seems to have taken on a wave, a motion that threatens to destabilize her. "Thanks."

"They asked me to take the stage, too, to speak against you, but I said I wouldn't."

"Right," she says again. "I suppose you can get away with that." She means that his mastery of Japanese makes Seva uniquely qualified to claim some freedom of maneuver, like refusing to take the stage to condemn a marked colleague. She means it as a compliment, but it comes out jealously reproachful. The floor continues its disturbing dance, and she finds the wall with her hand.

Seva makes a motion to keep walking. "I just wanted you to know," he says, and leaves her behind.

For a month now she has known she is marked and probably doomed. Actually, no: it has been longer, since the summer, when she first saw the new head of Glavlit. Omelchenko had been purged as a Stalin hand. Ruzya felt it was unfair: although he had served the tyrant well, Omelchenko had never exhibited more than the necessary zeal in doing his job. The new director, Pavel Romanov, carried the last name of the last czarist dynasty but was in fact said to represent a dynasty within the Communist Party. He had an angular profile and a bearing that seemed more imperious than bureaucratic. He came through on tours of Glavlit facilities, dispensing quick evaluations that foretold the fates of his ever-edgy subjects. When he came to the foreign correspondents' department Party meeting, he declared, "I have reviewed your personnel files, and I have concluded that some staff members do not belong in this department due to their lack of professional qualifications and some due to their application data." That phrase encompassed the pages upon pages of personal information employees had put down on their job applications: addresses and professions of relatives, and, of course, their ethnic origins. As soon as she heard it, Ruzya knew she was finished.

Soon after, Max Frankel, the new *New York Times* reporter in Moscow, wrote that the Soviet Jewish Autonomous Region was "as Jewish as it is autonomous," and she let it through. She may have preferred to be fired for a professional shortcoming, but this infraction proved too subtle.

And then there was the knitting incident. Days later it occurred to her that she may have done this intentionally, to bring on the inevitable ending she had tired of fearing. Ever since Romanov marked her, she had known he would get rid of her— but she also knew his task would prove initially difficult because of her status as a war widow. The morning of the knitting incident she had gone to a general staff meeting—attendance mandatory— after a night shift. She sat in the far-left chair in a middle row, a bad location if one intended to stay out of view of those onstage but a good one for making it out the door quickly once the meeting was over. As the agenda was announced, she glanced to her right and saw a mousy young woman who wore the kind of servile expression that immediately put Ruzya off. There was no chance of exchanging comments or playing Hangman with this one, and Ruzya suddenly feared she might fall asleep during the meeting. "Do you want me to show you how to knit?" she heard herself asking her neighbor, who surprised her further by nodding her acquiescence.

Ruzya, it should perhaps be noted, does not knit. She had never knitted before and would never knit again. But just the day before, a friend of Batsheva's had shown her two basic patterns and given her some hooks and yarn. She was exactly twelve lines into what she imagined would be a lavender scarf for Yolochka, and this was what she now took out to share with her nameless companion.

This pleasantly mindless activity occupied her for over two hours, until she was jolted by words that—she knew before she even heard their meaning—were for and about her. "I am out-raged," Romanov boomed, "to see that some of our Party com-rades disdain issues of importance to the entire staff, acting in a manner inconsistent—" His voice faded out again, but she knew then and there that her career at Glavlit was over.

Now the deplorable knitting incident is on the agenda in Part Two. They stand up one after another—the same people who were once itching to condemn her as a "rootless cosmopolitan" for bringing Yolochka to see the Central Telegraph dentist. Now they talk about her abhorrent attitude, her disregard for discipline, her immense irresponsibility. To conclude this well-orchestrated trashing, Romanov stands and sums up: "The department in ques-tion is the most scrutinized of Glavlit departments, since its staff members work directly with foreigners. It is therefore clear to all of those present," he continues, "that a person like this cannot work in this department."

Two days later—paperwork is never instantaneous—Romanov will summon her to his office on Zubovsky Boulevard. He will tell her he has signed an order transferring her to another department. She knows this is a veiled firing, and she does not want to bargain with the man who is taking away her job. Without asking which department, she will place her letter of res-ignation on Omelchenko's old desk.

CHAPTER TWENTY-THREE

FEBRUARY 1957

For a few months after the Glavlit meeting, Ruzya felt like she had managed to stay admirably ahead of the curve, rejecting the humiliation of a transfer, stepping away into the dignity and well-earned security of her second marriage. She and Semyon moved into his room. Yolochka, old enough now to manage on her own, stayed behind in that basement apartment populated by her many squabbling relatives. But now Ruzya lies on her back at night, studying the cracks in the ceiling of her new home and wishing she had kept a bit of the old life, where she had a job and an identity. She has never before been a no one, and though she tries to reassure herself that she is still someone now, she cannot feel it. She thinks of her old job's despicable nature, and she hates herself for thinking it is better to be a gendarme than a nonperson.

Even though the Doctors' Plot is over and the specter of deportation no longer haunts Moscow's Jews, finding work has scarcely become easier. Old anti-Semitic attitudes, rediscovered and recast as policies during the anti-cosmopolitan campaign, will last for decades more. There are now strict quotas, established by secret documents that are common knowledge, on hiring Jews and admitting Jews to universities.

Hope comes from a friend, as usual: she is given the number of one Vladimir Shamborg, a Jew who heads some department in the Economics Research Institute. He is looking for someone who can translate from German. Shamborg, she is told, used to be an executive of the Jewish Anti-Fascist Committee. In a conversation the day before Ruzya goes to see him, her friend Ester produces a bit of personal trivia: Shamborg was the man who approved Ester's own hiring at the JAC.

Shamborg, disturbingly, turns out to be a tall man whose features seem cut from a whole piece of some very expensive material. He hangs back slightly as he speaks and shocks Ruzya into near speechlessness with his long thin fingers that tap a little dance on the table before he begins his uncomfortable speech.

"I can be honest with you, right?" he says after showing Ruzya some sample texts.

She nods: she has a feeling she would prefer that he would not.

"I cannot give you a staff position."

" 'Application data'?" she guesses.

"Good, you understand." He blows out a relieved cloud of smoke. It would be very discomfiting indeed to have to tell a fellow Jew he cannot hire her because she is Jewish—or that he, being Jewish, cannot afford to risk his own job by hiring her.

She did freelance translations for him for a year. Gradually she grew used to this plodding new existence, which lacked the air of risky importance she had known for thirteen years. She broke her habits willingly and willfully, developing a reverence for the copy she handled, even if it was coarsely written economics texts. After a year she finally found a job elsewhere.

Shamborg blushed beet-red and sweaty when Ruzya told him she could no longer wait to see if he might finagle a staff position for her. When he begged her to wait a week so he could get her hired, she realized that it was his personal caution rather than clear directions from above that had kept him from hiring a Jew. She cared little anymore: this Jew was now going to become an editor at the Publishing House of Eastern Literature.

Soviet literary authorities used to boast that their country published more books in translation than any other. This was probably true: during much of the Soviet period, large numbers of titles in translation were published with huge press runs. It was an industry of sublimation: thousands of people who, under different circumstances, would have written, edited, or published original literature were instead engaged in the field of translation. They were heavily censored, of course: many books had chunks excised, many more were never cleared for translation, and still more could not even have been considered. Even so, more books were published in translation than in original Russian. Certainly the participation of writers and poets who could not hope to publish their own work contributed to maintaining a culture of extraordinarily high-quality translation—a tradition that dated back two centuries, to the beginnings of the Russian literary culture (and censorship). Still, the real workhorses of this industry were not repressed writers but people who were born translators. One of them, as it turned out, was my grandmother Ruzya.

She was originally hired to edit other people's translations from English, German, and French. Her job was to check the manuscripts against originals and edit them for accuracy and literary quality. After a couple of years she got up the courage to tell her favorite among the publishing house's stable of translators that she would like to try her hand at the job. He made no promises, but some months later he handed her an assignment he had turned down: the memoir of a man who had sailed across the Pacific alone at the age of sixty.

It was just as she had hoped. Her fingers tingled when she typed a sentence that seemed just the perfect match for the original. She went to sleep at night turning phrases around in her head, and she awoke in the morning itching to get to the typewriter. She wondered how friends who did this for a living—Ester, for example, had been a professional translator for a dozen years now—treated the work so casually. She, at forty, had found her calling.

Eventually she met other translators who felt as passionately about the art. Her daughter would turn out to be one of them: Yolochka did her first translation just a few years later and went on to translate from eight different languages. A while later, Ruzya's niece, Yasha's daughter, also confessed that she had what she termed "the sickness"; she is now one of Russia's top translators from French. In another couple of decades, when I translated my first book, from Russian into English, I, too, felt the tingle. I had been reared to love translating: when I was a teenager my mother gave me a book on the art of translation because she sincerely thought it was engrossing reading—and I agreed.

There was a tight focus to Ruzya's new field: once she began, she continued, for nearly three decades, to translate books by and about explorers. As she neared fifty, she became an explorer herself, taking up mountain climbing, which was the escape hobby of choice among the "internal émigrés" of the sixties and seventies. To risk her life, she conquered a fear of heights that had afflicted her since childhood. The heroes of the books she translated, of course, took risks that were much more dramatic. She can still recount in great detail the struggles of men who froze, starved, or tumbled to their deaths—all in an effort to touch a patch of soil no one had seen.

In the mid-1990s I came across an American magazine article in which the author confessed her passion for explorer stories. I clipped the article and brought it to Moscow for my grandmother. She loved the conclusion: that dying because of a bunch of rock samples that weighed one down made at least as much, if not more, sense as dying in the name of religion or ideology or nationhood.

"That's exactly it," my grandmother said. "Exactly."

CHAPTER TWENTY-FOUR

MARCH 1957

This time Ester does not feel guilty at all. She is practically a free woman. A couple of months ago Boris shocked her by announcing he was finally willing to divorce. It did not take Ester long to learn the source of this sudden change of heart: apparently, he had fallen for another woman, and she had set his divorce as a precondition for any sort of relationship. Ester came full circle in the last five years. First, she had decided to have another child with Boris, resigning herself, in effect, to spending the rest of her life with him. Then, in April 1953, her daughter was born, making Ester, quite simply, the happiest woman on earth. Whatever the cost, it was worth it—or at least she never thought about the cost. At Boris's unexpected news, Ester felt no more than a momentary jab of jealousy—and that mostly because he had related details of his burgeoning affair to their entire social circle.

Their mothers' reactions were more volatile. Bella, who had nursed a near hatred of Boris ever since she moved to Moscow a dozen years ago, was suddenly despondent at the thought of Ester becoming the single mother of two children—even though Boris was moving out, leaving to Ester, the children, and Bella the three-room apartment on Gorky Street to which they moved just last summer. Meanwhile, Boris's mother, Miriam, for whom this year marks the fortieth anniversary of marriage to a man every bit as meanly overbearing as Boris, made no effort to hide her own jealous joy. "You are doing what I have dreamed of doing for so many years," she told Ester. "If only I could hold a job and survive on my own, I would break free myself." Ester, who has been the breadwinner in the family for five years, stands to lose nothing but her chains, and Boris's flagrant infidelity relieves her of guilt.

Now once again she is at a resort, and once again romance is in the air. This time his name is Oleg, and he is tall, talkative, her age, and a colleague as well—an editor at the State Publishing House. They cross-country-ski together, and they talk of their marriages in the past tense—he has been divorced for two years, so he is far more practiced at this—and trade stories from their lives. Though he is an ethnic Russian, he can sympathize with Ester's experience of looking for work in the late forties, that decade-old fresh wound. He finished his education around the same time, and he found himself similarly stonewalled: interviews would go well, but following an appointment at the personnel department he would be rejected. After half a dozen such rejections a senior editor at some house took pity on him and pointed out that it was Oleg's wedding band—a clear sign of someone with leanings either toward the bourgeoisie or the foreign—that knocked him out of the running every time. Oleg removed his wedding band before his next personnel appointment and was promptly hired. When he told this story, Ester said something about her origins being, unfortunately, rather more firmly attached to her person than his wedding band, and they both laughed at the system's absurd, rigid ways.

Oleg and Ester have not rushed things. Theirs, it is clear, cannot be just another resort romance: two divorced people in their mid-thirties assume themselves to be choosier and more serious about their attachments. They have made tentative plans to meet in Moscow and pursue their acquaintance on that more familiar territory, in real life. On their last day at the resort, before they board buses that will take them, like children returning from camp, back to the city, Oleg invites her for a walk around the spa.

"Nice place, this," he says.

"Yes, I think I'll try to come here again," she responds. *Will they come here together?* she wonders.

"I'm not sure I'll be able to finagle a trip here again," says Oleg, apparently answering the question she did not voice. She looks over: he is walking slightly hunched, hands deep in the pockets of his gray coat, long nose turned downward, chin hiding in the space created by the two halves of his raised collar.

"You never know," she says in a noncommittal tone meant to let him know no commitment is expected from him.

"You see," he begins, stopping to face her, hands still in pockets, shoulders still scrunched up around his face, as though he were either very cold or very embarrassed. "You see, I like you very much. I mean—" His eyes trace the outlines of her body and his voice trails off, but she knows what he means: there are just not very many gorgeous, intelligent, well-read, self-sufficient, available women in their mid-thirties. "I mean, I like you very much," he repeats. "But you are just too Jewish. Jewishness is just too central for you, too important. It would come between us."

It hurts. She knows he is an idiot for saying what he said. She knows he is also right: it really would have come between them.

And she knows she is better off without him. It still hurts. She liked him very much too.

DECEMBER 26, 1957

Sasha feels very pleased with himself, Ester can tell. In anticipation of his thirteenth birthday, he developed what he apparently imagines are manly ways: he lowers his voice when he is serious, he spends long minutes in front of the mirror over the bathtub in the kitchen studying the darkening down on his upper lip, and he has taken to making pronouncements. He celebrated his birthday yesterday, making a production of drinking—though she never forbade alcohol before, he still seemed to assign a new significance to it—and today he went to see his father for lunch. Ester is not given to doubting her credentials, personal or professional, but she felt a twinge of insecurity when Sasha left in the early afternoon: he is so pointedly becoming a man, and here he was off to see his newly estranged father.

Now he is circling the kitchen, agitated but silent. Ester feels another pang of anxiety—slight, but it makes her realize she is on guard.

"So, how did it go?" she asks casually.

"He wanted me to come to live with him." Sasha plops down in a chair, spreading his legs in a manly way.

"Really?"

"Yeah, he said you were a woman—"

"Well, this is true." She visualizes Boris, decisive and already furious that the conversation may not go his way, making this obvious argument, and she suddenly feels relaxed.

"Yeah, and then he said you won't raise me right!"

"Really?" She does not expect an explanation, but one is apparently coming.

"He said two years ago you wanted to take me to live in Poland and then Israel and he said no and saved me from leaving the Soviet Union."

"Well, yes." This she did not expect. It is true: in 1956 the Soviet Union once again opened the exit door to former Polish citizens, allowing them to return to their country of birth. One of her close friends left, and she wanted to go too: Poland's border was not as tightly sealed against the West as Russia's, and she knew that sooner or later she would be able to make her way to Israel. Boris would not hear of it and she thought at first that here was a perfect way out of their marriage. If she left the country, they would not have to divide up the flat. All he needed to do was sign a release to let her take the children. He refused—because, she knew, he feared that having children abroad would damage his career prospects. Not that he aspired to much, by that point—whatever potential he had was canceled out by his indifference to his work—but he did want to keep his job, which her leaving could have jeopardized.

"So I said, 'That's the one thing I will never forgive you!' "

She laughs. She laughs because she is relieved, and she laughs because she is happy that her son shares her opinions and her pathos, and she also laughs because she can imagine Boris's face when Sasha said what he said. It is a very funny face.

NOVEMBER 1959

This time, setting off for another resort, Ester entertained no romantic notions. She has been too alone to think of company. Two months ago Bella died of a stroke, the last in a series that had rendered her progressively less mobile and more belligerent, and Ester sank into a state so hopelessly dark, so unlike anything she had ever known, that she wondered how and why she had ever survived war and hunger and mortal danger. Finally her friends at work arranged for a stay at a Black Sea sanatorium. She went in good faith, intending to do the resort bit of taking in the air and the sights and whatever conversation might come her way—for the sake of her two children, who needed a mother who could hear and see again, even if it was through the fog of loss.

Were it not for this gray filter that seemed to come between her and life itself, she probably would have become aware of Sergei's presence sooner. He is tall, with wavy light brown hair and looks that fall just short of beautiful: soft full lips, a broad nose, light green eyes surrounded by a net of fine wrinkles. He has a chip-on-his-shoulder eagerness about him: at forty-eight, he is well past the halfway point in a life that has consistently shortchanged him. The son of an Orthodox priest, he has been relegated to a lower caste for as long as he can remember: in postrevolutionary Russia the children of clergy were officially designated second-class citizens, banned, among other things, from most secondary schools and all colleges. After getting his allotted seven years of education, he worked as a builder, until 1936 when, in a fit of magnanimity, Stalin said that "sons do not answer for their fathers." Since the leader's word had the force of law, universities immediately opened their doors to the likes of Sergei—no small comfort even in the year when his father was arrested, never to return. He was in his last year of studying to be a civil engineer when he was dispatched to his first job: the construction of a new military airport in Western Belarus, which is where he was a month later, when the Germans attacked. He joined the crowds of refugees moving eastward, but German troops overtook them within twenty-four hours.

He was neither Jewish nor a Communist and so was able to settle in occupied Belarus, get a job, find a wife. But within a year he made contact with guerrilla fighters and, after several more months, joined them in the neighboring woods. He finished the war a Red Army officer. After the Soviets liberated Belarus and the guerrillas joined the army, he was given a job as a bridge builder. He returned to Moscow to complete his university degree. He was thirty-four by then, a late bloomer but a contented one: he had a young wife, two small sons, and a career of traveling around the expanded empire building bridges. Within a couple of years his wife was diagnosed with multiple sclerosis; by the time he traveled to this Black Sea sanatorium, illness had wrung nearly all the life out of her and the compassion out of him. Forty-eight—and he still felt like he had yet to start living.

When Ester finally noticed him, she was in no mood for the small talk of resort romances. "I am very Jewish," she said. He fought back a half-smile and said seriously, "My father knew Hebrew."

Three weeks later, it is the end of her stay. Sergei is leaving, too, to go to Lipetsk, an industrial city an overnight train ride away from Moscow. For the last dozen years he has moved his family from bridge construction site to bridge construction site, and Lipetsk is the fifth or sixth place they have lived. He tells her all of this in a hurried monotone: he has mostly listened, not talked, over the last three weeks, and now he is giving Ester all the necessary information in a speech he rehearsed overnight.

"My sons—well, this you know. Valery is sixteen and Alexander is fourteen. Your own son is right in between them. I will be working on moving to Moscow. I have been told that is an option, though I have not pursued it, you know, because there was no reason. You should also know that I have promised my wife I would not seek an official divorce. And, of course, I will always have to support them. But I make a decent living, there should be enough for all, if you have no objections to the situation—the arrangement, I mean."

Ester has been fiddling with the flowers he brought when he came to her room. She put them in a two-liter glass pickle jar on the bedside table, then, remembering that she will leave this room in less than an hour, took them out, then, realizing she will not spend the hours on the bus and days on the train clutching a bunch of white-and-yellow whatever they are called, put them back in the jar, which she decided to move to the large square dining table. And now she freezes with the jar and the flowers in her arms. She thinks—no, she distinctly hears—that, after a convoluted and twisted fashion, this man is proposing to her. Does she have any objections to the arrangement? Would she like to become the unlawfully wedded second wife of an aging Russian engineer with a disabled wife, two teenage sons, and a swarm of fears and resentments of his own? Yes, she supposes she would.

"No," she says. "I would have no objections to such a situation. Or the arrangement, as you say." She turns to face him. He embraces her, working his arms uncomfortably around the glass jar with the white-and-yellow flowers.

It was almost two years before Sergei brought his family to Moscow and moved in with Ester and her children. He soon commenced his pleading for a child. Ester, who had always planned to have a big family, found herself resisting: her two children plus his two seemed quite enough, and anyway, she was about to turn forty. Finally she gave in. At forty she found herself carrying a full-term baby, tangled in the bureaucratized Soviet medical system, which, because of some paperwork error, insisted she had another month to go. The boy inside her grew and grew, until he was too large to be born naturally, but the doctors insisted it was still too early. When they finally performed a cesarean, it was too late: the baby died within minutes of being born. Then roles were reversed: Ester felt that unless she had another child she would never move past the nightmare of losing one, while Sergei begged her not to risk it again. In 1964, at the age of forty-one, nearly twenty years after her first child was born, she had a son, Leonid, who grew to be an almost-exact copy of his father, with his very nearly perfect looks.

Ester and Sergei married officially in 1970, after his first wife died. They were together for twenty-seven years, until his death in 1987. It was a peaceful, happy, uneventful union. Temperamentally, Sergei proved the opposite of Ester's first husband; she quickly grew to appreciate his distaste for conflict and eventually learned to take charge where his accommodating nature left a vacuum. There was always just one thing missing: Sergei was not Jewish, and though she loved him all the more for being the rare Russian not infected with anti-Semitism, she could never make him understand how it could be that a fact of her birth, of an unused language, an unheeded religion, and a faraway country made up the single most important part of her being.

And so it happened that at the close of the fifties both of my grandmothers began their second lives—with new men, a new profession for Ruzya, and, a few years later, a new child for Ester. I have been tempted to link their new beginnings to that of their country, emerging slowly and uncertainly from the three decades of Stalinist terror. This connection would have been facile, and possibly insulting: both of my grandmothers, each in her way, had struggled not to march in lockstep with the country. Still, it seems no mere coincidence that as the regime loosened its hold, Ruzya, Ester, Semyon, and Sergei picked up their lives, banged up but essentially intact, and fashioned a second act: new fates and new families. In these families there were no longer any heroes, believers, or saviors—just people.

PART SEVEN

FAMILY

1958–1987

Ester and Ruzya

CHAPTER TWENTY-FIVE

JULY 1958

This is the second year Ruzya and Semyon have rented a dacha for the summer, a general's opulent country house in the same village where Ester, Bella, and the two children have their rental house. Ester started spending the summer here soon after the war—it was a tradition initiated by the elder Gessens—and keeps renting a dacha here even after her divorce, commuting the half hour it takes to get to Moscow by train from early June till late August. Ester's house is closer to the forest, so anytime they both have a free afternoon—and they have both arranged a good helping of so-called library days this summer—Ruzya wheels her large black bicycle out the gate and cycles the five minutes to Ester's dacha so they can take a walk in the woods. They walk slowly, their feet sinking slightly into the blanket of browned pine needles on the paths, and, as always, they talk.

"You know, I sometimes think I should not have left Yolochka behind when I married." Ruzya does not like to discuss motherhood with Ester, for it is a source of constant anxiety for her. She has never felt competent as a mother, and any joy she derived from communicating with her daughter has been shadowed with fear—no, with certainty—of failure. Ester's mothering is superior, both women know, if only because she herself never doubts it. This knowledge makes it hard for Ruzya to bring up the topic that most concerns her this summer, and makes it difficult for Ester to offer words of comfort.

"What choice did you have?" she tries. "You were moving into a single room with a new husband." This is true, of course.

"Lots of people share a single room with their husbands and their children and their parents as well." This is true too.

"But Yolochka was old enough, and perfectly independent."

"Too independent," says Ruzya, getting to the point. Yolochka, who will be sixteen next month, has so visibly and attractively come into her womanhood that the mere sight of her talking to a young man can make Ruzya cringe. Yolochka has been staying with them at the dacha this summer, in an arrangement that has proved less than perfectly comfortable. Yolochka and Semyon get along beautifully—she provides a willing and responsive audience for his myriad stories, and he pitches his tone just right for a very intelligent child who is also a very young woman. Largely thanks to Semyon's happy acceptance, Yolochka feels confident enough to invite her own friends to the dacha—like the young man named Zhenya, who was visiting the house next door late last week but then mysteriously transported himself to Semyon and Ruzya's downstairs couch, where he can be found now whenever he is not by Yolochka's side in the garden or anywhere else her fancy takes them. Because everything that is connected to Yolochka is, for Ruzya, a potential source of danger, this liaison frightens her.

"I'm afraid," she tells Ester, "that she will do something silly, move too fast. Girls are getting pregnant all the time now, you know, and then they marry and don't go to college—" She trails off.

Ester cannot muster words of comfort. Truth be told, early marriage and generally irresponsible behavior are what she thinks of when she looks at Yolochka. She has been so much luckier with Sasha, who, even being two years younger, is immeasurably more responsible. She should not be surprised: this is a boy who, at the age of eight, walked himself to the hospital to have his appendix removed—he did not think it appropriate to disturb his grandmother for an achy belly. At Ruzya's request, he took Yolochka sailing a couple of weeks ago—Ruzya is perpetually worried about her daughter's lack of exercise—and seemed a little turned off by the older girl's inappropriately lighthearted approach to the serious sport. It seems they may have capsized because of her. In any case, Ester, who is so often reproached for her lack of tact, searches for a way to acknowledge Ruzya's parental concern and reciprocate with something of her own that will, she hopes, lead them to another topic.

"I worry that Sasha is so stubborn," she announces when they reach a clearing and stop to look up at the sun over the pine trees, to confirm their bearings.

"Stubborn? What do you mean?" Ruzya is genuinely surprised.

"He has got it in his head now that he wants to be a physicist," Ester grumbles.

"But that's wonderful. He is such a capable boy!"

"Listen, everyone knows that they do not accept Jews to the physics faculty. I keep telling him this, and he just says that he will be the best and they won't be able to reject him."

"Oh." Ruzya does not know what to say. In Ester's description of Sasha, she recognizes her friend's spirit, and she cannot bring herself to criticize what she most admires about Ester: her insistence, her certainty even, that she has the right to live and do as she wants.

"I so wish we had left two years ago, when there was the chance," Ester continues. "If it weren't for Boris, we might be in Israel by now."

Ruzya twists her head at her friend's words, checking quickly that no one could hear Ester's dangerous words. The risks of such speech have lessened in the last five years: Ruzya now fears for her livelihood, not for her life. Still, she fears. The forest is thin in these parts, and she can be sure there is no one lurking for hundreds of yards. So what she says now is for her friend only. But what she says is, "I had the chance, you know, in 1946. But I decided not to go. I had a friend from school, Sonya, who was born in Germany, so they were allowed to repatriate. Her mother was dead, and her father proposed to me. I liked him. He was an interesting and handsome man. He was forty-six, but still, you know. Anyway, I didn't want to go. I think that was right. I'm not sure I would want Yolochka to be growing up in Germany now."

Well, here Ester can agree: she certainly would not want her children to grow up in Germany. But she can see how it could have worked out for her friend. "You could have left him and gone on to Israel, though," she proposes.

"Why?" Ruzya is surprised. "What would I do there?" Ruzya, to be frank, does not quite believe in the reality of Israel, and to the extent that she does, she finds the idea of a small Jewish nation at war in the desert at once absurd and unappealing.

"What do you mean—why?" Ester exclaims.

They go on to make the obvious arguments. They disagree, as usual.

AUGUST 1959

"I'm going to apply to the Pedagogical Institute." Yolochka is resolute. Ruzya and Semyon expected her hours ago—she was to have gone to Moscow University's Philology Department to submit her documents and then come out to see them at the dacha. But it is early evening now, and she has just arrived, looking tired and slightly disheveled: Moscow's summer dust like a brown powder over her black shoulder-length hair, dust also on her feet in open-toe shoes, a tiny pea of an oil stain on the chest of her blue-and-white summer dress: she must have spent hours walking around the city, eating doughy street fare when she got hungry.

"Why are you not applying to the university?"

"It's too humiliating."

"What?" Ruzya realizes this is a stupid question as soon as she asks it, and Yolochka's exasperated look makes her want to disappear.

"What? Well, I'll give you an example." Yolochka sits down on one of the brown plywood kitchen chairs and places her meaty elbows on the green Formica table. "They called me in for a quick interview. All very nice and civilized: 'Why do you list German as your primary foreign language when you took English in school?' So I'm about to answer when I look at the paper in front of him, and it's got a list of names on it, and opposite mine, in fat script— you know, like someone was writing it over and over—it says 'Jewish.' And a fat exclamation point."

"Oh, my girl—" Ruzya moves to hug Yolochka, but the girl has placed her hands over her head and the mother stands awkwardly by her side, unable to conjure a way to get her arms around her daughter.

"So I said, 'I've changed my mind,' " Yolochka continues. "I don't want to study philology. I want to be a teacher."

"But you have always wanted to study philology!" This exclamation escapes before Ruzya has a chance to realize that this, too, is a bad idea, that it makes Yolochka think she does not understand the situation. "I mean, I understand you had to do what you did."

"No," says Yolochka, tired. "I didn't have to. I could have gone through the humiliation. Hey, maybe they take one Jew in a million?"

"Oh," says Ruzya. She does not know what to say. The Pedagogical Institute sounds like a good idea: it is not easy to get into, but at least they do accept a certain number of Jews every year.

JULY 1961

This is probably only the second time Ester has felt any unease about being the mother of a boy: the first time was when Boris tried to lure him away. Now Sasha has been locked in the toilet for two hours, and Ester is growing convinced he will do something to himself in there. She has been sitting in the kitchen visualizing the tall ceiling in the toilet room and the long chain used to flush the toilet, catching herself visualizing them and telling herself to stop, and then wondering whether she can go and try to open the door to the toilet when her seventeen-year-old son is inside. And she sits in the kitchen, immobile, waiting.

He comes out after two and a half hours, red-nosed and flushed, looking very much like a child. Then he fills in the details of what she already knows must have happened today—what she has known for months would happen. Sasha went to take his oral mathematics exam at Moscow State University's physics department. He had been warned by well-wishers and others not to waste his time trying: that department is one that does not accept

Jews, regardless of ability. He refused to believe it: top of his class, studying for years toward his dream of becoming a physicist, he simply could not fail. He thought there were limits to what they would do. The examining professor kept him in the room for hours, solving problem after problem, until Sasha said, "Just a second, let me think"—"You should have thought before you came here!" the professor shouted. Sasha failed.

"You know, I thought they might trick me or give me problems that would require days to solve—but I never thought they'd exhaust me into failing!"

"I know," Ester says. She is furious, but also immensely relieved, as well as just plain tired after waiting for two and a half hours for him to emerge from the toilet room. She stands at the stove to warm up his lunch as she selects a Poland story to tell him. She thinks she will tell him about the ghetto bench. Or maybe the Catholic priest who was sent to their school to administer state exams and try to fail the Jews. Sasha waits. He will eat and listen gratefully.

CHAPTER TWENTY-SIX

MARCH 6, 1965

The large rectangular wooden table from the kitchen has been maneuvered through two doorways—in the four years Ruzya and Semyon have lived in this beautiful new two-room-plus-kitchen apartment on the top floor of the Writers' Union building, she has learned there is exactly one way to manage this—and now the kitchen table has been added to the dark polished-wood dining table, which is already unfolded to maximum seating capacity. The couch and all the chairs, armchairs, and stools in the apartment have been arranged around the table, and Semyon has gone to fetch more from the neighbors. Ruzya draws the curtains on one of two large windows to shield the furniture from the merciless afternoon sun and surveys the scene. She feels a remote prickle of panic. What if there is not enough food? She has made all her best dishes—the cabbage-and-eggs pie, the gefilte fish, innumerable salads—and Semyon has used his charm and connections to procure a cornucopia of cold cuts, but what if this is not enough? This is the first time she has undertaken a celebration on this scale: in the Russian tradition, forty-five is a significant age, especially for women, whom lurid folklore credits with gaining unprecedented sexual power at just this age. This is not why Ruzya has invited over twenty people to dinner: it simply seemed the thing to do. Now what if she cannot feed them all?

The doorbell gives one hoarse ring. An early guest? God forbid. Semyon with the chairs? He has been gone awhile now, probably drinking a toast to her health with the neighbors. Yolochka, who promised to come early? She should have been here an hour ago. Ruzya opens the door to find the concierge. This building has concierges, but, for reasons of socialist propriety, they are called "lift operators"—though the elevators are fully automatic and operated by the residents themselves quite successfully. The concierges are two identical overweight women of about fifty who sit on a stiff little couch next to the elevator with their knitting, watching all who come in and out of the building. At night they use a sticky dead bolt to lock the glass front door; the rest of the time their function is not exactly clear. Now one of these "lift operators" stands in front of Ruzya in her dark-blue chintz uniform, holding a huge black metal baking pan that looks like an absurd extension of her protruding stomach.

"A big date for you today!" she exclaims good-heartedly, exposing two missing teeth when she smiles. Before Ruzya can respond, she pushes the napkin-covered pan at her: "I made some *pelmeni* for you. Just stick them in the oven to heat up!"

Ruzya quickly asserts that the woman shouldn't have, but won't she please come in, and she is so touched, she does not know what to say, surely—surely what? The woman has already turned around and is waddling off toward the screened elevator door, dismissively waving a plump hand at Ruzya as she recedes. Ruzya stands in her own doorway holding the baking pan. She feels lost in the rituals of inhabiting the Writers' Union building, the complicated dance of tips and small gifts for the help and the help's generous offerings to the residents' social superiority and presumed fame. What is she to do with the pelmeni? This is not her home's usual fare: ground pork and beef wrapped in tiny pillows of dough. Who will eat it? She feels another tiny panic attack.

"Hello? Ester?" She is holding the lime-green plastic receiver and speaking too loud, as though the party's hubbub had already commenced. "Is Sasha home? No, no, I don't need to speak to him. Would you bring him with you when you come, though? I need a young man with a healthy appetite."

"Why in the world did you invite *him*?" Yolochka has just been forewarned that Ester will be bringing Sasha, whom Yolochka, as the closest in age, is expected to entertain. A quick reel of adolescent memories unwinds in her mind. She saw Sasha mostly during the summers, after Ruzya launched the tradition of renting a vacation house near the Gessens' dacha. He was the boy-child who pulled her back from her purposeful march toward womanhood. He took her out in the tiny one-sail boats of the local club, and one summer, when she decided to sign up too, he named her sailor on his ship and dispensed officious orders to her for nearly two months. Her most vivid Sasha memory is of his twelve-year-old mortification when she, his fifteen-year-old sailor, took an unintended step off the pier and shouted to him that it was his fault she was wet up to her very panties. That was—what?—almost eight years ago. Since then Yolochka has married and divorced twice, has been expelled from college, reinvented herself as a bohemian and a femme fatale and then again as a student, now at the Foreign Languages Institute, and the fiancée of a succession of intelligent, worldly, and talented older men, all of whom failed to hold her interest long enough to go through with settling down. She spends her days working at the Press News Agency and her evenings at the college, and the rest of her time writing, reading, typing, and reciting poetry. She is part of an informal group of young people who gather at the Mayakovsky monument in the center of the city to recite poetry, their own and other people's, and are always passing around typed sheets of paper. Sasha, from what Yolochka has heard from Ruzya, has followed a path straight as an arrow, entering college right after high school, studying to be an engineer or some such thing. (There is not a single man in Yolochka's life who is not a poet or an artist or both, and the rest of the world's occupations have grown indistinguishable.)

She senses him moving through the room before she really sees him: their childhood familiarity makes his walk instantly recognizable. Still, she is surprised when he reaches the empty stool next to her. She must have known he was grown, but still she expected to see a twelve-year-old boy. He is short—about five-foot-six—but that still makes him half a head taller than Yolochka. He has a broad and sinewy build and a very quiet confidence that masquerades as shyness. His nose—well, his nose is a problem, a bit too large and fleshy. He has the most sensuous mouth she has ever seen on a man, with an upper lip that looks drawn with the point of a feather and a full, surprised-looking lower lip. It feels obscene to look at this mouth, and she raises her eyes to his, light brown and smiling even as he appears to stand uncomfortably next to the stool, waiting for an invitation or at least an acknowledgment. The eyes are where she reads the confidence. Just like that, she knows. *This man will be my husband.*

Sasha gets a familiar feeling. His small but significant sexual history
is a succession of seductions—and it is always he who is seduced.
It seems for as long as he can remember he has been handsome
and quiet and desired by older women, each of whom casts him in
a different role. The most recent older woman is the secretary in
his college department, where, thanks to some strings pulled by
Ester's friends, he fulfills his work-while-you-study requirement.
The secretary, a mature woman of twenty-five, was herself the
mistress of the department's head administrator, and she cast Sasha
as the last temptation of youth. Now he feels Yolochka is casting
him as the proverbial Russian stone wall, the personification of
stability that is every woman's ideal. This strikes him as unobjec-
tionable.

He will learn, over the next days and weeks, that Yolochka is
the center of a complex system of suitors and admirers. He will
summarily be placed at the head of the line, and he will accept this
as his due. She will hint that he should pick her up after work,
and, having bought the requisite flowers, Sasha will wait for her
on the steps of the Press News Agency alongside a forlorn-
looking character, also with a bouquet—and Yolochka will acknowledge the other man with a smileless nod as she hands Sasha
her bag to carry. She will suggest they go to the French film festival, and he will spend a night in line at the ticket booth for the
pleasure of not only taking her out every night but hearing her tell
the telephone she is busy. In a few weeks, she will take ill with
some mysteriously debilitating infection, and Sasha will stare
across her bed at a red-haired young man, who, he will learn, is a
promising violinist and chess player—until Yolochka tells the
prodigy she is too tired for company, nodding to Sasha to indicate
he is expected to stay. After about six months, when she tells him
she is pregnant, he will acknowledge that it is time they got mar-

ried, and he will feel satisfied somehow that things have gone just as she intended.

By this time he will have guessed why she picked him. He has never known a person who was so frightened. It must have been the fear that drove her into a library hall for all of her childhood. Her inaccessibility, what others take for seductive conceit, is really a pervasive fear of people or, rather, of anyone who is not thoroughly known, anyone who is not family. Sasha has been her family almost as long as he can remember; in the way of relatives, they have fallen out of each other's sight for long stretches at a time but could still always be taken for granted. When she saw him at that party, she must have realized he could continue to be family: he could be her family. This strikes him as reasonable.

OCTOBER 1965

It is only the second time Ester has gone to see Ruzya since the baby was born. Motherhood the third time around, at the age of forty-two, has proved more limiting than she remembered, so she has not gone out much, preferring to have friends come to her place instead. Most of them have been only too happy: their own children are grown but have not yet given them the grandchildren their hearts and hands already demand—so they love to come and touch her little son's bursting pink thighs, his magically smooth cheeks. But now Ester is on the metro, on her way to the redbrick nine-story structure of the Writers' Union building where Ruzya lives. Ester is on a motherhood mission of a different order. She has to save her older son.

Her friends, modern women all, have sometimes expressed surprise verging on disapproval at her herding and hoarding ways, but Ester is not bothered: she did not raise her children to send them off into the world come what may. She herself lived with her mother until the moment the older woman died, and they were both convinced that there is no relationship stronger, closer, or more important than that of a mother and her child. Ester resolved to be different in one way only: she would have more than one child. Instead of the tense straight line that connected her and Bella, she wanted a taut, unbreakable circle that would hold her and all her children.

Not that she wants Sasha never to marry. Just not now and not this woman. Sasha is the perfect child. As though mindful of the terrible time when he came into the world, of Ester's youth and confusion, he never let his existence be a burden. When he was as young as two or three, he could be reasoned with: if Ester said she had to go to her college, he ceased his crying and pulled himself into a tight, controlled bundle. She did not know what a child's temper tantrum could be until her daughter was born. When Sasha was five, he was already going to the library alone to pick out books, and his only failing was that he read them all on the way home. When Sasha was eight, he took himself to the hospital to have his appendix removed. When he was thirteen, he confidently dismissed Boris's heavy-handed attempts to lure him away after the divorce.

How can it be that the first wedge in their easy relationship comes courtesy of her best friend's daughter? Ester has nothing against Yolochka, who is clearly a bright and talented young woman. But she is of a different mold. She leaves men in heaps of despair after a year or less; she careens wildly from one pursuit to the next; she burns and bursts and disappears at will.

Not to mention that Sasha is too young to marry. She suspects he may still be a virgin. If he marries Yolochka now, he will never find his own way as a man. And if he will not be reasoned with, maybe Ruzya can make her daughter see the sense of what Ester is saying. Yolochka, after all, cannot be all that serious about taking away Ester's son.

Ester holds little back as she describes the situation to Ruzya over the other woman's green Formica kitchen table. Ruzya brews tea the way each of them likes it—a cup of boiling hot, so-strong-it-is-black liquid for her friend, a cup of lukewarm golden-colored liquid for herself—and listens quietly.

Ruzya has always envied the confidence with which Ester parents. She is unshakable in her conviction not just that she is right but that her children are always right too. Ruzya's own suspicion that she is generally mistaken only gets amplified when she thinks of her child. And it doubles back on itself, making her think of all the things she has done wrong. At night, thinking of the baby Yolochka is carrying, Ruzya tallies up the wrongs and makes resolutions. She never should have made it her business to track down all those reading halls and cancel Yolochka's subscriptions. She should not have left her with her grandmother and the rest of the relatives in the old apartment when Yolochka was fifteen and Ruzya herself went to live with Semyon. She should not have threatened to disown her two years later, when Yolochka said she was going to marry an insulting, insane artist. And she should not have said "I told you so" when that union cracked predictably soon. She should not have made a production over Yolochka's expulsion from college over—of all things—her failure to attend physical education classes. She should always have presumed her daughter to be right, just as Ester does.

She reminds herself of this as she listens to Ester. She objects, of course; she speaks of the unborn child, of the love that surprised her. But she knows Ester must be right, as she usually is in

matters of parenting. She promises she will talk with Yolochka.
She will put another measure of distance between herself and her
faraway girl.

Ruzya did relay Ester's request—that she not marry her son—to
Yolochka, who never forgot it. She could hold grudges, and this
one she held against both her mother and her mother-in-law.

As soon as winter began, Ruzya talked her into joining her
and Ester and several other friends on a cross-country skiing trip.
Yolochka fell, hard, and miscarried that night. She told her
mother it was all her fault.

Still, she and Sasha did not change their wedding plans. They
were married on March 26, 1966. Nine and a half months later, I
was born. I was a difficult child in every respect: born premature,
I was sickly through my teenage years; very precocious, I was
painfully withdrawn with both peers and family—with the sole
exception of Ruzya, at whose house I spent many weekends and
vacations. At the ages of twenty-four and twenty-two, my parents
were hardly ready for parenthood, especially for severely challenging parenthood. I left home at fifteen, angry at them for sins
real and imagined, and we did not make real peace until I was in
my mid-twenties. My brother, Kostya, born eight years after me,
was, while no less talented, a joy for his parents and his grandmothers and an easy and well-done parenting job.

My parents' temperaments—my father's stubborn stoicism
and my mother's histrionic swings—made for a difficult match.
For the first fifteen years of their marriage they fought frequently,
shamelessly, at the top of their lungs. But they never seriously
considered separating, except once, about seven years after they
married. That time Ester intervened, more in the interest of truth
than in the interest of keeping them together: "You may find a

wife who is better-looking," she told her son. "You will definitely find one who is easier to get along with. But life with any other woman after Yolochka will bore you." They stayed together.

By that standard, theirs was a heavenly match. They read and learned, together and apart. They raised two children. They changed professions. They emigrated. They switched roles within the marriage. They could have kept at it forever. My parents were together for twenty-six years, until my mother's death in 1992.

Chapter Twenty-seven

June 1978

Ruzya must have taken this walk about a thousand times. She has been living in the idyllic little town of Dubna for just over three years, ever since she married Alik, a nuclear physicist. Semyon died in 1971. Their fourteen-year marriage had proved no refuge from the overwrought ways of her own family. Soon after they were married Ruzya realized Semyon could not stop at the three shots of vodka that made him a brilliant conversationalist. He drank secretively, whenever and wherever he could, morning and night. Empty bottles clinked whenever Ruzya opened or shut the closet door. Semyon deteriorated slowly until finally, when he could no longer work, he consented to treatment. His doctor used a strong medication, and Semyon's heart failed: he had been sober about two weeks when he died of a heart attack.

A couple of years after Semyon's death an old friend named Sara promised to set Ruzya up with someone named Alik, a recently divorced and therefore eminently eligible physicist and mountain climber, but Alik had ruled her out on the basis of age: he, at fifty-six, was counting on a young woman. Ruzya then met him accidentally, on a mountain-climbing trip—it was an even smaller world up there—and kept their romance secret until the wedding. She asked Sara to be a witness at the wedding without telling her whom she was marrying. She was making a point.

The point was there to be made. Once the wedding was scheduled, she became something of a celebrity among a small circle of women translators. She was doing research for a translation at Yolochka's place of work, the Foreign Literature Library—her daughter had worked there since graduating from college—and the door of the reading room opened at regular intervals: a woman's head, different each time, would show in the opening and disappear: everyone wanted a peek at The Woman Who Is Getting Hitched at Fifty-four.

It was, in addition to love and luck and that surprising sense of inevitability that makes a marriage between two adults suddenly a necessity—aside from all that, it was a personal triumph. Ruzya had always known how to squeeze every possible bit of happiness out of the worst of circumstances, but with Alik's arrival, she realized how hard she had had to work at it the last ten years: Semyon's drinking and then his death, followed by the zigzagging of Boba, her old friend and now lover, tortured by his inability to leave his wife, had relegated her to the world of small but passionate joys; her contentment with Alik is broad, stable, and generalized. After the wedding they moved into his studio apartment here: her work can be done anywhere, while he is tied to his lab. Dubna, just a couple of hours outside of Moscow, is a small town of yellow two- and four-story apartment buildings, surrounded by a pine forest. She and Alik make a nightly ritual of praising the air while they take a walk in the woods, to the Dubna River and back. She loves these strolls, which remind her that moving to

Dubna—where the apartment is cramped and so is their social circle—was about love and beauty.

Today she is taking the walk alone, early in the morning: she
is on her way to see her visitors—Yolochka, Sasha, and their children. This is the first time since Ruzya moved here that her
daughter has brought her entire family to visit. Ruzya and Alik's
apartment is too small to house all of them, and the hotel demands
the sort of connections and money they do not have, so they have
set up a tent in the woods by the river, a half hour's walk from
Ruzya's building. Ruzya walks fast, as she always does, though she
realizes Yolochka and her family may not even have woken up
yet: they rise late, and this is just one way in which their lifestyle is
mysterious to her. She feels the usual joy laced with anxiety at the
thought of seeing Yolochka, and the tiny threat of jealousy at having to share her grandchildren with their parents. Since she
moved here she has had Masha come and stay with her every vacation, and the baby, Kostya, has been sent to stay with her a few
times as well. Alik, who has no grandchildren of his own, strains
to conceal his discomfort in the presence of small children, but
their visits are the only times when Ruzya really feels at home in
Alik's town and his apartment.

"Grandma, Grandma, stop!" Three-and-a-half-year-old Kostya
is shouting and running from the tent. "Don't come down until I
help you!"

He runs up the short but steep incline that leads to the tent
and extends his tiny arm gallantly up to his grandma. How did her
distant daughter with her careening marriage ever produce such a
perfect child? Their older one is a prickly girl, sometimes affec-
tionate, often withdrawn, and always perceptibly alone. But the
boy, round-faced and dark-haired, is genuinely happy and evenly
open to the world.

He gets her down to the tent and offers her a chair, a gimmicky and uncomfortable folding number: she will never understand the way these two spend money. Their messy apartment has no real furniture, just bare-bones bookshelves from floor to ceiling—and here they have splurged on a set of camping furniture. They could at least have bought a proper camping stove instead: Sasha is now fiddling with a jerry-rigged contraption they use for cooking while Yolochka waits, holding a blackened aluminum pot by its long handle. Ruzya starts talking to them, and the conversation, like all their conversations, finds its way to their future, the question of whether they plan to set themselves up in a more stable manner, which, in her mind, has become synonymous with whether Sasha will ever finish his dissertation. That would mean more money—his salary at the research institute would automatically go up—but, more important, it would mean he is a man of serious intentions, of at least minimal standing. Ruzya has been alternately teasing and nagging him about his dissertation for years. Last time he told her he had put something down on paper. This time Yolochka answers for him.

"We have found a different solution to this problem."

Ruzya knows instantly what this means. At varying levels of awareness she has been dreading this moment for six years, ever since the government began allowing Jews to emigrate. Yolochka's first husband had been among the first to take this exit, once and for all establishing emigration not as the stuff of rumor and dreams unfulfilled but as a possibility. Yolochka has occasionally brought up the subject since. Sasha used to show little interest, but that must have changed. All this flashes through her mind so quickly it is as though she had been preparing to hear just this news for a long time. Her first thought, and her first gesture, go to Masha, her gangly eleven-year-old granddaughter, who returns the look from under a mane of hopelessly tangled black hair and reaches in her ready but slightly misdirected way to meet the embrace.

"This means I might never see you again," Ruzya says, pressing the girl's head to her shoulder.

JUNE 1978

For Ester there are no tears, though she wishes they would come. Sasha told her calmly, almost matter-of-factly. The unfairness is strangling her. She will be left behind because she has failed.

"Why have I succeeded in bringing up my children as Jews but not as Zionists?" she asks Sergei at breakfast and again at supper and at bedtime, and he smiles a lost smile. "If only they wanted to go to Israel . . ."

She has said the same to Sasha and Yolochka, and they have smiled, knowing and dismissing: it is not up for discussion. They are going to America, and if she does not want to come, she will have to stay behind.

This is the third time. When former Polish citizens were first allowed to leave the Soviet Union in 1946, she felt no pull. Where would she have gone? She was a woman from nowhere and she had no one, save for her mother. Her marriage to Boris was still too new then to think of leaving, and non-Polish spouses were not allowed to go along. She stayed.

She did not regret it exactly, but when the same door opened again in 1956, she wanted out. She had been through the anti-Semitic meat grinder of the late forties by then; that memory lived inside her and—she knew—it lived in every person in the country, Jewish or not, and this made her want to go to one place only: Israel. Boris would not let her—and Sasha swore never to forgive his father for that.

So in a way she knew he would leave eventually. She wanted him to—never more than that day almost exactly seventeen years ago when Sasha came home from his oral mathematics exam at the university's physics department. If he can spare his own children that kind of humiliation, then, by God, he should go. But she also knows something else: there is only one guarantee that Sasha will not have to watch powerlessly, as she did, while his children discover that they were born to pain—and that is to go to Israel. They can say what they want about America, but it is not a Jewish state, and that means Jews are never fully safe. Should she be consoled by the fact that Sasha has not been hurt enough to realize this?

"Why won't they listen to me and go to Israel?" she asks Sergei at bedtime.

"I don't know, love," he says. "I would."

She knows this is true: Sergei, who gets restless at any talk of Jewishness, would go to Israel for her sake, for the sake of their young son, and for the satisfaction of finally leaving the country that robbed him of his youth. But she also knows it will not happen: at fifty-five and sixty-four, they are too old to pick up and move if their grown children are not willing to come, are in fact moving somewhere else altogether. Still, the knowledge that her husband would try to share her dream with her soothes her. She lies down next to him and turns and turns the variables of the future in her mind. Soon enough the thoughts close in on her again and she longs to crawl out of this skin or at least to cry, but she cannot.

The tears will come three years later, when Sasha, Yolochka, and the children do finally leave the country. The moment she returns from seeing them off at the airport she knows that she will never see her son or her grandchildren again: stripped of their citizenship for the desire to leave the country, they are now considered enemies of the Soviet state. They will never be allowed to visit again, and she will, of course, never be given an exit visa to visit them. She will cry for three days.

June 1978

Odd, but for Ruzya the decision to stay has never been about the country. Some people torment themselves about the language, about staying inside a culture they love. Ruzya understands, and she can well imagine herself haunted by the loss of the familiar, but she has no experience of such loss or such fear. Still, she has always stayed. The first time she decided not to leave the country was in the hungry, cold year of 1946, when a school friend's father proposed to marry her and take her to Germany. He was offering himself, a solid man of fifty, plus the opportunity to leave the Soviet Union, and he hoped that the sum of his parts would make him attractive enough. Ruzya was twenty-six and hoping for more. This was how she did not move to Dresden. Will she move to Boston now?

This would mean leaving Alik: as a nuclear physicist, he is a living repository of state secrets, and he will never be allowed to travel abroad. She thinks of her marriage and the years that preceded it. There was one person who was privy to the fact and the particulars of her relationship with Alik, and the relationship he finally displaced, and to all that pulled and spun and sometimes snapped in her life after Semyon's death. This person was Yolochka, the daughter who had been so much the stranger as a child and who as an adult became Ruzya's confidante. Ruzya needs her daughter; but does Yolochka need Ruzya?

What would life in Boston be like? She would be the perfect Russian grandmother, the one who lives to cook for her grandchildren and tries her child's patience with her very presence. She can envision herself waiting for the children after school, worried if they are late and thrilling to their footsteps on the stairs (or would they live in a house in Boston, rather than an apartment— she has read about that, but it seems hard to imagine). Kostya is three; it will be over ten years before he longs to escape her attentions. Ten years is a long time.

What would happen to Alik? He would look for another wife. Oh, he loves Ruzya. Every time they have been apart he has written letters so full of longing, so extraordinary in each word's struggle to connect his reality to hers, that just thinking of them makes her feel loved. And she always feels married, perhaps more married than she has ever felt in her life. Within months of starting to live together they developed a routine that she knows will stay essentially unchanged as long as they both are alive. He naps in the afternoons, and then they both work at home, he in the large room and she in the kitchen, where her typewriter has taken up residence atop the refrigerator. In the same kitchen she cooks three meals a day: he needs his hot meals. When he eats, he sometimes remembers, his voice filling with retroactive horror, the way he had to eat in the cafeteria when he was between marriages. She hates it when he talks about how much he needs a wife. But, of course, it is true: he needs her. *He* needs her.

She will not go to Boston.

She will never doubt that decision.

FEBRUARY 18, 1981

For the most exquisitely torturous part they line up along a waist-high chrome barrier. For the next hour they can see their children but they can no longer touch them or talk to them. They can hear bits of the conversation between them and the customs official, a huge woman in a dark blue uniform who subjects all of their possessions to a thorough examination. She pauses over children's drawings, brassieres, cigarette packs. Kostya, jumping up to be seen over the woman's booth, declares, "I have gold!" She asks to see it in a tone of condescension but with a glint in her eye. He produces a scrap of tinsel and the morning's only smile. "You are golden," the customs officer says.

Ester and Ruzya stand next to each other. Next to Ruzya stands Samuil's mother, Batsheva, Samuil's sister, Zhenya, and her daughter, and then there are another dozen and a half red-eyed friends and relatives.

They spent the night pacing Sasha and Yolochka's large apartment, empty of furniture now but full of people. Sasha and Yolochka had announced an "open house," and over seventy people had come through, most bold enough to affirm their association with the newly minted enemies of the state by putting their names down on sheets of computer paper taped to the wall—memory's sign-up sheet. By midnight they had left and the closest relatives commenced their vigil. They sat in the kitchen, drinking instant coffee. Samuil's sister said she wanted to show Masha his letters from the front. Yolochka said the children had to sleep. Masha locked herself in the toilet to read the letters. Ruzya objected—rightly—that Masha would retain little, under the circumstances. Ester kept checking her watch.

The last of the suitcases—cheap cardboard ones, intended to be used just once—makes it to the other side of customs. They wave. Samuil's sister blows kisses, and Kostya returns them. Yolochka says something to Masha, who looks back again, straight at Batsheva. Ester and Ruzya lead the procession out of the airport. What a way to cement a thirty-year friendship: losing their children on the same day.

EPILOGUE

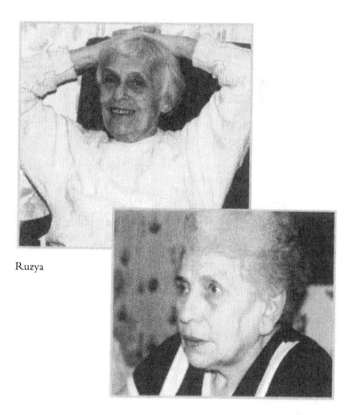

Ruzya

Ester

NOVEMBER 1987

Ester has worked here for nearly forty years. She has worked with the same people for most of this time, and all of them tried to talk her out of what she is about to do now. She is planning to go into the chief editor's office—and they are all convinced she will come out of it unemployed. As she starts her way down the long wide hallway, her black pumps drumming a slow beat on the shiny parquet floor, her colleagues sit in their large shared room, immobilized by the inevitable, like the comrades of a soldier who is running toward enemy tanks with grenades strapped to his body.

For Ester the decision to go to her boss today was not a difficult one. There was a letter from Sasha and Yolochka. Sasha writes infrequently—after an initial rash of letters he has stayed silent for months on end—so Ester is accustomed to getting her news from Ruzya, who gets at least weekly updates from her daughter. They have long since developed the habit of reading their children's letters out loud to each other and other relatives.

But here was a jointly written letter actually addressed to the family at large. Apparently the children had learned it was now possible for former Soviet citizens to secure visiting visas; all they needed was a properly executed invitation from an immediate relative—an official piece of paper with all sorts of seals and stamps.

They all know what an invitation entails. Aside from queues and the humiliating struggle for bureaucrats' attention, there is the matter of obtaining a "letter of recommendation" from one's place of work, certifying that one is trustworthy enough to be allowed to invite a foreigner to enter the country. Ruzya says she cannot even consider it: coming out about having a child abroad would spell immediate professional death for Alik. She has managed, admirably and all but miraculously, to keep the fact of her daughter's emigration out of the Dubna rumor mill. For the last seven years she has lied whenever asked about her grandchildren's whereabouts, ultimately inventing an entire parallel life for them. She wants nothing more than to see her daughter and grandchildren; she and Yolochka have been discussing the possibility of meeting in a mutually accessible place—Budapest, perhaps, or Sofia. But she cannot, simply cannot, risk her husband's livelihood to invite them to Moscow.

What the hell. At sixty-four, Ester is nine years past the minimal retirement age for women. She could start drawing a pension. She could continue to do some freelance translating—though she might lose some assignments, from editors who would be scared off by her newly marred "application data." What the hell. A job is a small thing to risk for the chance to see her son.

Or so she has been telling herself. Still, her breathing is growing more tentative as she nears the editor in chief's quarters. She reminds herself she has faced worse in her life, and the thought sticks on the way down, leaving a rough and bitter taste in her throat. Remember to breathe. The editor in chief is not here. Would she like to see his deputy? No. Yes, of course.

Bochkarev is square all over: shoulders, head, hands. He sits behind a square desk of light wood. He looks at her from behind square black-rimmed glasses. What would this be regarding? She fires her speech, memorized in advance, and wonders after she is finished whether she may have mixed up the order of words.

Bochkarev looks down at a square piece of paper on his desk, then back up at her. "When did he emigrate?"

"Nineteen eighty-one," she says. He must want to know how long his organization has failed to exhibit the necessary vigilance: they did not even know an employee had a son abroad.

"Nineteen eighty-one." Bochkarev's thick eyebrows move closer together. "You must miss him an awful lot. To not see your son in six years!" He extends his hand for the piece of paper she has brought: the text of a recommendation.

They were incredulous back in the department. They stopped working and ran out to get a bottle of wine. They were celebrating a victory much bigger than Ester's keeping her job, and even than her being granted a chance to see her son. The seven or eight women—it was all women—gathered in that editorial office that day were celebrating having proof that something in their country had finally changed, for surely Bochkarev's magnanimity came on instructions from above. Later that day, Ester and Ruzya continued the celebration. This was when perestroika began for my grandmothers.

My parents and my brother went to Moscow in February 1988. Asking my grandmothers about the visit is of little use: both women respond with airy superlatives. It was the best thing that ever happened, in part because no one believed it could. Miracles continued: in the fall Ester and Ruzya went to visit their children in the United States. My father and I were able to arrange for Ester to take a trip to Israel from the United States—more than forty years after she sent that telegram to Poland: "Next year in Jerusalem." It was everything she had imagined.

In another year it became possible for Russian citizens to visit Israel with impunity, and my grandmother Ester has gone to visit again. She follows Israeli politics, collecting details from television, radio, and, when one of her children or grandchildren helps, the Internet; her own views have grown increasingly militant. Today, at seventy-nine, she is no longer able to travel to Israel as a tourist—she walks with great difficulty—but she continues to dream of one of her children or grandchildren moving there and taking her along. She envies the Akivises—Max and Lyusya, the friends at whose house she and Ruzya used to keep their skis: they joined their younger daughter in Israel in the early nineties. Her own daughter disappointed Ester by choosing to move to America with her son in 1990. Every year for a decade now Ester has spent three months in the United States, visiting her daughter in Connecticut and her son on Cape Cod. She jokes that her best-laid plans have come to naught: despite having had three children, she can count on having only one of them, her youngest son, Leonid, by her side. He is a journalist in Moscow. Ester herself retired in 1990, when her magazine closed, though she still takes the occasional translation from Polish or English.

My grandmother Ruzya, on the other hand, says that if she ever emigrated, it would be to the United States: she likes it, and unlike her friend Ester, she has a strong aversion to nationalism in general and Zionism in particular. She disliked Israel intensely when she visited in 1993—mostly, she admits, because it was "too Jewish." In the early 1990s she traveled frequently to America, not only visiting my parents in Boston but also making her way to New York and to the West Coast to see San Francisco.

She went to Boston for the last time in August 1992, for her daughter's funeral. Yolochka had told her about the breast cancer in a letter two and a half years earlier; she had already had the operation, and the tests had already shown the cancer had spread to the lymph nodes—though she had kept that detail to herself. Ruzya went to Boston for three months then, and watched the early stages of her daughter's deterioration. She felt, alternately, that she could not stand another day of going through life's most cruel and unnatural process—preparing for her child's death—and that she could be nowhere else. At one point Yolochka suggested a book her mother might like to translate: Ruzya had retired a year or so earlier. Ruzya took it up and, from that point on, "saved herself a little" by sitting at the computer in her daughter's study, doing what she loved.

She returned to translating after that. In the new Russia there was little demand for the tales of obsessive explorers that so captured her imagination, and Ruzya switched to translating romance novels. Her friends have reproached her for participating in the corruption of Russia's literary tastes; she defends herself vehemently: "I translate books that promote the values of love and sex at their best, and there cannot be anything wrong with that!" Plus, the romance novels are usually printed in larger type, which is easier for her to read. She will be eighty-two in a few weeks, and poor eyesight is just one of the obstacles she overcomes to work: her neck becomes unbearably stiff if she sits over her typewriter (my brother's and my attempts to switch her over to a computer or an electric typewriter have consistently failed). So she reads the original while lying on her back on the couch, turns the phrase over in her head, and then gets up to type it. Getting the phrase just right can still thrill her.

APRIL 1993

"Hungarian! Who invented it? My brain couldn't retain a word—not 'thank you,' not 'hello,' not 'one,' 'two,' or 'three.' I've never felt so much like a foreigner." I have just come to Moscow after reporting a story in the Balkans, and I am complaining.

"Ah, Hungarian," my grandmother Ruzya says as we step off the bus into the sleeting grayness of a Moscow spring. "Never could wrap my mind around it either. Italian, Czech, Romanian, Polish—none of these were a problem. German, French, and English, of course, I knew. But Hungarian—no matter how much I struggled, I couldn't get past the dictionary."

I stare down at my grandmother—she has always been shorter than I, but lately the difference seems to be increasing—and grope for the right question to ask. I know she translates books from English and German and that she knows French. But Czech, Romanian, Polish? What's with all the languages?

"What's with all the languages?" I ask. "I never knew you translated from those." This book began as my grandmother and I walked to the market from the bus stop that day, our shoes swelling with the melting mess of snow and ice, and she told me about her work at Glavlit. How much of this had I known already? I knew she was a member of the Party. In the late 1970s, when my mother was reading a smuggled copy of *1984* and retelling the plot excitedly to her mother one evening at the kitchen table, I heard my grandmother Ruzya say she had once held a job right out of that book. But I did not learn until I was twenty-six that my grandmother had once censored people like me—American journalists accredited in Moscow.

And what had I known about Ester? That she was a hero who would not bend to the secret police. Not that she ever made a secret of the Major Ivanova story: I had heard it, but my mind could not make her near miss at working for the NKVD fit in the heroic narrative, so I edited the story out. That had its benefits, of course: each time I heard the story of Ester's Lubyanka visit, I listened with amazement, as though I had never heard it before.

DECEMBER 1, 1999

I am in Vienna on a three-month fellowship, working on this book. My grandmother Ruzya, an inveterate traveler, has made the thirty-hour train journey from Moscow to visit me here. My younger brother, who now goes by the name Keith, has flown from Boston. Days, they brave the freezing wind to see the sights while I sit at the computer. Evenings, we spend in my kitchen, and the interview continues. I collect the little details that feed my daily work, but, really, only one question remains. Keith and I attempt to reframe it every evening.

"So Grandma Ester agreed to work as a translator for the NKVD, and if it weren't for an accident of fate—"

"Someone who works for the NKVD as a translator is not letting anyone else down," my grandmother Ruzya interrupts me. "Whereas an informant is a lowlife."

"But you were never an informant!"

"I was not an informant. But my work was less decent, less moral than Ester's would have been had she become a translator."

"Meanwhile, she would have become an NKVD lieutenant."

"That doesn't mean anything. Lots of people may have been

NKVD lieutenants. The doctors who worked at the NKVD—they also had a lieutenant's rank—doctors and nurses, all—and this did not demean them in any way. Am I right?" She is now seeking the support of my brother, who is silent. "I guess not. If he is not saying anything, he must think I'm wrong."

"I think it's not so simple," I say, attempting to interpret my grandmothers' choices—a trap that my brother has wisely just avoided.

"True," Grandma Ruzya grants.

"Grandma Ester was a real hero, the way she resisted the NKVD's attempts to make her an informant."

"True again."

"But she was risking not only her own life but the life of her mother, who may not have survived without her."

"True, true."

"Meanwhile, you raised our mother, without whom we wouldn't have come into being."

"True, certainly."

"So where is the moral high ground here? I mean, what if that Major Gurov, who was always threatening to shoot Grandma Ester, had shot her? What if you had listened to your conscience and quit Glavlit, leaving yourself and your child without a livelihood?"

"But still," my grandmother says, in the weighty tone of someone who has thought through to a conclusion, the pain of which she does not relish. "I see her actions as a display of civic courage. For a person who commits a feat of heroism, or simply a moral act that brings with it a certain danger—right?—the whole point is that he is not thinking of the consequences. Because if there were no threat, then it would be neither a heroic feat nor a highly moral deed. Do you understand?"

She looks at the two of us, clearly forgetting at this moment that we owe our existence to her compromise. Our silence now leaves our grandmother alone with her compromise, again.

FEBRUARY 3, 2002

It is nearly four in the morning. Through my window I can see the illuminated gilded onion dome of a small neighborhood church and the neon sign of Russia's largest oil company. I have been living in Moscow for nearly eight years. I came back for the first time in early 1991, on assignment, and felt at home in ways I had forgotten existed. For the next three years I returned more and more frequently, for ever longer stretches of time, and finally decided to stay. My grandmothers did not know quite what to think of this. Ester and I clashed over her initial insistence on being kept abreast of all my late-night comings and goings: she constantly worried something would happen to me in the streets of Moscow, though when I was away in New York she presumed me to be safe. Ruzya worried too: that I would stay in this horrible country; that I would leave.

For most of the last ten years I have been accredited as a foreign journalist in Moscow; right now I am the *U.S. News & World Report* correspondent here. The joking awareness that, if time were collapsed, my grandmother might censor me occasionally surfaces between us. The practice of censoring foreign correspondents openly was abandoned in 1961, just four years after Ruzya left her job. Of course, Soviet authorities continued to expel any journalist who violated rules written and rules unspoken. In the last couple of years, that practice has reared its ugly head again: several foreign correspondents have been asked to leave, while

370 ESTER AND RUZYA

many more Russian journalists have found themselves unemployed and unemployable for running afoul of the current post-
democratic regime.

Ten years after the collapse of communism, Russia is restoring
many of the old regime's symbols and some of its repressive ways.
Conventional wisdom has it that this retraction is our punishment
for failing to do what Germans did after World War II: search our
national soul, purge and cleanse it. A prominent human rights activist marveled a few years ago at how this could have happened
after tens of millions of people were killed or crippled by the
regime: "Amazingly, none of the dead turned out to have children," he wrote with morbid irony—meaning that if any of them
had had children, surely these children would never have let the
injustice be forgotten. That is not the problem. The problem is
that all of those who were in any way, large or small, responsible
for holding up the murderous regime also have children and—
more relevant now—grandchildren. The victims of the terror
were also its perpetrators—mostly, but not always, willing. "In my
sleepless nights I can hardly find solace in the knowledge that I did
not participate directly in murders and betrayals," wrote Yevgenia
Ginzburg, a onetime devoted Communist who spent eighteen
years in Stalinist camps. "The killing was done not only by those
who dealt the blows but by those who supported Evil. It does not
matter how they did it: whether by thoughtlessly repeating dangerous theoretical formulas, or by silently raising their right hand,
or by cowardly writing half-truths. Mea culpa . . . And more and
more I come to think that even eighteen years of hell on Earth
cannot relieve me of my guilt."

We who did not spend eighteen years or even a day in that
hell, who did not bruise our own souls in the search for the decent
compromise that does not exist and for the right choice when
there is no choice at all—we have no right to sit in judgment of

our grandparents. I am not even sure we can presume to tell their stories. Still, writing about Ester, Ruzya, and Jakub is my best contribution to ensuring that nothing like the terror with which they lived ever returns. But for most of the time I have spent writing this book, I have feared that it will.

It is perhaps a measure of my reassimilation that I have done what Russians do in times of stagnant fear: I have retreated into the cocoon of my family. I have done less and less journalism over the last couple of years. A year and a half ago my partner, Svenya, and I adopted a three-year-old boy, whose name is Vova. Three months ago I gave birth to his sister, whom we named Yolochka. Unlike both me and her father, she has light eyes and hair, which is a brown reddish color; I trace that and her straight, flared eyebrows to her great-grandfather Samuil. Since she started sleeping through the night, I have been able to work while she sleeps.

It is almost five in the morning. Today was a big day. Vova seems to have gotten the hang of reading: he will be able to move on to books in a few weeks. Yolochka is big enough to have sat, for the first time, facing forward in the baby carrier Svenya and I take turns wearing. I am finally finishing the book. Downstairs, the work is almost done on my grandmother Ruzya's new apartment: she was willing to give up the Writers' Union flat to be near her great-grandchildren, and we bought and renovated the apartment directly below us. In a couple of weeks, Ester will return from her annual stay in the United States. That day or the next I will take Yolochka the dozen blocks or so to Tverskaya (as Gorky Street is now known again) to meet her other great-grandmother and welcome her home.

Printed in the United States
by Baker & Taylor Publisher Services